I0132714

Speeches of Hyo Jin Moon

2006 - 2008

Delivered Sundays at Belvedere Estate in Tarrytown, New York

Edited by Frank Kaufmann and Peter Ross

Copyright © 2010 by Hyo Jin Moon

All rights reserved

All material in this book in all formats and media, unless otherwise stated, is the property of Hyo Jin Moon, and the family and estate of Hyo Jin Moon.

Copyright and other intellectual property laws protect these materials. Reproduction or retransmission of these materials, in whole or in part, in any manner, without the prior written consent of the copyright holder, is a violation of copyright law.

Cover photo 2007, Tokyo concert performance courtesy of Canaan Station copyright, 2007

Back cover photo, Hyo Jin Moon speaking from the podium, all rights reserved

With grateful acknowledgment to the
True Family of Hyo Jin Moon

Table of Contents

Editor's Preface

This book is unofficial and unauthorized.

These 80 sermons were given by Hyo Jin Nim Moon at the Belvedere international training center, Tarrytown, New York, from January 1, 2006, until March 9, 2008. The final speech was given one week prior to Hyo Jin Nim's unexpected passing.

Each Sunday morning speech without exception began at 7 AM sharp in an environment of minimal liturgy with one or two holy songs sung for ten or so minutes prior to Hyo Jin Nim's arrival.

Once Hyo Jin Nim entered the room, a brief representative prayer was offered. This was followed by a bow from the audience to Hyo Jin Nim, and he would bow to us simultaneously in return. As he then stepped onto the stage to take the podium, Hyo Jin Nim quickly muted the spontaneous applause that greeted him. Then he would speak.

Hyo Jin Nim's speeches were delivered entirely in English. They were professionally videotaped, and audiotaped from a podium-mounted microphone. These raw transcripts from tape were edited into their current form, governed only by two criteria: to retain the author's voice and content, and to enhance readability.

Frank Kaufmann and Peter Ross
March 17, 2010

Introduction

These speeches came about following the ascension of Shin Gil Nim, Hyo Jin Nim's eldest son on December 28, 2005.

Shin Gil Nim lost his physical life in a car accident near Boston. Hyo Jin Nim's stated reason for starting to speak was to educate Shin Gil Nim in the spiritual world as Hyo Jin Nim had been separated from him for many years. On January 22, 2006, Hyo Jin Nim said:

> *When I think about Shin Gil, I feel sorry. In my heart, I feel sorry that I couldn't spend much time with him. I wasn't allowed to. The court wouldn't let me. It was a unique circumstance, unprecedented. In a way, I know that is my victory when it comes to what had happened. But I feel sorry that I couldn't spend much time with him. I really wanted to. It was just about to be at the point where I could spend some time because he was just days from legal age, legally independent. That's the kind of thing that gets you. You're planning all this stuff, and well, I just have to wait a little longer.*

The first speech was on January 1, 2006. Hyo Jin Nim had planned to speak for one full year. But, week by week his attachment to his faithful and diverse audience grew.

Immediately after each speech Hyo Jin Nim went back to his studio near the Holy Rock on the Belvedere grounds. Usually, only his assistant Janine went back and spent time in the studio with Hyo Jin Nim after the speeches. He would ask about all the different people in the audience, especially new people. He wanted to know if he was appreciated and if people were getting something from what he tried to give each person who came.

As he reflected on the teaching that just finished, often he would suddenly get the title of the sermon for the week to come. Then, throughout the week he'd work on his speech based on that title. As he did, he looked forward to seeing everyone again.

We were coming toward finishing the one full year that Hyo Jin Nim had set for himself. At the end of his November 19, 2006, speech, "Repentance," Hyo Jin Nim caught the audience off guard. He asked us if he should keep going past the original plan and time he set.

> *Do you want this to go on? Do you want me to come every Sunday?*
>
> [Silence.]
>
> *How long?*
>
> [Silence.]
>
> *Give me the days. How long do you see that being?*
>
> [Silence.]
>
> *You give me a time and I'll do it. Whatever. How long? That's what I'm asking.*
>
> [Finally the soft voice of a Japanese sister, barely audible,
>
> "Forever Hyo Jin Nim"—the audience laughs,]
>
> *I'll be here as long as you need me.*

For Hyo Jin Nim himself, the experience of consistently speaking publicly had an impact on him. On May 27, 2007, at Belvedere, Hyo Jin Nim said:

> *I'm speaking every Sunday because I'm getting attached to certain things—physically, intellectually, even certain faces. But to make this into a duty that I want to carry on,*

now that's the next step. I might have initially done it because of extraordinary circumstances. I forced, I willed myself to do this stuff. But in the process I changed.

It was a precious and blessed opportunity for those of us who attended Hyo Jin Nim's speeches. And however he may have been changed, he changed us forever by what he so greatly gave of his life and experience.

On March 17, 2008, Hyo Jin Moon ascended to the spiritual world at the age of 46, as medical efforts to respond to sudden health complications proved insufficient .

Essence of a Life of Faith
January 1, 2006

Hello, everyone. It's been a long time. I think it's been about ten years. I can't remember your faces too well except for those who have been long time members. Looking at your faces, it seems people's faces change as they age. Except for some of you, I can' remember too well. During this time I would like to share content coming from my heart.

I would like to dedicate my determination and commitment to Shin Gil who recently passed away. I know Shin Gil will go to a good place. I know his uncle Heung Jin will look over him. So there is no worry about that in my mind. Also, shouldn't I send him off well? Shin Gil went before us to where we all will eventually go.

Living a life of faith is about learning how to die well. We all eventually go the path of death. What is the true value of life? It is understanding how to die well through living. Some people, unfortunately, send their children to the spiritual world first. Now I am one of those parents.

Nevertheless, I receive some consolation in that the spiritual world is the ultimate destination of life. The greatest lesson we should remember while living on earth is how to die well. There is something I want to share with you from that perspective.

This past December 29th, I woke up early in the morning, took a shower, and was packing to leave to Korea. That is when I heard news of my son's accident. I was getting ready to leave from JFK at 9 that morning.

There is rarely anyone who calls me early in the morning. But that morning, a call came early, and when I answered it was my older sister. She asked, "Did you hear the news?" and so I asked "What news?" And she said, "I think Shin Gil had a car accident." I asked her again, "What did you say? What are you talking about?" At that moment, I could not understand at all what was happening. It was entirely unexpected news.

It was harder to understand because I had met Shin Gil a week ago. I finally had found out his phone number that had changed several times, and met him after a very long time. When I met Shin Gil one week ago, he said, "I am so happy because I have been looking forward and forward to this day." He told me that when he turns the legal age of 18, on February 13, 2006, he was planning to come to New York to live with me. He told me that he had applied to all the colleges in New York and nearby so that he could stay close to me. And he proudly showed me his driver's license with his name Shin Gil Moon on it. I was so proud of Shin Gil.

That is why I could not even guess when I heard news of the accident from my sister. It was news I could not imagine with my head. I found out the cell phone numbers of my other children and called them but no one answered. So I called here and there and my sister In Jin found an article in the internet about a car accident of a 17th-year old on December 28th, 4 AM. I called the police station of that area and confirmed that it was Shin Gil. I did everything I could to find out the funeral location and information I should know as the father but could not find out anything. So I received only the basic information through a lawyer.

And there is even more things still left. I do not know what will happen from now. It does not depend on me. It depends on how they respond and answer. However, one thing is certain. Shin Gil will be buried in Paju Wonjeon. That is all. It does not matter what it takes. He is my son. Even if something happens, I hope that you will understand. Shin Gil is my son, my father's grandson, and my lineage. Shin Gil will be buried there.

Anyway, Shin Gil transformed me. I was born anew because of him. I became a different person. I became a different person from who I was five days ago. I became a totally different person from before. I will become a better person from now. Shin Gil made me into a better person. I will become a better person for Shin Gil.

I will come by to speak with everyone once in a while. Is that okay? [Yes.] I want to keep it short today. I do not want to preach. Thank you for your prayers and *jeongsung*. I know that Shin Gil will go to a good place. Please do not worry about me and do not worry about Shin Gil. Please have conviction. Thank you.

What Father Is Doing
January 8, 2006

How are you doing? *(Good.)* Good, I'm doing fine too. It's been a while. It's been, what? Ten years, something like that? I didn't come here to talk about me. Me—that's my problem, not yours.

I want to talk about, "What Father Is Doing," and I'm here to help you. So, where should I start? Have you been attending Father's speeches, Father's rallies? What do you think is Father's main point? Why does he think that speech rallies are necessary? Do you know they're necessary? Do you feel it? Do you feel it in your heart? Do you feel it in your gut? Do you feel it in your body? *(Yes!)* Well, I don't think so.

Let's start with the bridge over the Bering Strait. It's close to 50 miles long over wretched waters, 48 miles or something like that. There was some kind of feasibility study done on this about 10 years ago shown on a documentary that still is being aired on the Learning Channel. They constantly update the costs, but it's doable, it is doable. If you can tunnel your way between England and continental Europe, it is doable, sure. We do have technology, it's just tremendous, astronomically expensive. How do you afford it? Many countries have to come into play and if you talk about the Bering Strait, basically you're talking about America, the Soviet Union, [and] China. All these must come into play. It's a big, big, big responsibility. And unless you have some kind of practical wherewithal in terms of politics and economics, it is very difficult, okay? But it is doable, and that's where we start.

How do you start anything, when you haven't done anything, and when it's never been done before? Where do you start? So, okay, in order to understand Father's reality, you have to understand a very simple concept, why is he here?! What is he here to restore?! And then, who are you? What are you made of? When you look at yourselves is there some kind of universal common point that we can all declare in unison, regardless of your culture and all the influences and background? You all come from different backgrounds and environments, and have different thought styles. Then is there something that is universal?

So, what is that? How are you made? If you have to define yourself, if you have to define yourself, how would you define yourself? *(Children of God/Child of God.)* Okay, well let's put all that together. Simply put, how many levels do you think you got? One, two, three, ... ten, ... twenty, ... million? Simply put, look at yourself first. You think you're a spiritual being right? You struggle to be one. Okay, we'll talk about spirit. And you want to be intelligent, right? You want to be smarter than the next guy who's sitting next to you, right? And you're a physical being and it plays out whether you want to be tougher than the other guy next to you or whatever. It becomes apparent that that matters to everybody. You measure each other based on those conditions. Very simply three conditions, spirit, mind, and body. I think that's universal.

If you're going to start anything, if you're going to try to reason anything and try to communicate to the rest of the world beyond yourself you have to find some kind of basic
commonality where you can create a focus from which you can create some kind of uniformity in the end. Some reason, some rationality. Without that basis there is no rationality, there's not even a birth of it. It doesn't matter, if you want to sell an icicle to an Eskimo, you have to have this basic pattern.

So, having said that, what's Father's condition? What's Father's life? What's Father's course? To me it's very simple. It echoes these three things. It basically echoes that individual manifestation only on a larger scale, that's about it. So, all you need to do is always focus on what that is. What that individual responsibility is that magnifies to whatever level. That's the key point of understanding what the hell Father's doing. Don't look at it any other way. If you do, you are an idiot. So, all this historical stuff, what is—what does it represent? It's just preparing the way for the messiah? Do you believe in the messiah? Okay, so I'm talking to this in-crowd here. You believe that crap, so be it. Excuse my language! So be it. Okay, everything exists to receive that spiritual entity. That's the beginning point. But Father's course goes opposite. Restoration is the opposite. That means it has to restore the intellect and the body, right? You can see that plainly in history.

With ideology, there are ideological wars. On the horizontal plane just put Cain and Abel into the scene. Why? Because it's a conflict! We went through the Cold War, right? Ideologically, yeah? That kind of stuff, that kind of stuff. That's the intellectual stuff, crazy intellectual stuff, right? Now it comes to the physical stuff, and that's about it. China will be the richest nation on earth in about a decade. Everybody knows that. That creates conflict with America. That's similar right? They all want to be rich. It's not like "I don't believe in God, and you believe in God—so I'm going to kill you, you mother ... ." You know I used to curse more. It's been a while since I've been here, but now I'm going to try to hold back as much as I can! That's about it. And when that happens, whenever that happens, it's a great time for us. Why? Because now we have something to work with, as long as there's a conflict of interests, Parents can always put it right. Isn't that sad but true.

Then what? It's interesting because then we'll be connecting pretty much every archangel nation—America, Soviet Union, and China. Any time you talk about amenities and prices of course there's gonna be interests there. Why? Because of oil. Why do you think you're rich? When you're rich, you have money to buy stuff and you can spend as much of it as you want. So of course, in these backward areas they know your weaknesses. They know the indulgent nature of capitalism. That's basically what they feed on. It doesn't matter whether it's theocracy or dictatorship, it doesn't matter. Why, because ultimately in the end they have to play to the people. That's what they're afraid of. And whether you like it or not there's no way you can stop that anymore.

I mean even 10 or 15 years ago there wasn't stuff to buy, it was too expensive, but now it's cheaper and it's global, you know? You're talking about 10s of millions of dollars and they're so goddamn— excuse my language!—available to all. So knowing all this you see that Father's incredible stuff is doable. It's not that difficult. As long as you believe in what you are.

How many Christians out there want to see Father as the messiah? I remember a long time ago, about 17 years ago, I was watching the 700 channel—I talked about this to you. Pat Robertson actually said on television, "How can that little yellow man be the messiah?" What the … , what does he look like then? Blonde hair, blue eyes? There was some TV show on that said that at the very least Jesus is not blonde haired, he's got brunette hair. That's funny. Do you think they really want to be judged, they want the messiah to come and judge them? What's he going to look like? What does the messiah look like?

There's a simple kind of step even when it comes to Father's course. And Father himself had to start with the whole spirit, mind and body stuff, kind of like teacher, parent, and now what do you say? It's very difficult for some of you to understand. Teacher is the body stuff, you understand me? I mean for many parents, I'm sure a lot of you had that parental experience. You don't even feel like a parent when you're dealing with these little monkeys, you know what I'm saying? They're little monkeys, they're not even humans. You try to teach them stuff, you know? You can't even try to be a parent to them, they don't understand what you're talking about. You're basically dealing with physical monkeys.

And look, just think about it, someone told me you understand, you have this guy in the church hierarchy, he used to be the president of Unification Church and he goes around to these seminaries and he's trying to make a point. After all this time, he finally comes to the realization of Father's success. He was trying to figure out why others of the 36 Couples failed. He gets his ideas from birth and from children, and he sees why there's conflict. The reason they failed, his conclusion is, is because their beliefs and thinking are trapped in children's mentality. They can't break out of that, even when they are trying to think about Father and Father's nature. Father was chosen, so they think somehow that they're the chosen one too. That's not how it is.

Why do you think even Christians think about birthright anyway? Why don't you play that to the man himself. You don't want to put that just on elder son crap. You know what I mean? You want to be a messiah, go ahead and be it, you jerk. Why would anyone in their right mind want to be that miserable? But misery is relative, right? Pain is relative, right? So is the opposite, right? Who gives a care?! What do you want? So, it's up to you too, that's relative too.

So, I didn't come here to be anything else. I've really have seen a lot of crap these days, just recently, I mean unthinkable crap. And I don't really give a curse. You know why, because I'm going to let someone else judge that, not me. I'll move on. I'll try my best to find some forgiveness in my heart. Okay? Okay. So how can we help America? Let's move on.

How can we help America? What the hell is America anyway? You know all my brothers have gone to school and got high levels of education. If only if we could use those kind of funds, all the blessings that we had in the past in a certain way. Okay, sure, but that's in the past. And Father did it for his reasons, not yours. I mean, I have more sympathy when it comes to that—when it comes to the Japanese members than American members, that's for sure. Because I deal with those interesting types. I like colorful things, colorful stuff. Even dealing with anything that's colorful, I don't mind. I think that's interesting, it's exciting, it's stimulating. Yeah, sometimes it's the absolute opposite and it's a pain in the butt, but that's the stuff, that's reality. So be it.

Now, having said that all this, why did Father do that, for what reason? Obviously to make the conditions of the spirit, the spiritual foundation. And what did he do? He absolutely tried every second, almost looking like wasting cash just to create all these organizations, all this stuff that's come and gone. Just to give, give, give to the intellect. You have no idea. I mean, if I talk about it, it will blow everybody's mind. It is astronomical, and where did that come from? That was the blessing that Father envisioned, even on just a physical level—it's in shambles and that's shameful. And whose fault was that? It's our fault, so we have to fix it, okay? This is nobody else's problem, but ours and that's about it. You don't want to be stupid. If you want to advertise, you go to school to learn how to properly advertise, you dumb monkeys. Don't do the obvious stuff. And we can go on and succeed because there is still a whole lot of blessing here. There is. It is doable. Why do I believe that? Okay, since you pushed me.

You know, I watch my competitors. I watch those people speak on Sundays, new comers like Joel Osteen. I pay attention to all those guys, saying all their deal, okay, okay. All packaging. Don't try to give me that. And what do they want to do? What do they want to do? They want to set an example, be an example of something for others. Okay, that's okay, we can compete with that. We can do that too. Let's just start with that. We can do that too.

We can start with the body first, we can focus on the body, the world of needs. The thing about materialism is that when that controls everything, whether you like it or not, you're not really thinking about anything, it just consumes you completely. The physical stuff. When you look at America especially, you know pilgrims stopped coming to America to find God hundreds of years ago, 17th century. People come to America to find opportunity, riches! They want to be God, they want to be rich. That's about it. There's no other reason to come to America. You don't find here, you don't find any other reason. That's about it. It's not even the freedom, it's about opportunity.

What freedom?—freedom to be what? I mean what if you were religious? American freedom is very offensive to you, you know what I'm saying? It has nothing to do with freedom. It just says that so many times. It likes to say it. And people, you know always like to put their best foot forward, whether it's true or not is irrelevant. When they think that they have the power to do so, then they will do so. Based on how they want to be perceived, because without that perception, you don't get accolades. America needs to have that kind of self-glorification so it can fuel itself, in terms of its need for consumption and excess, so be it, and that's reality.

Okay, so when you're talking about America's freedom, in essence it's basically capitalism. What does capitalism create? What's important in capitalism? Opportunity. But if you're so obsessed with opportunity you're obviously going to become an opportunist. If you become an opportunist, you are not going to be a very caring person for other people. You're going to be self-centered, and if you're a self-centered s.o.b. you're not going to be a good role model for the rest of the world, because you're so caught up in your own individualistic need. You're a pure individualist.

Then what? When you create a frickin' climate of that stuff and you encourage that stuff, how do you think that society will end up? Do you really see a future in that? No, I don't think so. Somebody will use the United States as the wrong example and try to modify it to somehow be better than your stupid dumb ass, that's about it. It might be a little bit, but still in the end, they'll succeed. Because you're going down the wrong path, point of no return and that's about it. It doesn't matter how much you try to deny it, it will happen eventually. It will start from you and it will go up the line of your family; you'll contaminate even your grandfather, your mother and your father, never mind your children and your posterity. Because that's all they see.

Is that the American dream? I don't think so. Somewhere along the line the American dream has passed away. I'm not American. I'm proud not to be an American. I can be called American technically because I've been living here over thirty years. But I came here because my Father had his mission, that's about it, I tagged along. I guess he carried me along so I had no choice about it. So be it. It doesn't matter. That's not the point. But Father spent so much time and energy, and so much stuff; if I actually started listing, line item by line item, it would blow your frickin' mind. But I'm not going to do that—not today. There'll be plenty of time for that crap later. But that's all in the past.

What's important is what's going to happen in the future. And what can you do. There are times that—I'll share since I'm in a sharing mood I'm going to share. Okay you know I let myself, normally I don't behave that way, but I did at one point in my life, and I do regret it, but that's why I'm telling you—I let it go. I just let it go. I didn't want to resolve it. I didn't want to deal with it. I didn't want a solution. I just let it go. I just let it go. I just let that anger just go. And it grew. And it grew. And I realized in the end why it was growing and started getting out of control. Because everything is connected. And that's the realization that I had. The reason that it was growing and getting bigger and bigger was because I let it go and it connected to all sorts of other stuff. And that's the thing about living, being a human being, is that you're connected. And when you know it's not good for you get rid of it as fast as you can!

I believe that in the future we can do a whole lot of good stuff. Why? Because we're unique damn it! We're absolutely unique! And we can prove that we got something better. Hey, we'll compete and we'll win. We're here to stay and we'll compete until the end. And let's compete, okay, it doesn't matter. In goodness, screw badness, in goodness let's see who's the better man in the end; you know what I'm saying? And that's why to a point there's an attraction to democracy. Because it's kind of brotherly, you know what I'm saying, right? Because that's also a very important part of restoration, not just restoring Adam's position but Cain and Abel too. Then, we can win. And let it happen. I'd rather have a democracy to work with than some kind of theocracy. You know what I'm saying? There're a lot of nuts out there—crazy people "la, la, la"—I'm not saying anything. If you know me, it's just a joke, okay? I'm just very direct, in many ways. The way I express is very shallow, and sometimes it works. Not all the time. That's about it.

Anyway, I believe we can do this, okay? You know what I'm saying? This is kind of the first time for me in a long time. I'm going to keep it short, okay? And I'll try to stay away from notes like I used to. If I have notes I'll speak longer, that's why I don't have notes! Anyway, you guys take care, I'm fine. You know things will happen the way they should. And I see tremendous hope for the future. And thank you for your concern and your prayers. And I'll do my best to help you guys as much as I can. To share with you, and be with you, okay?

Thank you.

How Deep Is Your Love?
January 22, 2006

How are you doing? *(Good.)* Good, nice to see you again.

Before I start, some people on the ground/underground told me that some people have problem with my colorful words. My advice to you is—stay home! Having said that, I'll try to make the choice of my words as dull as possible. Can't guarantee anything, but I'll try. Today, I came back from spending some time in Hawaii. It's kind of a new start for me, and I'm volunteering to do this, and it's important for me. And that's why I might as well start with something general. Let's start with something big. Let's think about love. "How Deep Is Your Love?"

I guess if you talk to people in general and observe how they use the language, the word love, they use it in a very secular way. On a surface level, they do use the word love a lot. "I love chocolate," "I love Gucci," "I love money," "I love to have more power," "I would love to have that position or this position," "I would love to spend just one night with that famous person." Love gets used a lot. In a way, secularly speaking, love is almost like a literary supplement to highlight or heighten the value or description of your needs. And that's pretty much what the word love has come down to. That's how people use the word love in their lives. And just think about it. That is the definition and description which people in general in society constantly share with one another.

But what is the true meaning of love? Does the meaning of love end with the definition and value that we at this point in time are comfortable with or accept? Or does it have something of a greater meaning? I guess that is why people seek religion. Because something inside tells them, maybe it's the inner voice. We have to understand in the individual self. We all understand through the Principle teaching that there is a spirit, mind, and body. You have physical body, you have intellect, and there is the spirit itself. Even in self, there are these three stages. We understand that because of Father's teaching. But in the external world and in the secular world, the understanding of even the simplest thing that we pursue, that we hold value, because of what we understand, what we believe—what others believe is pretty foreign for us. We understand why they want those things, why they love those things because at one time or the other you loved those things too. But you want something more. That's why you seek something greater. That's why you try to understand God. And it's a lifelong process. It's never ending.

How do you understand the depth of love? You know, because when you look at God's way of love, many times you have to accept a lot of things that you don't want to accept. You don't want a definition or a value of love to be something with suffering, pain, and misery. You have to be sadistic to like that kind of stuff! If you are a prize fighter, maybe you can teach and train yourself to love pain because that's how you make a living. But beyond that, it's very difficult to accept. Because in many cases, in the life of pursuing God's course, or God's ways, or learning about God's definition of things in life, it is opposite of what people consider love to be in a secular world. I like chocolate, too, but if you like chocolate too much, you are going to get fat. Yeah, money is good, sure. You can buy a mansion, you can buy not just one, buy 10 of them. Have it strewn all around the world, take time out and go to those places, juice up, try to conquer the world again and be the richest man on earth. All those things, you like to talk about it, and you like to think about it at times. Sure!

There are many ways to go about if you just don't think about those things. Maybe it's because I have learned about those things, almost even to the point of brainwashing ever since I was born. Maybe I can't, or it's very difficult for me, to part from what I learned, just cut away from it. Because I don't want to go down in history as such and such and such. Because that is ingrained into me. There are ways to go about pursuing that kind of stuff, but if I do, I'm going to go down in history because of my lineage, what I belong to, something that I can't ever change. I mean, just because you change my children's name from Moon to Hong, that does not mean they will forever be Hongs. People can do that. Crazy people do those kinds of stuff. Without my permission, they can burn my son's body and deprive me of my last right to see my son. They can do those kinds of stuff. And what happens after that? I think about the consequences. No matter how, at times, how difficult it is for me to accept certain things, I have to think about those things because I believe in it. How I came to accept that, that's not the problem. The situation is that I believe in it. That's the problem. Because I accept that I have to deal with that issue. Because I believe in the consequences. That's why I have to make and interpret things based on that direction. And that's why it's very difficult for me to try to go the opposite direction. I struggle with it. I wish, in a way, sometimes when you think about giving excuses and stuff, you can rationalize things. Yes, I could do those kinds of stuff, too, but why? What am I doing it to? Who am I doing it to? Why? For what reason? It's just better to go, "Hey, get off," and not talk about it at all. But that's not important. That's not important.

Anyway, I'm here because I want to be here, not because it's my duty. So, no matter what, I'm going to make the best of it. I know what duty feels like. Pretty much I was there for a long time every Sunday for eight years. But this is not something of that nature. This is something different. I feel that I have something to share, and I'm going to do my best to do so.

So having said that, how do you go about trying to understand God's love? First of all, I have to understand my parental love. If you want to go up, everybody has somebody above, right? Even messiah has a father. So, immediately, that's where I would start. Let's say, that's your first starting point. Of course in life, you have bosses and stuff and other subject and object relationship, but let's just be intimate. The best way you can start in general is that we all have parental relationship with our own self. So that's the fundamental, that's primeval subject and object relationship that we can start with.

In order to understand your father, you have to understand yourself first. You have to understand, 'Where is my limit?' and 'Where do I belong?' in this relationship. Many people I see in the secular world, of course, they like certain positions, and they will do anything to attain it. But many times, just getting it is not the end of the story, it's only half of the story. Then you have to fulfill. You have to understand the responsibility, be accountable to the position, the demands of the position that you have just acquired with any and all means necessary. So even just having the position is not the end of the story. That's just the beginning. So just start with yourself. Don't think about any other position that you would like to achieve or attain. Think about yourself. I'm father's son. Okay, what am I? Who am I? What is my limitation? How should I define myself? When you talk about definition of yourself, you have to understand the limits of your responsibility. And what is that? What is the main nature of my responsibility, what is the merit of my responsibility? What is the expectation? When you talk about merit, you have to connect it to your expectation of the position. Otherwise, there is no meaning. So, when you talk about expectations, how do you go about trying to understand the meaning of that stuff if you don't begin to try to understand who your subject in a relationship is? I mean, who is your subject? Because that is the basic starting point of the relationship you are trying to achieve. That is the beginning of understanding everything greater, ultimately God. If father is too far from me, then I'm going to start with my mother or something. You know what I'm saying? I have an older sister. If my older sister can be a guide, an indicator for me to understand or familiarize myself with the basic go-about or direction as to how I should approach understanding my mother, then maybe that's where I should start from.

Sometimes you have to take things step by step. You can't always think big all the time. Especially if you are really serious, if you want it to be meaningful. If you really want to find quality, and achieve quality, then you really have to take caution, right? You have to do things step by step. You can't always take giant leaps. Maybe in general as humanity we can, but not as an individual. So that's where you should start. And if you get to know that, then maybe you'll have a little more understanding about how better to approach things, what kind of direction you should choose to make that contact. And from it and through it, you can start to build something out of it, something more meaningful. And if you have this kind of prepared knowledge, then you can try it out. It can be exciting. And it can be more stimulating for you because you have these kinds of properties that you can bounce things off from. And because you have all sorts of greater options, then maybe you'll hit the mark. Because ultimately in the end, you have to make it work somehow. That's your responsibility.

We understand God as a suffering God, and He's trying to make it work. So in long waiting, of course it can be perceived as something painful, miserable, tremendous suffering, never ending agony, and concern, worry. But you have to start somewhere. So starting somewhere, I feel that you have to understand who you are. And try to be better, make the best preparation possible. And try out all sorts of different things, and find the thing that works to make that connection upward properly. In the past, I just did it. I just did those kinds of things. I did what I was told to do. And I was kind of a crazy kid. I knew all things about the world when I was young. There came a point in my life I changed, and I did everything I was told, and I did my best. That's about it. I might as well. I don't like it. I really don't like it. But if I'm going to do it, I might as well do my best, try my best, give it all out. What you see is what you get. Why would I hide anything from you? The only reason I don't talk about it is because I can't. I'm not afraid of men. You can kill me. You can shoot me dead. You can poison me. I'm not afraid of you. Why should I lie to you? Well, you know what? I think about myself first.

Let's just talk about men, mankind. The things that I have, the things that men have problem with, dealing with in relationships is, I simplify it to, it comes down to three words, three definitions. 'Triple A,' I call it: arrogance, aggression, and ambition. That's pretty much the basic premise in which that we deal with in terms of subjectivity. In femininity, in women's stuff, I call it 'Triple S' to make it simple: sensitivity, sensibility, and seduction. Why do men have problem with aggression, and arrogance, and ambition? Put it nicely, ambition is, "Oh, he has high goals." Arrogance is, "Oh, he's proud." Aggression is,

"Oh, he's so tough and powerful." When you look at the physical self, and intellectual self, and spiritual self, that 'Triple A' stuff has a different meaning in each, but all the different kind of words have a similar value in the end. There is a simile in there. When you talk about the messiah, you talk about him as arrogant, ambitious, and aggressive, but it just has different words describing that basic nature of it. The words that I have just used, that's about it. How would you want to put it? Absolute? Person who demands absolute obedience? Absolute faith? All those properties that we have, have meaning behind it. But we abuse it, we misuse it. Many things, when it's mishandled—it's not the gun that killed people, it's the people who pull the trigger of the gun that kills people—everything that we have as a tool, we can misuse it. Our intelligence, first of all, is a tool. Therefore, all the words that we create to enrich our lives beyond monkeys, are tools so we can enrich our lives and grow harmoniously in an infinite way in all sorts of possibilities. Even music, everything that we have, it's a tool. It's only a tool. A tool to do what? Of course, that's what we have to figure out. It can take a lifetime.

You'll go through the journey of defining, redefining, and revising the value of words that we normally use in our day-to-day lives. And hopefully, everyone can always enhance the quality of it. I mean, that would be the ideal world if everybody pursues that kind of endeavor and if they never ever stop enhancing their quality of the things that they understand. Trying to enhance the quality, the value, and the definition of even the basic things that we understand till the day we're there, when we die, never stopping. If we can push till the day we die, yes, we can change the world. Yes, that would be the beginning of the ideal world. Because we struggle with the things that we describe as our needs. That is why we want to have religion, because we want to unify that stuff. The basic stuff that we rely upon to create community, to create society.

Think about yourself. Think about yourself in just dealing with a basic understanding of words that we use to communicate with one another. I mean, there is a difference when you use certain words in basic language with your children and your immediate family. And even the same meaning will have a different kind of tone. You will choose to use different kind of words that have similar meaning, but you use it in a different way or choose different words when you go to a tribal meeting, a social meeting, or on a national stage, or on a global stage. This is kind of informal for me, that is why sometimes I would curse. But if this were a public rally, then I know it's for the public I would choose not to use certain language. Do you know what I am saying? Who cares if I use colorful language at times? I don't think that would demean the value of what I'm trying to say. It's the point that I'm trying to make that's important. I don't think you should be distracted by such frivolous things. Most of the time that kind of a person doesn't really make it in this world. People who are like that—I don't think you are going to be somebody one day. It's very easy to criticize, but it's very difficult to create something. If you understand the value of that, the basic things that are important in life, and know how to go about achieving it, you wouldn't be that critical, that cynical. Because what's important is the essence of the stuff that you are trying to create. And why do you try to create anyway? You try to do it for God. You are not doing it for the money, right? You are doing it to help your fellow men, right? And money is secondary. It's not a primary concern. If blessing comes, so be it. And if I have more, I can give more. That's about it. I'm not going to take it with me. I see my sister come and try to fundraise for Colonel Park. Did you guys give? I gave a long time ago. And I see people sometimes trying to justify yourselves. You try to pick and choose what is favorable to you. I don't like to make excuses. I'd rather just go.

Anyway, if you talk about all this love, there is so many things that we have to work out even within ourselves before when we paint the picture upward, try to advertise as who we are. But, you have to put up real stuff, you know? What you are has to be in the stuff. You have to put the proof in the stuff. When I think about Shin Gil, I feel sorry. In my heart, I feel sorry that I couldn't spend much time with him. I wasn't allowed to. The court wouldn't let me. It was a unique circumstance, unprecedented. In a way, I know that is my victory when it comes to what had happened. But I feel sorry that I couldn't spend much time with him. I really wanted to. It was just about to be at the point where I could spend some time because he was just days from legal age, legally independent. That's the kind of thing that gets you. You're planning all this stuff, and well, I just have to wait a little longer. That's about it. We all know. We just have to know how to die well. That's what's important.

Even when we look at our individual lives with our own family, we all are trying constantly to understand the value of love. Normally, you start with language, all the words that you use. Basically that's where everything begins: with an idea, and the exchange of that idea. We have to understand the eternal concept of divine love, so we have to begin somewhere. It starts with words. Words are very, very important to little kids, and the meaning of them. They are constantly asking, and if they somehow pick up certain words, they try to use it in their language. When they communicate with each other or with me, they are constantly trying to expand their understanding of more and more words. Many times in that expansion, they feel love. It's kind of interesting because it has to be something personal, something for which they can recognize the value. If we talk about something of value, because they are little kids with their limited understanding, it's important. They feel loved. And you somehow promise them stuff, that "I'm going to give you more, more, and more stuff," and the promise of that expansion of their needs that they like that gives them all sorts of tingling sensation in their heads and they are happy. Because they understand the importance of that possibility. Because it's going to give them some kind of fulfillment, some joy.

Of course you start with the physical self. Pretty much it's these needs that have value to those little kids, very, very tangible stuff. That's where you begin. Then as you grow, as you mature, normally you start to see when teenagers reach a certain age, cut close to about maybe fifteen, sixteen, or seventeen, their friends become more important than your whole family, your brothers and sisters, your father and mother. They start to become tribal. They go beyond a certain phase, they go beyond the family and they start to be tribal, then they expand to society, and nation. And that matches something in Korea. Their big age is 60 years old. So that means if you give yourself from 0 to 10, 10 to 20, 20 to 30, and so forth, one decade at a time and spread it out like that, it will take about 60 years to get to the global stage of some sort. If you have a defined pathway and you have preplanned some kind of program, if you are successful at it, most likely you will reach that stage, that phase. So, in Korea, when you reach 60 years old of age, that's where you begin again. Most likely, in the past, people didn't live that long, so if you reached 60 years of age, obviously you're getting a second chance in life. That's kind of past stuff, but there is a philosophy behind that. And that's pretty much where your life begins. That's my interpretation.

So the value of the needs changes as you move up in matter, right? From family to tribe, society, to nation, and to the world, the value will change. As you go beyond it, of course the value will change in terms of your needs. It might have started with a bunch of toys in the beginning, but it changes as it moves up the value of your needs, the definition of your needs. Because you ultimately have to understand what God sees defined as love or how God values love. That's what you have to understand. That's what we're trying to understand. We constantly have to upgrade our values and definition of our needs. That's the most important thing I feel if you try, if you want to understand God's love, you can't just get stuck in certain kind of level and say, "This is God's love." I think that's stupid. I think that's blasphemy. Because in the end, the basic direction of love, all that plus and minus, good and evil stuff and the tree of love, it all was there as part of the Garden of Eden.

So the important thing is, what is the next step? You just have to choose one direction. That's what being absolute is. Why? Because that's what's in yourself. If selfishness is bad and living for the sake of others is good, that's plus and minus, and that's what we start with. That reality will never change. We'll always have the individual self to deal with. We have to try to accomplish that task forever. Certain things can be habitual. We understand there are some properties there. There are tools out there, even built-in innate tools. We just have to trigger them. We can use these to automate that kind of process. But all those things have to be triggered. They have to be connected and triggered. We do have all the tools. But you have to understand what that is, and trigger it, keep it moving. Then you can automate it, you can become habitual. That's the basic stuff, you just have to know how to use it in a functional way. You can give yourself a lot of bad habits, but you can also give yourself good habits, too. You can teach yourself to give, right? Because there is great joy in that. There is pleasure in that. It's better in your pocket than my pocket, and you see that person just light up and you get a kick out of it. Even with the simple kindness of giving stuff, there is pleasure in it. And you can make that into a habit. You can get addicted to that kind of stuff, too, and not only the things that will kill you. It's how you choose it. You have all the stuff. Even things that can kill you can also save your life, right? Like vaccinations, for example.

There are all sorts of stuff we just have to understand the meaning of, understand why it exists, and define it properly. And as we heighten the definition into greater truth, greater sensitivity and sensibility, then yes, everything can benefit us based on right choice making. Everything. It's up to us. Some people get there a little earlier, that's why you have to share this kind of stuff, right? You have a social duty to do this if you are civilized, right? So everything is that basic, we already have it, we just don't use it properly. We don't stress it enough at times. It gets buried away because someone is vainglorious. That's about it. That's the only reason we struggle.

Let's think about it. We can focus on the kind of resources that we have. We are absolutely unique. In certain ways, we can have more cash than any large corporation in the world in a given year. People will envy it. All right. That's something for people to envy. That's reality. At the same time, we are a unique church. Why? Because we put emphasis on blessing. And we actually have this kind of reality. All those international blessings coming together, seeing the importance of being engrafted, understanding the importance of lineage, and trying to establish that kind of foundation of substance based on the ideal of who we are. That's very unique. We can talk about all sorts of stuff, racial propensity or any other thing. There's a lot of stuff that we have to push forward and challenge the world with. But you can't do it alone, you need an army. We can always start a television network with certain amount of money, and certain kinds of characters. Yes, we can make it work if we have some kind of a prepared investment capital and we are willing to use it solely for that reason. Sure, we'll make it work one way or the other in 10 years. Yes, if they can do it, we can do it. Absolutely. That time will come. Father will do his best to complete his mission while he's breathing. Period. He has the right way. That's about it. Do the best you can. Father, I hope you are successful. That's all I can do. I'll try to help you, though, if I can. Sure, okay, I'll do that. But taking it to the next step? Sure, we can do that stuff. We already have that foundation. We just have to act upon it. And that day will come. I know. I absolutely believe this. It's not that difficult. It's just we already have it. We ought to do it. It's a matter of doing it. We can win. That's about it.

You measure your love. How deep is your love? How far away from God are you? What degree? What kind of love? How do you define love? How do you define your needs? Measure yourself. I don't know you, just as you don't know me that well. If some of you think you know me, you only know me because I had my obligations. I had my duty to stand in front of you before a long time. That's about it. Pretty much, that's about it. To me, the reason I like creativity is because it keeps me simple. Some kinds of process is a pain in the neck and very complicated. So I like my life to be simple. I need that balance. That's why I can't really understand people who criticize. They don't really understand the creative process, they have so much time in their hands and they have so much energy. They criticize, spewing out this nonsensical garble and superficial analysis. Do something meaningful. If you really want to use your head, make something meaningful. Then you will truly appreciate the simplicity of life. You can't start to see the essence of stuff unless your life is somehow balanced. When it's all jumbled up, you're not going to find it.

If you want to understand and find God's love, find something, bring some kind of balance into your life. In order to do that, you have to try to do something meaningful, make something meaningful, create something meaningful. You can start to recreate even just the basic definition of things that are important to you, the needs that are important to you. Do something that can actually be meaningful to you that can change you. If you can't really stand outward yet, then start with yourself first. Only then, you can start to see some clarity. Otherwise, everything is jumbled up.

You only have this cynicism, criticism, all these jumbled thoughts in your head and you're not going to find anything. Simply start with the basic things first. First step first. First things first. Find the new definition of life, the things that are important to you, the needs. I don't want to say love. That's too big for me even. Even I am trying to redefine the basic stuff. I don't even want to talk about, or even think about love, but I'm leading up to that. That's about it. That's my faith. I hope I have given you something that you can use.

Anyway, take care, okay?

Family
January 29, 2006

Good morning. *(Good morning.)* I'm in the process of debugging myself, so if I'm slow, just bear with me today, okay? Today, I want to share with you about, "Family."

How many people come from a large family? More than 10? I have an older sister, older brother, and many younger brothers and sisters. When you look at my family situation, there is always an issue all the time that resonates all the time, somebody has a little more than the other guy. I guess it's a general tradition. Even in Western culture too. There still are many countries in the West that continue to hold on to a certain kind of historical tradition. For example, let's say, having a monarchy. They do have certain very strong attachment to that monarchy line and way of thinking in terms of government and social structure. So there is a basic structure that we pretty much accept. I didn't mention Asian societies because there it's pretty much a given. In China, Japan, Korea, certain traditions are untouchable. They're permanent, and always will be permanent.

There are certain things that we all understand basically, even when it comes to speaking, only personally, about my family situation. My older sister always complained, even when I was growing up, "He gets it more than me. I want to be equal. I want more fairness." Of course, all my little brothers and sisters are like that too, they want that stuff, more than anything. Because I guess, someone, some unfortunate soul like me, ends up being the primary cause of all that ruckus. So when you think about that situation, I don't know, is that a blessing? It depends on how you look at it, I guess.

What if you have nothing? I don't think it's a blessing. What if you have everything? Is that a blessing? I don't think so either. You can call it a primary source of greater conflict, as people can't really accept certain things just because they're there. There is always a story behind the story, always. Because we're human. As a human society, even on the microcosmic level of simple family, that stuff is real. There's a story behind the story. Why? Because we're individuals who make up something greater. And it moves up. So as you move up, obviously the story gets larger and more complicated. That's because there's a story behind the story behind that story, blah, blah, oh, I don't know. So that is the basic complex reality that you have to sort through if you want to do something to make change in a society. So you have to try to understand it basically, even when you talk principle. You talk about principle in a very simple way. We were the first ones to stand on principle. But you must go up through the rigors of the basic workshop up to this workshop. We need to try to understand the reality of that subject-object relationship. That's where we have to start. Let's just start with that. What is the point of trying to go through the rigors of being educated about that relationship of subject and object, which is fundamental in the Divine Principle? Because, it reminds us how to think, how to approach, how to analyze, and how to understand, not just myself but that guy, the subject. That is the endless effort of trying to pound the basics into you. That's the essence of what we have to walk away with after hearing those things over and over and over again. Not just knowing myself, but also about that other guy.

That is the basics, the primary reason why we go through the rigors of those workshops and being drilled with things over and over and over again. Because it's difficult. Why? Because it's ongoing. Many times, the greater difficulty in practical reality, the more intensely things begin to happen. You have to understand and learn at the same time in real time. And it's changing constantly. It's not always just linear and stagnant, it's constantly in flux. Many times the peaks are higher, many times the valleys are lower—it's not always consistent even if it were nothing more than following the course of a ripple. It is very, very organic. That's the problem that we face. So based on even a simple measurement, or standard measurement, we have difficulty because sometimes reality defies even something as simple as that. Sometimes peaks are above it, sometimes valleys are under it. So how do you measure yourself when things like that happen? In most circumstances you can answer that with the simple question: What is my duty? What is my responsibility to somehow secure myself, to give me some kind of stability? Because in the end, you are the one who has to be in control of yourself in terms of your stability, right? Because it's you who have to be in control of your actions in the end. Right or wrong, you have to face the consequences. If you don't want to be responsible, then go ahead and deny your own self. You can do whatever you want. But if you want to be responsible, then you have to take the responsibility to create stability for yourself.

How do you go about building that? Let me just start from myself. I have an older sister. I know she wants to be me. And I have a lot of younger brothers and sisters who want to be me, too. Some have that desire more than others. That's fine with me. So I think about, "How am I to fit in this basic family situation that we all have?" As a person who is standing in front of you, who has a position whether I like it or not, this is not voluntary stuff. It was given. I had no choice. I didn't make it. I let myself in for that? It didn't come like that. Hey, you're there. You're stuck with it forever. All right, so what can I do with this stuff? So on the horizontal level, I find it amazing. My little sisters constantly complain, "I want to be treated like the boys, I want equal treatment. How come all the boys get preferential treatment?" Blah, blah, blah, on and on. I don't care, okay, no problem. You can have it. But then some of the other boys might not agree. Pretty much, the girls want what the boys have whether he's younger or older, but the boys, they want what the older brother has. And together we're in a unique situation because we have Cain and Abel families and children centering on Father. Cain families, they want what Abel family has. There's all this kind of chasing around stuff. What are you chasing basically in the end? That's about it. That's the cause of the problem, much of it. Pretty much, general conflict, 99.99 percent of the time, it's about that. It's very rare to fight over something else. That's it. And it starts from your family whether you like it or not. I'm not special, we're not special in this case. Do you understand me? Everybody has this problem. That's the sad part. That's the problem that needs to be resolved.

So, how would you go about that? What would be the ideal position of an ideal elder son? Let's say the boys are over here and the girls are over here. If I'm stuck in the middle, because I pretty much have to stand in the middle, I have to allow them to come in and have access to what's above, to the vertical. That would be the ideal elder brother. Not always hogging it but more than that, the selfless thing. If you can do that, always, then you pretty much can create peace all the time. Would you say that fits theoretically? It seems so simple, but it's so hard to do so. Why? Many times, we have different things that we like. I guess because there are character differences or personality differences, we like certain things more than other kinds of things. And many times, it's difficult to accommodate all that difference and that's what causes the problem. And because everybody has their own demands—and of course the reality is constantly changing, and hopefully it's moving forward—and those are expanding, growing larger and stronger, sometimes that growth is not fast enough to cover the demand. And you seem powerless or you seem, I guess, not caring to the people who are demanding. That's about it. If only those who are demanding something could at times just be a little patient, we could recover from that kind of potential crisis. But sometimes, everyone becomes distant in these kinds of situations.

What's the stuff? What do you think? You fill in the blank. Why do you need to have it so quickly? What are you going to do with all this stuff when you finally get everything that you want? What are you going to do with it? I see what you do with it. That's about it. I don't think that's a good thing. That's going to come and bite your behind any time soon. And I worry about that. It's not because I don't know how to do that—if you think of it, you try to avoid it. But, you have to know your limitations. You have to know your circumstances. And for some things, it's not going to work so well. That's why you don't do it. That's why you should avoid it. You walk around crap, not because you're afraid of it, it's because you don't want to step on it. I mean, if you get pissed off, you can do that, step on it. But you walk around it to avoid it because of obvious reasons. That's about it. And sometimes, we just get too hurried, and we want too many things, all the time, too quickly. Just walk away sometimes. Just step back. I don't really need it now.

If you give yourself a little more time and try to think about more positive things rather than selfish things all the time, maybe all those things, even the stuff you think you want now, might end up not that important when you mature. Give yourself a proper time to grow. I know the world is in a hurry. And if you follow that, you become obsessed with it and sensitive to that stuff. Then what do you think you're going to end up with? You'll end up being just like that, that's about it. You'll be chasing the same thing that everybody is chasing. The way they chase it, and the strategy they use to chase that stuff is nasty. It's not something you can be proud of, that you want to hold in your heart to be proud of forever. I don't think so. The glory might be temporary, but if that's what you choose, okay, I can't stop you, right? So that's about it.

So how do you start with creating an ideal world? You start with yourself, and use basic understanding of your basic family that people grow up with, and even the family that you have. If you have unresolved issues, try to make it up. Try to do something about it, start from there. Don't argue. Don't look off too far. All of you have to have that answer cleared up and properly. That's the only way we can start to influence society, alright? So if you want to go about it properly, then let's be proper. Then we can talk about it. We can make strategy that is real, that can make things happen. Otherwise, it's just talk. No one cares about just talking. There are plenty of people who can talk. Now let's talk about something that can make a difference in the end. I think that's important. That's the kind of stuff that needs to be said, and people need to talk like that. More people talk that way than try to walk it. And yes, we can have that foundation and start making things better because we have an army. We can stand on the line and cover each other's back. Some fights, you just can't do it alone. That does not mean that just because you have numbers, that you are going to automatically win, either. It's not this triangle of quality, quantity and speed, like in competition. And you really have to home in on work and sacrifice. If you don't do that, it doesn't work. Very simple.

That's all I want to share with you. What's family? Family is about learning about what's proper, proper order, subject and object relationship, and how to live with God for crying out loud. If you can't live with each other in brotherhood just because you have this elder son stuff, how do you expect to live with your parents? How do you expect to live with God? Brotherhood is just horizontal stuff. This is where we work out that ultimate quest for living with God. Rather than just shooing away these little sisters, I'm going to be an old boy and let's see what good you got. That kind of simple stuff. You do more of it, all that other stuff goes away. It's not that difficult when you have a good family.

And this is a lot of work in certain situations, because there are walls of no communication. Jump starting it is some tremendous challenge. It becomes the greatest problem and challenge. But it can be done and if it is done, no matter how difficult a hand is dealt to you, maybe when you get a moment, you can do it. In the end, it can be resolved. No problem. But given that stuff, ironing out that stuff, I think, is important at every level. One way or the other, it has to be done. And the clearer we are and more focused we are, the better soldiers we will be. No doubt about that, I believe in that stuff.

Anyway, I'm just here to perform the beauty of a pep talk, right? So that's pretty much all I have to say, I guess. Not much, as far as this topic is concerned. For a year, I said to myself, I'll be here every Sunday from here. But I have to go away for a few days, and next week, I don't think I can make it. But the week after, I'll be here. So take care.

What is Love?
February 3, 2006

How is everybody? (Good; good morning!) Good morning. When you think about love, what is love? You will die for love or you will kill for love. It can happen, right? When you really love something, it makes you want to die for it; at the same time in the extreme opposite, you will kill for it. That's what love is. Right? And everything that exists under the Sun pretty much has both extremes stemming from it.

Why is it like that? Is it for you, or is it for me? It's that stuff: it's that struggle; it's that basic struggle. I'll die for something, or I'll kill for something. It's that stuff. It's the "we" or "I" struggle, because when I'm dying for something it's not "me" it's "we." It's as simple as that; everything starts from that. And that you need to know how to answer. That's your quest in this short life. However long you think that you can live, it' short! It's not long enough for me! I know I'm dying, getting closer to my death than to my living, and that's for sure. And that is the truth that I can never deny.

And that's how it begins. Know what you want to do with your life. Is it going to be "we" or is it going to be "I"? You make the choice, and understand that life is what you got, and what you got isn't that much. And that's where we're equal. So, it doesn't matter what you got; it really doesn't matter.

Okay, you have to do your own thinking. Look, I'm not going to read a story book for you. Okay? You make your own stories - that's your life. You write your own songs. You write your own stories. That's all we do. That's the best we can do. And hopefully somebody can be inspired by it. Okay? All I can do is what I do. That's it. It's up to you what you do.

So you take care. Okay?

I may be gone for a few weeks so I'll see you later when I come back. Okay?

Something in the Middle Called Life
February 19, 2006

Good morning. *(Good morning.)* You guys like it short, right? No? What does that mean? What's a good life? I guess I have demand for a specific quantity of time. Okay, anyway. Today's topic is, "Something in the Middle Called Life."

Did you know, if there is anything you have no choice over, I guess that's birth and death, right? It's all based on birth and death and between there is something called life. People can say, "Ah, because we have a lot of technology and science, you know, you can literally create babies!" They have in fact, through in vitro fertilization; you can literally create something in a Petri dish. But there's an argument, you know, because all your fame that you achieved in understanding how things work, it's all knowledge. But the nature of the knowledge is knowing what works based on a blueprint of how things work. That is all it is.

So you know, you can't really take credit for that. Think about it. What about the kid who's born out of that circumstance. Did he have a choice to become that kind of person? Without a father or mother, going through those natural processes of becoming a child? That's why this causes a moral issue dilemma. When you take certain things out of context just because you have certain knowledge, therefore power, just because you know how to manifest certain thing that does not always mean you come to a good conclusion, right? So.

But the same is true with death, too. You can kill yourself, right? Honestly if you go, if you prepare that moment of departure, you know, get rid of whatever problem by committing suicide, there will be no more lonely children. Or even people if they're old they're doing it because they want to separate from a kind of humiliation, and indignity that comes from, I guess, social pressure or rejection. So you pick your time and you know exactly how you're gonna depart. But what does that mean? It means that you can argue that even in birth and death you can have control. But even so, there are still certain things you have no control over.

But that funny thing is called life. We think we have something in control. That's where all sorts of interesting stuff happens. Many times it can be good but many times it can be completely different from how you want it to be.

Let's talk about that stuff, that stuff in the middle. That something in the middle that gives you that power, that control shown by the ability to make choices. So, you know, when we talk about that 'choice making stuff', you start from young age and you move up and mature and get older and older and older. Then you are faced with a lot of challenges and the pressures that come from having to make the right choice. Let's think about just the pure practical, physical level. Just try to define life in itself.

Let's say you live 90 years. Most people basically sleep off one-third of it, okay? So, if you sleep off 30 years, you got 60 years left to work with. Another third, 30 more years, you use it to put stuff in your body and pass it through your body, and clean it. And then there's waiting for things, you know, move your body from point A to point B trying to be somebody. So basically out of 90 years you're left with about one-third of stuff to try to prove yourself. What is this proving and defining who you are? If you are defining yourself, obviously you have to define it against your limitations. You have to know your limitations. You have to know your capabilities in order to do something.

So think about what most kids go through before they enter so-called society. That takes I guess like 20 years or something, 18 years, 16 years in what I would call educational institutions. This is how they prepare themselves, learn how to act, learn things. Learn a trade, learn some skills so that they can know how to make a living, take care of yourself, and ultimately find your quest in life. Defining yourself and becoming something that's good, and [doing something] that you want to do, whether it's taught or comes from inside yourself— that's pretty much the process that everybody must bear. And I don't think there's an exception to that rule. Somehow, some way, you have to meet that measure in order to be something in society, to make a difference.

Let's not even talk about making a difference—just starting. Let's look at that as the kind of challenge you have to face. Based on those challenges, you have to make choices. Who's the biggest employer? I guess it's the government. That's the biggest employer in any kind of nationalistic setting, right? And then after that I guess, the market now, the biggest corporation in the world is Wal-Mart, right? That's pretty sad start.

But of course there are bigger corporations. You know corporations that have military contracts. They do a lot of technical things. These are for the most part engineers who work for government-owned agencies. In engineering, these government-controlled agencies, control pretty much anybody who's anybody.

But even those people know that without government support, systems and necessary things they cannot succeed. They cannot compete with the rest of the world in technical, technological, and engineering areas. They need to, the government to, create a competitive product. You can't make it without government support. It takes tremendous time to make a meaningful discovery, development, and innovation.

Yeah, I know all about this free market stuff, but I think the free market gets overrated. I don't think the desire for money is the fuel of human effort. Creating is the basic essence of betterment. Competitive people know how to take certain things and apply them. Quantity, quality, and speed matters. The market based on supply and demand, you really need to churn, that's why you take whatever knowledge there is that is out there, that is meaningful, and then somehow apply and implement it into your product. That's how to make money.

But even when you talk like this, what happens? What's the end? Whether money is the most important thing or whether it's because money can give you a lot of personal stuff. I guess it's indulgence, and also at the same time money can translate into power. So, what does that mean? That power and money is everything? No, I don't think so. Because when you talk about power and money, power is only good when you understand how the power system works. Why is that? Why does it exist? Power exists because you want to move a greater self into a certain direction that's about it. That's all it is.

But people abuse it. How many people in power, in high places really like to spend time with people at the bottom, eh? Do they really care about common people? Do they want to live with them? I don't think so. What about people who want money? Let's say you have all the money in the world. Then what happens? You buy stuff for yourself. But if you do have something of a good nature, then I think the best investment at the start is investing in people.

How many people want all the knowledge and all the money and to control the entire universe right off the bat, as their initial goal? People don't do that. That's why it is smartest to strive for the basic stuff, just what you need to make a living. People don't want everything all at once because ultimately they want to climb up. They want to be something and then through something called desire, move up, up, and up and up. Without properly defining why we have things and why we need to use these things in certain proper ways, for the sake of something greater, and to maintain right standards. Unless we have clear benchmarks to identity higher standards it is very difficult to achieve a greater society. Why? Because definition gets lost, and then everybody is either on their own, or else will start to define their own standards. When that happens it becomes very difficult to come together and unify. Even just a single leaf, never mind the world.

The biggest employers are governments, then who's next? Wal-Mart in America? Oh my goodness. You walk into Wal-Mart and what do you see? Bunch of clothes. Sam's Club is also part of Wal-Mart. You walk in there and you see bunches of TVs, clothes, foodstuff. I guess that it's all about just putting something in your body, putting something on your body, and just kind of keeping this body occupied, preoccupied with something. That's all it is. And they're the biggest employers, next

to the government. That's a sad commentary when you look at it, when you look at a nation of this magnitude.

You know, people with a certain level of tradition normally tell you they want their children you grow up to be a doctor, lawyer, or an accountant, at least an accountant, something that people need all the time. Koreans do that. I think lot of Jewish parents do that to their children. I don't know about Americans, but people in a kind of historical, traditional country that has kind of deep tradition and put tradition in the forefront, they demand that kind of stuff. Why do we demand that kind of stuff of our children? What are we expecting, what does that mean? Why do you need to be a doctor? Why do I have to be a doctor? Why do I have to be a lawyer? Why do I have to be an accountant?

Because that's the safest way, I guess, you know, a thinking parent, a concerned parent, I want my children to have some kind of safe situation. That's about it, isn't it? And then, as long as you have that, I don't expect much but as long as you have that, you know, I'm happy. I don't think I'm sending my children to be a doctor so that they can create a cure for cancer, I don't think every parent desires that. Maybe they desire it but I don't think they expect it. Maybe, you guys, maybe you want to send your children to become a lawyer, but maybe you want your children to go out and defend God and ultimately win. In your favor, maybe that's your desire but I don't think that's what everyone thinks.

So inside of about 90 years is 30 years or so to find who the hell you can be, you have to know your limit, you gotta know your capability and you got to prove something. And hopefully, if you believe in something that you do, then you can use that time to make a difference.

But how do you make that kind of difference? How do you become somebody? When you have the stuff just like everybody else, how can you become somebody who can actually make a difference? I guess the only way is to have something, and some kind of direction or value. I like to call it a direction that outshines something else, outshines other things. In the realm of competition, do we have such a thing? You have to ask yourself that question. If we do, how do you utilize it in your life? What can you do with it?

Those are the basic questions you have to ask yourself, give answers, and give actions. Many times it's very easy, you know, to be a cynic when you have to deal with this kind of dualistic reality. But in reality because you can be very pessimistic, you can be optimistic, or you can be kind of critical. You can be really trying one thing, and at the same time the opposite will be trying to come up with something or solution. You can love and hate all of this. You have all this duality that you are dealing with constantly and every aspect of life. Your whole life can be like that. Everything you interact with and experience. It all demands a response to these kinds of questions.

The challenge is that many times things force themselves on you, and you have to give an immediate answer, you're forced to answer right away. And that's the difficult challenge. This is why you have to have greater principle, right? That's why you try to believe in higher power because that demand, that challenge of immediacy is overwhelming. Because many times, if you goof up, you are going to pay for it. You're gonna stand and face the consequences that you just created. You. They can't blame anyone else.

That's why it becomes necessary to understand the reality of God properly, the demand of God. That's called responsibility. That demand issue is called responsibility. I wish I didn't have to be responsible. It is fun to be irresponsible, isn't it? It's fun to not care. Wahh, wahh! I blow things off. I'm really trying not to curse, okay. I know there are children here. It's kind of natural for me, because that's how I grew up, you know. That's the kind of people that I know and was part of, the kind of people I saw most of the time. But I think I'm okay. I know how to behave if I want to.

Anyway, so how do you, how do we actually live up to that demand? That ultimate demand? We worry about the people who make stuff, worry about supply and demand, oh, my product has to be such and such so that I can, you know, put it to the market and demand will come forth and I'll make tons of money! Of course demand is important to everybody whether you believe God or not. Because that's how you make money, that's how the world goes around, right? Whether you make money or you shoot up a lot whatever ladder of success you are part of. Because every boss has a demand.

Then I think about the free market. People say it creates a kind of openness and that creates betterment—betterment in what? Better safety in car? Guess that's important but beyond that, what? Better fashion? You know, better whatever. There's a limitation to that. What if everybody can do that? What if [the] whole world can do that? What happens to those parts of any given industry? What happens to the marketplace in that kind of situation?

It pretty much will be end up as kind of nationalism, quite obviously. I'm American, so I should buy American products. I'm Korean, so I should buy Korean products. But if everything's the same, there's no need to buy from this country or that, from Korea, or American products, or anybody else's stuff. That's about it, isn't it?

So let's say we reach that point. And the truth is that it's not that far away, then just think about, it in a short period of time Korea's just kind of competing with the big boys selling big items, huge items, pretty much anything that is big that's carried things on water whether it's oil or merchandise, you know, they build it, and you drive it around. Even in America, if Koreans can do it, so can everybody else. Then what? I know it could take about 10 generation, but in very short period of time, we'll be faced with that kind of reality. When everybody becomes nationalistic, then what happens?

That's why we have to focus on greater value. Remember? Because you have to make choices everyday and sometime it's overwhelming. Everybody feels that stuff. That's called life. And pretty much the reason that Father says certain things in certain ways. He explains how things are done, and that is that it's because of this reality I'm talking about. It's not that far before what I'm telling you is going to be manifested. When that happens, that's about it. Who has a greater value? Whose value out of the greatness is the greatest? Who are the ones that can tie everything together. The answer is very simple, but there is a different kind of simple. While transcending all this basic stuff we can talk about those this higher way. I could go on about this but like I said, I like to keep it short because you like it short.

Practically speaking, this kind of stuff is only good for about a week. That's about it. And if you have something, if I give you something for that week, that's all it's worth, period. It's over. Game over. You gonna move on. It's always that way. You can't try to pray, maybe you do it as a condition for spiritual reasons, you know, heavenly conditions, but in all respects, in practicality, it doesn't work. At best, if I can give you one or two thoughts, that's about it; and you can think about for a week. That's all it's worth and everything else is overrated. That's why if you're gonna be anybody, you gotta do those thing, you got to be somebody who can do this for life. That's about it. Anyways, I don't think so. You gotta know your limit. Everything has a limit in life.

Many times, that's another personal, individual challenge. Know your limit. You know, there are many things that can overwhelm you, and sometimes it's that vainglorious stuff that can really hurt you. That's why you have to understand why you are doing something. You gotta define everything that you do. You want to be right? You literally have to define everything you do. Don't think about other, don't judge other people. Define what you do. And stand by it.

You have no time to worry about other people. Because they have to do the same thing. And knowing this, keep it true. That's your only chance. There's no guarantee in life. But as long as you're willing to do it, make it so. Make it into a short term goal. I'm going to try to do that every day. I wake up and try to think like that. The long term goal? I'll die for that. Look, whatever it takes. If you have something of that nature, I think that's called a personal value. I think it's safe to call that a personal value. Because whatever you do, you will face it one way or the other. Right and wrong. Right or wrong.

This thing called life in the middle is just doing that, knowing who I am, finding what I can do, what I have to do for greater power, higher goals. And know how to die well, I guess. That's the greatest control I guess, right? That's the greatest choice you can make. Every choice you make is what you control.

I made stupid choices in my life. I'll pay for till the day that I die. That's about it. That's my problem. That's about it. I don't need your sympathy. I can take care of it. I was always like that. When I was a little, a young buck, you know, I always tried to be a cool guy. Anyway, take care of yourself, okay? Is that short enough? I'll see you next week, okay? All right.

Can True Love Be Addictive?
February 26, 2006

How are you doing? *(Good.)* That's good. Today, how should I put it, I want to talk about something interesting, "Can True Love Be Addictive?" How can we make true love addictive?

When you talk about addiction, I guess, people have a kind of negative connotation right off the bat, right? Why? Because it's a kind of human behavior, or a human action that if you get addicted, ultimately in the end you go out of control. It's a human behavior that cannot be controlled. That's the general understanding when dealing with the addiction factor. Is there good and bad addiction? Do you think there is such a thing? Does every human behavior demand a certain outcome in the end? Whether you demand or not if it happens it results in consequences, consequential action. Is that right? I guess so.

So what is the nature of addiction? As a parent, you know, when your children are growing and running into teenage years and you see all sorts of stuff happening out there, you worry about that factor. You worry about children going out of control. That's the most important thing as a parent, a concerned parent, who has children growing up and reaching the teenage years. These are the years when they are constantly exploring because they need to know. First they have to figure out what their limitations are. But in a free society there are many treacherous things out there whether you like it or not. Many times children's greatest argument to their parents is, "How can I know my limit if I don't try it?" Based on that kind of argument, everything starts. And how are you going to stop them? If you are truly concerned and if you think that you can be a good parent, how are you ultimately going to have control over your children. You know you need this control until the day they can be free to choose and be what they can be, all they can be. Until that day, you know, you will never rest easy. You know, even when people are old, say you're 80 and have a 60 year old son, you still say, "Hey, be careful when you cross the street." This kind of silly stuff people always make jokes about. But that really does happen, maybe in a different way but with the same magnitude, that's about it. With the same intense, how should I put it, intent.

So, how do you deal with that kind of reality when every action can be turned into an addiction? Because think about it, addiction comes from nothing but an action that gives you some kind of pleasure, that's about it. That's the nature of addiction. There is some kind of action no matter what it is, if it gives you certain satisfaction, certain pleasure, however stupid or however great it might be it doesn't matter. It's just based on your limitation, that's about it. But to you, it becomes addictive because you feel the pleasure. But not everybody's the same, right? Some people look at certain things in certain ways. Somebody looks at the same thing one way, the next guy looks at it in a different way. Take the cliché of 'glass half empty or half full.' So based on that kind of reality, the addiction factor is part of life. Why? Because it happens. Because you want to feel joy, you want to feel pleasure. At the final point in our life we question whether that intent was good or bad. But think about it. Who are you talking to? Are you talking to yourself, are you talking to somebody else? Are you talking to a certain community? Are you talking to a Hollywood crowd or are you talking to neo-capitalists? They each have a different perspective when it comes to self-pleasure. Even just on a geographical level, people's pleasures are all very different. For those of you who grew up in the South or Midwest of America, I mean, I like, I used to love hunting. Only reason I stopped it is just because I didn't want to do it anymore. I had my own reasons and I didn't like to kill anymore for my pleasure. That's about it. But people do, people do that stuff, and they get whole lot of richness out of it.

As a father, you wait for a son to grow up, reach a certain age and then take him out for the first time and you guide him to shoot a deer. And when the son scores, that's a life-long experience, that'll last until day you die I guess. And that's the kind of momentous kind of stuff that you look for in having that kind of union with your own kid, based on your preference, I guess.

Now, when you talk about love, what the hell is love anyway? What is true love? If you can forgive the devil himself and bless people at the same time, you know, yet the primary ancestors can be cast from the Garden of Eden for their sins. That is the kind of promise in the extreme of love. And love is nothing, it's just a concept. How the hell do you make a concept into something that is actually, you know, in actuality means something to you and affects your daily life? What is true love? True love is law, law of something. What is that? Law, what is that something? It's God's law, right? It's God's idea. It's God's concept. God's will. And we have to somehow figure out God's concept, God's will, the idea, the pure thought and then put it into practice. You can't practice a certain concept unless you have a counterpart. That's the thing. You can't really love because ultimately in the end, love too has to bring about joy, pleasure and happiness. That's why you have to manifest things, right? So everything that can be manifested has certain law that is somehow correlated to the law of God, and God is the God of true love we say. So be it.

So how do you take that concept and make it work in your life? You have to question that. How do you feel joy? How does one become addicted to something? What happens in that process? You know men have to be macho right, individual, independent, self-sufficient. You try your best to be subjective and be forthright in your own ways, and you try to show the world that your decision is better than the other guy who's next to you. So how do you go about that process? Obviously you start with a need, right? You need to feel something. And you have a goal called expectation. Expectation is a goal, that's about it. I want to be this because I need this, but the goal is over there and I expect to be there one day. So you create, you give yourself the opportunity, you train yourself, you give yourself a routine. Routine is nothing other than orientation toward what is required. You start with a basic requirement and you move upward, and then it depends on how far you want to move up the ladder. This is inborn, why? Because everything in the physical world has to show itself. When you say 'merit'—it's nothing other than that physical manifestation, and people judge you by what you manifest. And then you try to make that into some kind of habit, habituation. You want to make the routine into a habit.

I'll talk about something else. There is something else in between that I think is important for us to try to pursue, to try to be addicted to true love! Normally what happens in a secular world is that they go right to habituation, you try to make that into a habit, you make the routine into a habit. When you get habituated it is nothing more than thinking that you are going to get pleasure in the end of the same stuff that you did to experience joy so far. You want that addiction factor. You want your action, every action that you have invested in your life to have some sort of self-gratification, pleasure factor. This is very important to you. So, it's easy to see addiction as the stupid stuff that people get addicted to and go out of control. But there are many, many other things because anything in action absolutely has an addiction factor in the end. You give somebody a little power they go crazy, they change. I've seen it many, many times. You give people a little of money, they do stupid stuff.

So, what is it, what are we trying to define? What is right and wrong? Before we talk about right and wrong, you have to truly talk about what your addiction is. Because when you talk about right and wrong you are putting yourself in the position of judgment which you really don't want to do. Trust me. Even if you are a politician, try to do that and you are not going to be a popular politician, how's that? So, what is your limitation? You have to understand your limitations. And you have to understand why you want to feel joy with that particular stuff. Why do you need that stuff to feel joy, to feel that you are somebody? Why is that important to you? You have to answer that. Not just to yourself, but to your family, to your society, to your nation, to the world, ultimately to God and forever.

Is it easy to feel joy? When you want to kill your enemy, destroy your enemy, you just have vengeance in your heart, every pore of your body smells that blood that you want to taste. Should I go ahead with it? There is pleasure in violence, yes. Sure, absolutely. I beat up a lot of kids when I was young. I had no choice. Look at that, I fought a lot. There's a pleasure in it—God's honest truth. Momentary, however it might be, but there is a pleasure in it. Whether you go for some kind of sports, kids go for sports, whether you become an academician or become involved in arts or whatever—kids do those kinds of stuff because they're just trying to figure out who they are. Everything is open to them and they want to feel something, and they want to feel that they earn that feeling.

I can prove something through my action. And at the same time it can be a pleasure and at the same time I can get recognition. Oh, man that is the greatest thing. But just because you feel whatever you want to feel, which is ultimately in the end some sort of self-gratification and pleasure, does that mean that everything is allowed? Is everything allowed? That's why I think that in love there is law, right? Especially, if you truly talk about true love there is true law. There is a very specific way in which you should feel those kinds of stuff, right? But can it be done, can it be achieved, can you condition your body, yourself, your mind—let's put away the spirit stuff as you normally don't deal with that stuff, right? So, can you feel joy doing a difficult task? It's very easy to judge, but everybody has their limitations, everybody. It can differ. That's about it.

It's a funny thing when you give somebody power, they try to consume you. They don't try to recognize you, instead they try to consume you. That's the kind of phenomenon that happens almost 100 percent of the time. Never fails. Why? Maybe because some kind of envy might be involved, some jealousy might be involved, who knows. They want something that you have that they don't have. That's about it, isn't it? Why do people become criminal? You know, people call me all sorts of things. If I take something that is not mine, that's criminal, right? So, where does it end? What's right and what's wrong? When you do certain things there are consequences, that's about it. It's no different. That's why in the end everybody's equal, right, equal in that. That's about it. But is there stuff, is there order? No, I'm not going to talk about that stuff today.

Look, I'm trying to get back into the groove of things. It's been 10 years, I guess, right? I mean I know it's something like riding a bike but hey, give me a break. Don't give me a hard time for crying out loud. I don't think I mislead you in any way. What you see is what you got, that's about it. You take it as it comes. Look, I had my problems. It's all my problems. Blame it on me, okay? It's easy that way. And I can live with myself. I really don't care what you think. But I'll tell you that much. That's all I think. And if it affected you, I am sorry. And it was beyond me. I understand what I have done wrong, and I know my son is listening. I want to make a difference. That's about it. That's it! That's it! Nothing else. I could care less if I don't have to ever stand here again for the rest of my life. Look, if I can live without it for 10 years I can do so for the rest of my life, trust me. Most likely I'd be better off that way. But anyway, most of all I'm grateful. This is something sacred, that's just how it is, but I'm doing it. I'm trying to do this because I want to do this for my reasons. Let me start with that. I'm not going to tell you I'm doing it for you. I'm doing it because I want to do this. That's it. I feel that I need to do this. I need to communicate something. You know what I'm saying?

What's important in making addiction work for true love? I think it's the ritual factor. You have to have some kind of ritual. You have to have some kind of rites of passage, stuff with symbolism and meaning, stuff with value, value that can last. You have to get into an expected goal and a steady routine. You have to stick the ritual stuff between that which eventually becomes routine and habituation. You have to put that something in there. Make it meaningful. You have to make some kind of symbolism work. I don't care what. It depends on you. That's because everybody's limitation is different, everybody's control factors are different. It depends on you. Make that, put that into that practice.

Ultimately, if you can make your own habit and pursue it, and begin to acquire in that a certain pleasure based on action, then when you're in that, there's, 'hey, whatever!' Forgive that little fool that you want to kill. Today, it's a new day. You wake up in the morning, you brush up, you do the same routine eating stuff, stuff down the throat, do that. Make that into a ritual. Put it in between the routine and habit forming process. Make it something valuable. Make it something meaningful. And if you can do that one step at a time you'll find out what love is, I guess, right? You are not going to understand everything at once, are you crazy? They're the craziest people I know. You give somebody power and overnight they change—they're the sickest, they disgust me. They don't know nothing. They think they are geniuses overnight. It's crazy stuff.

Look, you want to change the world? You got to have good communication, people you can interact with, people you bounce stuff off with. That's human spirit. When you have plenty of that you can bounce off the energy and then you can really multiply. And that can be very addictive to people who don't see that stuff at the secular level, trust me.

There are a lot of good people in the secular world. But they want more too, just like you. After all, those kids out there, there's a lot of young … teenagers. You got to know your limit and take your time. Those stupid arguments, 'how can I know my limit if I don't try.' Don't use that kind of stupid argument. A bunch of them make that, don't do it. Learn about yourself and your limit properly.

Some kid says, some second generation, "Make me a star." It's cheaper over there. That started just recently. It took about five years to settle—stuff. I put myself in some kind of, and I put myself in a kind of, you know, how should I put it—anyway it was just kind of meditated form, for him. I just wanted to disappear and do the 10 thousand stuff and start at something around two thousand a month. And this boy, "Make me a star."

They really don't understand how things work. Just because you think you have something they want everything. But how can I give you everything when, if I spent the little stuff that I got, invest it in you and it doesn't pan out. That's crazy stuff. Why, if you become something, if you can artificially do something ultimately in the end, for you to become a star, you have to prove it to the rest of the world just like anybody else. That's crazy stuff. They just want something and think that's it, that's the end. What's now?

Doesn't work that way. I had two cases like that, second generation. They gave up. It's too difficult. Oh my. It is nice and pretty when you were thinking that you want to be a star someday. When you go through all the stuff that you have to go through, oh, it's difficult, what, and have what, somebody else sacrifice for that nonsense, you understand me? You have to know your limit. Don't be stupid.

And think about it. It's not like, it's very difficult in that what I'm like around Father's son, I can't do certain things, certain stuff. I can't let it be just for the sake of capitalism stuff—I can't live like this. I got a lot of flap for just investing an old boy.

Anyway, I wish you can do this right. And we will, I know. I know what's important in the 21st century. Ecumenism. Ecumenism. And that is everything in the end. Trust me. Anyways, step out of there.

You can wait, if you really love something, right? If you believe in something, right? So that's what I guess love is. Do that stuff, little stuff everyday in your own way. It matters to you and if you shine, it matters to the community. That's about it.

Okay? All right, that's it.

I'll see you next week.

Why Do We Want to Love Somebody?
March 2, 2006

Good morning. *(Good morning.)*

"Why do We Want to Love Somebody?" Why do you want to be loved? What is love to you? What do you love? If you have a definition of the love that you want to have, how are you going to get it? There's a need and want in life that drives us into action to make life. What we do is because of that drive, no other reason.

So, what is that drive? History tells us that we seek the highest love. We all want to be the best in whatever we do. You want to be number one! We don't want to be number two. Well if you live long enough, you at least want to be in the rankings. It's not that simple always to be number one.

So, what is love? What is love for you? What do you want, why do you need, why do you want love? If you can't answer that for yourself, then you haven't understood much about yourself. Because the next question, the next step is that if you need and want love you're not going to be able to have it alone. That means that something else comes into your picture, and when it comes, what do you think is going to happen to you? What word will occur to you? It's called sacrifice. And that's going to mess you up for a long time, until you get it right. That word is going to mess you up until you get it right. I know what I want. No, I know what I need and I know what I want. But, sacrifice? That's a different story. That's going to mess you up.

So, how are you going to make that right? There's no magic answer. You have to persevere. You have to understand where you stand, and you have to persevere. That's the only answer, till you make it right. You have to make it right. Because in the end, you stand alone in judgment.

I wish I could have had a little more time with my son. I'm not the kind of guy who regrets things, but that's one thing that I regret and that's going to hurt me to the day I die. Why? Because I loved somebody.

You don't live that long you guys. I will be fifty soon, you know. I'm trying to take care of myself, you know. But, in a few more years you'll be dead! Right? What the heck is that? What are we learning in this life.

Find yourself, okay? And die well. Because you don't live that long. And I hope that you want to be good, okay? Because we can learn from each other, okay?

Find good, find you, and die well. Okay?

How Many Are Still Serious About Going Out and Spreading the Word?

March 5, 2006

Thank you. Please sit down.

Are you concerned about all this sectarian violence around the world? It's bad, isn't it? It seems like it's getting worse. I think it's only going to get worse before it gets any better. That kind of sectarianism, the divide will increase on the religious level, economical level, and political level. We will just see more of it before it changes. So, how did you join? How did you join this church? Why did you join the church? How many people are still going out there and trying to reach out and still keeping the faith and doing the duty of trying to spread the word, spread the news? How many people are truly serious about that mission of educating the rest of the world based on the principle that was taught by Father? You see, even in our church, of course Father wants to institutionalize more and more. Why? Because he's 86 and in 2012 he will be 92. As days go by, he's only going to get older. He's not going to get any younger. That's for sure.

But it seems like we still have to hold on to certain things because of who we are. It doesn't matter if the recent climate is political. That does not make everybody just run out and try to be a second-rate politician. I've seen that kind of stuff many times. There is this hoop-la and everybody rolls over there, and next everybody wants to get into business. Whether it's in politics, business, trying to become an educator or whatever, those kinds of fads exist even in our church. I don't think our lives should be governed and dictated by fashion.

Think about trying to make a change in somebody. It's going to take a long time. If you ever had to take care of some young members, it takes years and years. Let's say that person has an attitude problem—arrogant and so pleased with himself. Dealing with that kind of situation takes a whole lot of effort. And change doesn't happen overnight. You have to be a parent, you have to be a teacher, and sometimes you have to be sometimes a friend, even a brother or a sister. You have to play a whole host of roles and do all sorts of work. You have to do just about everything under the sun including a whole lot of stuff, like counseling or therapy. Whatever it demands at any given moment, that's what you have to do just to save one soul, just to help one guy, some young guy, a new guy, or a new gal. That's just the reality.

And how can we expand if we lose something that is so true and valuable, something that just doesn't change? It's just like the concept of rearing children as a parent. Parenthood, it is universal. What works never changes. Regardless of what your religious beliefs and disciplines may be, it doesn't matter. Some things are universally true. And there are universal truths. Yes, it works. What we are trying to do, and what we are trying to say is that we are unique, and our uniqueness represents God more than anybody else. So be it. Before you say that, you have to apply universal truth to our life and to our actions, to our belief and actions. Otherwise, all that stuff, unique stuff, doesn't matter. It will not sell. How can you move somebody with this if you can't convince them or persuade them? It doesn't matter. Even in just trying to sell even a cookie or cereal, somebody has to see the value in it before they purchase it. Even in business, it's trying to make money, dealing with inanimate things, and you are going out there trying to make money. So be it. That has to be proven. By what?

By the quality of your product. How can we prove ourselves as what we say we are? We can never lose sight of that fundamental universal truth. If you are going to make a difference, that's how you have to do it. If you are going to institutionalize, certain things have to be bedrock. Certain things have to be fundamental before you start expanding and growing.

You hear so much information out there. There are so many human stories and life stories. There's a lot of stuff. I read it sometimes, but it gets lost in translation, I guess. Some people just don't get it because it's not translated properly or not translated in time. There's such a long delay of things. When you are living in a world of expediency and convenience, that becomes a real serious problem because you can look like an idiot. You look like an inefficient system. How do you prove to the world that we are better? And all the while more and more people are just becoming more fashion oriented based on whatever is given at hand in one moment. Those things are important things that we have to always address because if we don't, we'll lose it all one day. The word might stay, but it's going to take a longer time to bring it back.

Father will go down in history. Yes, sure, absolutely. He will. But what about you? What about your children? I guess the only solution is to practice that stuff, isn't it? You have to go out and try that again. That's the only way. Do it, and bring more people, and try to reignite that fire that was once lost. Step by step, one person at a time. If that's what it takes, that's what you have to do. There is no shortcut to greatness. There is no shortcut to success. Maybe there is in America. You may win a lottery, how many people do that stuff? Think about it.

Because of all the separation and misunderstanding people have perpetuated against each other, therefore this kind of sectarian violence is back. It's observable all around the world. Even when you think about all those crazy so called Muslims who hate America, they do have an issue that we can understand. Why? Because America is the land of the most powerful capitalism. Based on that and freedom, so many things are guaranteed and protected even if you have questions about certain methods, certain ways, and certain things that are accepted. You can understand why they want to blow up Americans, "the great devil." Of course, you can't give condolence to those kinds of things, but they do have a reason for their action. And we live with them. It's difficult for us to change. So, that's why they try to blow you up. That's all they know I guess. But they want change. People want to be better. People want to feel joy in life and have something to be proud of. They want something that gives them those things. They want that kind of prosperity and whatever happiness that comes from it. Sure, no problem. But there are ways in which you can go about achieving that, and there are questionable methods. And as long as there is a questionable method, it's going to be very difficult to bring about any kind of permanent stability.

So, how do you go about changing that? How do you change America when so many things have gone wrong? Freedom is guaranteed and protected absolutely, but that ain't going to change it. It's religion, sacred stuff. They'll die before they try to change it. They'll die fighting for it. How are you going to do that? How are you going to change that situation? It's going to take a long time to inspire even your children. In other words, you absolutely have to inspire generations on and on and on unendingly, until it happens. Until the change that we can see and feel happens, that we can guarantee it ourselves and say, 'Yes, this is the change. This is the change that will stay.' You have to start with something. You have to start somewhere. It's something kind of silly. I have been doing stuff and going into China now. And you try to think about, 'Oh, I need to do something, I need to make it.' It's silly. It's insane. But if I have to do this on my own, hey, stuff costs. How's that? That's why I try to do my best to not cross that line. There are opportunities that, yes, I know I'm going to get more return on this stuff if I take that opportunity, but I can't. Why? For me, it's just because of my name. That's about it, because I don't want to be an idiot.

But you have to start somewhere and you have to try to do those kinds of stuff. And your children need that kind of stuff. The more we have the better. Multimedia is very, very important. Why? Because if you have to sell our 'product,' you are going to have to master your communication capability. Things are out there for a reason. Things are given to us for a reason. That timing is here for a reason. That's the first step, obvious step. Everybody is trying to take that.

Look at how Fox has succeeded in America. It has pretty much taken over every level in such a short period of time. The trend was in the way money was invested, much less than the way we would do it. When you look at Fox News, it is literally run by a few character-driven shows, and they cycle it three times a day. That's about it. And they have a little live stuff in the morning and in the mid afternoon.

Everything else is just a few character-driven shows. The format is very simple. "Your World with Neil Cavuto," "The O'Reilly Factor," "The Sean Hannity Show," and "Brad of Banaster." It's a few shows, a few character-driven shows, and they pretty much take on the world, and they influence so many people. Just one single person did all that. His radio show has a few points measuring his audience. Every point is like a million. People religiously turn his show on every day and listen to him just blab for four hours long.

I was just watching the news the other day. I see some guy who made money on fast food and donated 250 or 300 million dollars or something to help develop a Catholic town because he's Catholic. A lot of people are giving their money. There is another guy who died and gave billions to charity. Well, they are not giving it to us, right? And they're doing that. They're trying to, in a sense, become more and more established and showcase their lifestyle, their tradition, their ritual, their religion.

Do you want to move to Cheong Pyeong now? That's funny, the story behind that stuff. Anyway, at least your children can help, as you guys are getting too old. But you know, you are not dead yet, right? You are going to die fighting, right? You will go out until your last breath, right? All right. For people who are actually going to make the difference, I would rather bet on the children. We'll die together. But if there's going to be change made, I rather bet on your children.

All those activities that we used to do, I think if we can afford it, of course, it should be continued because it's important. Science, medicine, and engineering committee has to be brought together. And it's very different. You can't really try to be intellectuals unless you can have a discourse with them and start at least. And create a much more serious, much more meaningful, much more useful foundation based on those committees. It is necessary to help what we want to achieve. What was the last year that ICUS [International Conference on the Unity of the Sciences] was held? Anyway, long time ago. There's a lot of stuff that's important because you need to communicate. You persuade people through communication. You need to have those bases formed. That's very important especially in democracy and for society. And Bush speaks about justice through democracy, that kind of stuff. Some people fervently believe in this stuff. So be it. All those things, we should take care of and we should nurture them, even if it's just an idea. It changes.

You can't just sit around idle. Those things are important. Fundamental things are important. And we have to master those fundamentals before we try to think about anything else. Without that, it is absolutely not going to happen. I would rather believe in aliens. Wouldn't that be great if some flying saucer lands on the White House lawn and say, "Hey, believe in Reverend Moon–otherwise we are going to laser you." We can change the world just like that. I bet a million dollars on that one. So, we should invest in ourselves because it's important. The fundamental things are important. We should encourage not just ourselves but our community. We need to act together as a grass roots movement too. Certain things are important and certain people, the powers that be, they need to know that. Then anything's possible after trying.

 Life is short, you know. It's about finding something in life. That's about it in this sorry life. It's about making the right choices and finding something—a value, an eternal value. That's life. Because only here, you make choices that can alter your life. This or that. Because think about it—we believe in spirit, mind, and body. Fate, faith, and fact. Control it. Know what that is. Make the right decision, right choices. Know how to control it. That's the best you can do.

It's not what you want that keeps your livelihood. That's just livelihood stuff. Ultimately, in the end, that is the question you must answer on your own. In your life, in yourselves, in your idiosyncrasy. Find it. That is your purpose. That's our job. Good luck. It'll take your life. It'll take a lifetime. It won't end. This quest will never end. Why? Because you want more. Trust me.

Okay, take care of yourselves. I'll see you next week.

Teamwork
March 12, 2006

Please sit down. How are you doing? *(Good.)* Okay. That's good. Another day of judgment. Today, I want to share with you something very basic, "Teamwork."

People think about teamwork in all sorts of relative ways I guess. I've even heard that teamwork is a sign of these changing times. For example, young people get together just to supplement their expenses. They become day traders, they get together as a group, and share information they gather during the week. After gathering at church on Sunday, they have a get-together and go through stuff, and that is how they get their little extra allowance. It is a different kind of a world. I guess the idea of teamwork has different meanings to everyone to a certain extent. For most people it happens on a physical level and on an intellectual level. But with people like us, if anything matters, it has to be spiritual, right? Because everything else is under spiritual, right? That's our priority. So, of course it is important. However, in terms of reality, and on a bigger scheme of things based on your faith, what's really important is the hereafter and dying well. Another way to put the 'dying well' concept is in the frame of ultimate control, controlling your life and living well for the inevitable death. So, let's control living. That's what we are trying to accomplish on a daily basis.

Everything that we are curious about leads us to gather information. It's all about how to achieve something before the end, ultimately. We just do that the best way we know how. And sometimes, some things are so tremendous because it's so expansive and difficult. You can't do it alone. You need community. You need extension into a greater family. But having said that, before we talk about independence and individual, idiosyncratic individuality, let us just focus on teamwork. Why do we need that stuff? Because certain things are very difficult to achieve alone, that is why. It is not just for the sake of taking care of your menial stuff or your livelihood. But it is because of your faith, because you believe in something greater. And basically your life—what you accept in this physical world in its full presence—is all about preparing you for that stage, the final stage. And you need that kind of support. You need people who understand that stuff, who can think in communion with you, who can take care of you at times, and who you can depend on.

Everybody belongs to some family. But even if you look at just a single family unit, if there is a standard, a test, some people do well, some people don't. Some families need some special help, right? That kind of stuff. That is why you need to have that kind of support group and teamwork. The most important thing is having that support base, something that you can depend on. Because that's the opposite of independence, right? Of course, you want to teach your children to be independent, but at the same time to be a team player. That's because you want them to go out into the world and be successful somehow.

Having that kind of stuff is important because without it, it doesn't work. Even on a physical level, things don't work without that understanding. You cannot try to become a team player if your ulterior motive is being selfish. In the Garden of Eden, prior to the Fall, there is the Tree of Knowledge of Good and Evil. If you believe that stuff, so be it. The main thing you need to know about the Fall is its aftermath. You have to know what that actually is. And what that actually is, is that you have to deal with your selfishness and selflessness—independence and teamwork. These will always exist whether you like it or not. It does not matter if everything is done and everything is perfect and restoration is over. That stuff starts all over again. And that's about it. That is the absolute truth.

But how do you go about changing that? How do you go about dealing with that issue? You look around the world and it is still selfish. How do you open up hell, if you do not contain hell? Hell is nothing other than just that selfishness gone out of control. Still, even if symbolically, let us say everything is done. So be it. Then we have to go backwards. We have to contain that selfishness intellectually; we have to contain that selfishness physically. It takes time. It does not happen just because of conditions. That is absolute. If you do not understand that, you should not be here. I should not be talking to you because that is basic principle that I understand.

So, how do we go about changing that reality? Oh, boy. Where should we start? Look at you. Look at yourself. What can you do? If that is the basic simple question that we have to answer, where do you stand? What kind of community can you make? Ultimately achieving that goal, that's the task at hand. Somebody has got to do it. Where do you stand? I don't know you that well. You don't know me. So, start from some place where you can create that kind of community, with some kind of passion. Find people that you can relate to, something related to your passion. I do not care whether it is physical, intellectual, or spiritual. I really do not care. That is not important. Find somebody and create a community. I think that is very healthy as long as we clearly understand why we are here. Because all that in the end should come together, if you understand that rule of thumb. And that should be absolute. Knock yourself out. Why? Because some people cannot do it alone. There are things, even the greatest man, even Father, he cannot do alone. That is why he needs you.

Do not feel shame, do not feel bad. Sometimes you need to reach out. Know your limit. The important thing about knowing how basic teamwork works is to know—what is the lesson being taught through the teamwork process? What is being taught is, obviously, you have to have a purpose. You set a goal. You set a realistic time duration expectation. Then you have to understand your boundaries. In other words, set your limit based on your capability, collectively, because we are talking about teamwork. And of course, like I said earlier, it is important to support each other because that gives you something substantial. It teaches you how to share ideas and about checks and balances.

For me, teamwork is important because it keeps me humble. That is about it. I have to keep myself humble if I want to embrace the people I am with. Why? Because it goes on and life goes on. Anything that has worth, anything that is meaningful should last forever. Why? Because love is eternal.

And what is the purpose of coming together? That we all grow up together and not just me, right? Secondly, it keeps me honest. Why? Because I live with those guys. You have to have that transparency. And it gives you that integrity. It forces you to stand up and check your integrity.

Lastly, it gives you a sense of security. It is like a helmet. So, in some way, it is three H's right (humble, honest, helmet)? Something like that. Secure me from what? Falling, hurting myself, and doing stupid things—I guess which I am known for. Look, I don't do stuff without reason. I react, that's about it. And sometimes, of course, you should not do that. Hey, I am not perfect. Did I ever say I was perfect? Perfection lasts forever. Do you know that? If you understand that concept, perfect is theoretically pure ideological stuff. That is about it. And that is pretty much where you have to start from, and that is how you have to approach it. Why? Because we ultimately have to deal with the real world. Your children are growing up.

There are three people very difficult for me to forgive: my ex-in-laws, and one monkey guy. I have two sets of family, but all those children got a job. One works in New York in some advertising firm or somewhere. And that is my reality. And how do you change that? Now, if that is difficult, how do you change the world? Do you think it is going to happen automatically? Because you believe? Believe in what? Believe in yourself, that you are holy? Why do you think that? Why would you think that you were holy? Because you have a bunch of holes like a sponge? Maybe then I will believe you. You have a lot of stupidity if you want to tell others you're holy. How do you help somebody with that kind of an attitude? Even if you were, how are you going to change somebody?

Look, let us say you can take the fault for somebody, you can take the blame, you can take the hit, and even go to the jail for somebody. But how do you change the world? Because there is something like that out there. The important thing is, why do I need teamwork? Because to me, like I said, it keeps me humble and it keeps me honest. And that is my helmet, my security. That is why. And it will take an army of people like this—a tribe coming together, creating a critical mass. Anyway, just start to change. And in changing, you have to reach out. How do you reach out? If everything ultimately evolves downwards spirals, down into physicality in terms of manifestation from an idea, we have to communicate. That is what is important. That medium somehow must be contained and controlled. We have to have that capacity. Otherwise, it can never be done. Others are doing it. It could have been done a long time ago.

Anyway, it is never too late. Some things never go away. Because if it is inevitable, it is never too late. You just have to remind yourself of that stuff. Once again, that is about it. Somebody needs to talk about this kind of stuff. You have to remind yourself of that, even if somebody else does not. You have to understand how society is changed. You know that. What are we doing? It is very, very difficult controlling the media. Yes, other people are doing it because they take all the smart people of the world, and they spend a lot of money and spend a lot of time to get there. And even they fail sometimes. No guarantee. Sure. But what is necessary has to be done one way or the other.

We can't quit. We believe in something else. We think that we can't do it and we quit on ourselves? I insist, you have to be kidding me! How do you win with that kind of a loser's attitude? If you really want change, you have to do this. Otherwise, I do not believe it is going to happen. I do not see the stuff that can make it happen. I am not just talking about physical stuff. I am not just talking about the mind stuff either. There is also spirit.

Because it is going to take a long time. If you believe it is going to happen in your lifetime, I think you are crazy. I believe that is just lies. I know what you are addicted to, you little power mongers.

Anyway, I believe we can do it. But it takes everything we got. If you are going to do it, if that is the case, I will be the team player, too. Some things you just can't do alone. There are a lot of things you can't do alone in this stupid life. Some things—you just can't do it alone.

Okay, I will see you next week.

Attraction and Expectation
March 19, 2006

Another day of judgment. That's just how it is. Today I would like to talk about, "Attraction and Expectation."

There are a lot of young people here. What are you attracted to? Physical things, mental things, spiritual things? Ultimately in life, we have to define where we stand at every step of the way in our lives. And we always have to contend with the reality that we face when dealing with ourselves. In ourselves there's always a conflict of mind and body. And we ultimately search for the greater spiritual truth when we look at everything, even a single word, for instance, a word that we use casually to describe things and communicate with one another. Everything should have some kind of connection ultimately to the main reality—body, mind, and spirit.

We have to know the process of how to go about achieving that union. Understanding that process, I think, is a kind of lifelong endeavor we all inevitably have to face and have to answer ultimately in the end—because if you don't, well, you are going to be lost. A lot of you bring your children here and if you are lost, then obviously your children will be lost too. It's important to talk about these matters to your children. Tell them why people get attracted to certain things, and what is the meaning of this or that. Start with the very basic things, simple things that are important and relevant to children growing up. Because, whether you understood it or not, it was important to you too. Maybe it's important that if you didn't question yourself to that extent, maybe it's time for the sake of someone else that you try to redefine what you think you have understood up to now. You can do that for the sake of someone else you care about. Everything doesn't have to revolve around you.

So attraction. What is it? Let's just talk about physical attraction for a moment. People are attracted to good looking people, right? We see beautiful people on television and in movies. Physical beauty is important. When looking at the physical we find that people are attracted to those who seem to have power, powerful things, powerful this, powerful that. Whether it's a creature out there in the wild kingdom or it is something that represents or is symbolic of power, if power is involved, people get attracted to it. In current civilization, money is also very attractive. Look at all the kinds of networks out there. These share information and advance various social settings. These are pretty much the things that rule today. It's very difficult not to see it. You see it all the time, constantly, because it's effective. Effective in what way? Obviously it's for the sake of color, but it's effective. People do pay attention to those things. People want those things, desire those things because they are attractive to them. Next you get into mental stuff, intellectual attraction. Intellectual attraction goes toward people who do creative things whether it's color, sound, wording and words, or mechanical things. Anything that involves creativity or having some kind of mastery over things, being a virtuoso or showing some kind of specialty or maybe just a wealth of knowledge in general. People are attracted intellectually to those types of people.

And obviously, finally, we come to the spiritual stuff. For something to have spiritual attraction it has to have eternal purpose and value, that's what we are taught to understand. Something that is spiritually attractive has that end. Something has to come forward and when that is given, when that is manifest, it enthralls you. That is the kind of stuff – inspirations, lessons, or the value you want to inherit – because that's what the spiritual represents. This spiritual quality can be in many things. It can be all the greatness that defines what is eternally great – true love. It can be in many forms. You can even see it sometimes in the action of a little child. It doesn't matter. You will know it when you see it because it will always ring true in you. It's not just you. Even after you pass, it will ring true for generations and generations. To people who search and seek out that kind of eternal truth, things of that nature will always resonate. It will always have some value. It will give you purpose from it. Okay.

That's the basic outline of what I think is attractive – physically, intellectually and spiritually. The next question is what are we going to do with this? If we have these kinds of things, what are you going to do with it? Before you get into even that step of questioning – do you have it, something that you can share with others? Do you have something that is attractive? And if you do, what are you going to do with it? When you watch television people, you see them use a lot of attractive things to sell stuff, right? Now election season is coming. People are going to go on television and try to make themselves attractive and appealing. They're going to sell themselves so they can get elected. You see all sorts of this kind of thing. Whether people are involved in politics, of course, obviously people are always selling stuff. They're always in our way, trying to pitch their product, making themselves look as attractive as possible. But is it true? Unfortunately, many times it's the consumer who finds out the hard way. I wish there was some kind of guarantee that you are only getting what you are promised.

Society really does not have a clear definition of what is true eternity or true love. Think even about orthodox religions, still they are waiting for the messiah. This is whether you are Jewish, Christian, Catholic, or Muslim – you are still waiting for something, a savior to come. The unorthodox, but also the 'second class' monotheistic religions, Mormons, Scientologists, the Moonies, right? But at least we believe that somebody's already here. We're not waiting for nobody, we just have to prove it. You just have to go out and convince people that it is. We are all right, but you need to have more give and take and learn.

People are out there selling their stuff every day, every day using attractiveness. The funny thing is in cities, all these smart people who can show their intelligence and intellectual brilliance, come to work just to try to move up the corporate ladder. They labor away every day just to show their brilliance, their specialty, and their excellence. But the funny thing is that in the end, they normally don't show any of these things. That's pretty much how it is in the end. That intellectual stuff, for them, that's the pinnacle, that's the maximum for them. They settle there. They like to have the horizontal stuff, but they don't want to go up any higher. They don't want to pursue spirituality. So, in the end, they pretty much come down again. They use their talent, their brilliance, to indulge in what? In materialism. When you have attraction it's very, very, very easy to be indulgent. It's very, very easy to exploit things because you have that power. You have that power to attract. And if you don't know how to contain that, that attraction can be devastating to civilization. Because what you are glorifying is pretty much self-destructive things such as exploitation, indulgence, self-aggrandizement, self-centeredness. Once you start exploiting and you get used to, and start enjoying indulgence, you are going to become self-centered very soon. It's pretty much a given. You can 100 percent expect that person to become self-centered sometime soon, period. You can't be exploitive and self-indulgent and be a nice person. You don't become a nice person by doing this kind of stuff. This is important because it's basic, it's the bedrock of trying to be decent, nice and honest. If you want your children to understand that stuff, you have to know how to define what tricks them into becoming that kind of exploitive, self-centered person. There are things out there that encourage people down that path, not just children but even you, even me, it doesn't matter how old or young you are.

You will learn until the day you die things that you can teach about how to become a better person by truly defining the meaning of attraction, things that are attractive to you. You have to make the list of do's and don'ts and keep them in your mind, and in yourself. Start from there. What kind of attraction is a "do" and what kind of attraction is a "don't." See what works for you. If it works for you, teach your children. Just start from there. You can do that, right? For the sake of your children. And try to compare notes. In other words, what you are saying and what you see on television, sit together and talk about it. Start there. Have a healthy discussion. That's the best way to get to know your kids and that's the best way to teach your children how to respect you and depend on you when it comes to deciding on the things that are right, learning what is moral and whatever. The only way they are going to come closer to you is when you have become that kind of figure in their lives. Right? That's why you come with your children. You're hoping to see somebody who is going to stand here to be some kind of a figure like that, that's about it isn't it? I'm not saying that I'm that kind of figure but that's what you expect. It's the same thing. You have to have that kind of relationship with yourself first. You have to define that stuff to yourself first. You have to say, does it make sense to me, can I believe in this stuff, do I accept this stuff? Yeah, okay, then if somebody needs sharing, I share it with them, hey man, what. How does it sound? Sound okay? Okay, let's tell our kids then. Like I said, last week I talked about team spirit and team practice. Hey, then you share it, do it with your friends and stuff.

That's what you should talk about, not stupid gossip. Because it is more important to us that we have a higher level, a higher quality. Define things this way, that's how you compete. That's what people look at when you are competing. Otherwise, you can't compete. You are going to lose. You are going to lose out on those things. And it's the small things that make the difference between first and second. All those things matter.

We need to control everything we define. So before we think about control, you have to define it properly. Please, if you don't define it properly, don't even think about trying to control it. You are going to screw up big. It's not going to last. Even if you think you have something, it's not going to last. So, start from something that people take for granted, but your children are interested in. Let it be true to you. Then you can die for it. Yeah, that definition—I vouch my life on that stuff. Start from there. And when your children want to look at you, they want you to be confident. How else? When there's so much temptation pulling them left and right, if you can't even define certain things with confidence, that's not going to give them any kind of confidence. So, it's important. All those little things are important and you must define it properly because that's God's expectation, that's Father's expectation to humanity.

Know how to take care of yourself and starting from your family, take care of them before you start going out with this 'I'm going to change the world' stuff. If you have that opportunity, use it wisely. It's great time for you to be learning, too. I'm grateful. I'm going to do my best. I don't think it's ever lost. They'll come back to me one day, my children. What I got, I'm doing my best. I'll do better. I have more to prove. I want to be an attractive dad.

Take care of yourself. I'll see you next week.

Addressing Problems
March 26, 2006

Thank you, please sit down. Today I want to talk about addressing problems.

We all have problems. Nobody has problems in this room? I'm trying to find some kind of universality in sharing.

I guess the way to approach the problem is to understand what kind of standard we set in terms of absolute, first on a primary level, the secondary level, and the physical level. For instance, what I mean by a primary absolute is like the law of physics. It's something we learn that's been confirmed. We know that it exists to the extent that we understand it, and we have verified it to the point that's basically within the range of our limitations about how we perceive certain physical laws. And even that has a certain absolute value.

As for secondary absolute, this is something that has to do with the intelligence that we manifest in our reality to create some kind of law and order. So, it's human made stuff—the laws that we live by. You break the law, or any kind of legal wrongdoing, and it will be dealt with and will be remedied.

And third is physical stuff. But to me it's a kind of etiquette. For example, some people get offended if I use colorful words. They protest to your friends or whatever. Ultimately in the end, because we have a small society, it comes back to my ears, blah, blah, blah. That kind of stuff.

So, basically we have certain things of universal magnitude in the realms of intellect and the physical parameters we set. Then we try to use those as some kind of a benchmark to regulate our lives. Having said that, the problem arises when certain individuals don't recognize the standards that get set as absolute, whether it's primary, secondary, or 'etiquette wise.' That's basically how problems arise. And when you talk about problems in society, most of you don't live alone, right? Even if you are single and don't have family, still you live in society to make a living. Like Jeremiah Johnson, or whatever his name was, living out in the hills somewhere hunting for life—unless you are somebody like that, maybe there is that kind of exception—but otherwise everybody, everybody, has some connection to society in general. You can't depart from that gregariousness because we need it. You don't want to be alone, first of all.

When you talk about that basic human reality, the problem arises by not understanding the nature of gregariousness, which can be complex. Why? Because it's individuals coming together creating a gregarious reality. And that creates complexity because we each believe that we are individually unique. We are idiosyncratic. However minute the differences might be, it's still difference. There is some sort of recognizable difference but many times because of the complexity, we blame the complexity because we don't take time to understand all the factors that are involved, even just dealing with your immediate group—never mind society in general—just in your gregarious sect. That's why problems arise. I mean, how many parents can honestly say that they understand all their children's idiosyncratic reality. Sometimes I want to ask that to my father. Well, I ask you the same question. Let's say, if you have more than two or three, how much do you really know about your kids? How much are you connected with them?

Problems arise when there is disconnection. In order to recognize a problem, first of all you have to understand how many factors are involved in the picture. What are the components, what are the vital components? There is always a vital component in any complex organism or complex things. How many vital factors are there? You have to identify them, recognize them, understand them, and know how they connect to one another. How do you make a relationship, in whatever reciprocal ways people act just to have a relationship. If you don't understand that clearly, you cannot go forward. If there's a problem, let's say, you can never address it. Many times, the problem goes unsolved or you say to yourself it's difficult to solve. But that's because you haven't fully identified all the factors. That's why it's unsolved, cannot be solved, it's difficult to solve. But the truth is, it can be solved. Just as with anything we are still learning, through science or whatever just to learn about the physical universe and the laws of physics, we still have a ways to go. Or even about healing our bodies for instance. There are many diseases that we don't understand how to cure because we haven't fully comprehended or identified all the factors that cause that kind of problem. Therefore, we don't have the ability to address and remedy the problem. We still have a long way to go even just to deal with the physical universe as we know it.

So, let's start with things that you can do. Let's not talk about things that it'll take years and years and generations and generations to fully comprehend. Even changing the world, it'll take generations. That's why you can't really take yourself that seriously. I'm in the process of things—that's about it. That's the best I can do, I'm not Father. I'm in the process of things, that's about it. So, when you address that kind of reality, face what's true, and what affects our lives. It has something to do with our future, too. However long you may live. Even just recently a member I know personally passed away. I hope she goes in peace, she settles in quickly, and I believe and have hope that her family will be taken care of by people who care about them. In other words, our life is very short.

Even with the short life we are faced with, we still have a ways to go. And there are many problems that we still haven't fully comprehended. Why? Because we can't control things. Just because you have the position of a leader, if you don't understand the people who work under you, you can't really become a good leader. Of course, there is a kind of cliché, a certain concept that is obvious, 'if you want to be a leader you have to lead the way.'

There are so many programs that try to teach you, whether it's governmental or religiously motivated, that try to help people. The U.S. government has a program called The Peace Corps, right? I think it was started in the 1960s by John Kennedy. And there are other organizations that have done a lot of good, mostly Christian-based organizations, that try to do charitable work. I mean even for crying out loud, Jimmy Carter with Habitat for Humanity. He goes and starts building these houses to give to people in need, people with low income, or in hard times in poverty. If you don't do something like that, it's very difficult even for that good-intended stuff and ideas, to last.

You have to know what your limitations are. You have to know yourself. You have to know what you are doing. You have to understand your position, yourself, first. Know your limitations, know your boundaries, know your responsibility and how it connects to others. That kind of reality should come down from above, right? We try to talk about hierarchy, law and order. If that is important to us then that's what should be passed down. That kind of attitude, that kind of way of living should be given. Otherwise, it's do your own thing. You don't want to pretend. You don't go far, don't last. What you see is what you get, you know what I'm saying? And it should be that. Because you can't change yourself if you are going to pretend. Obviously, you are not going to help people around you and certainly you are not going to change the world. You can only get better when you understand your limitation. Then you can try to expand it, increase your boundary, your potential.

As in many things, the thing that gives us a problem is this kind of immature confidence. Arrogance. Quick judgment, jumping into judgment without fully grasping the issue at hand. That's the problem. If we can just step back before making any decisions, if we talk about that basic stuff, I think we can solve many problems that we have. We can tackle them with our own hands. We don't need God's help. We don't need Father's intervention. You can solve it. We can solve it. We can take care of those problems. If we can't do that, don't think you are going to change the world. Because that is just—that's a lie. That will never come true.

But, we can do it. Start from yourself. Understand your limitations. Know you and try to connect to the people around you, and try to get to know them, understand all the factors, including the ones that create complexity. So, work small, you don't have to always think big. Everybody likes to do that, I know. But work within your limit. Start, if you want to understand greater computations, start small and try to understand it, see how it works and learn. Have life experience. That's more important than just the theory stuff. You can talk about stuff until whenever. But look, you have to know how to work it. If you don't know how to work it, you are not going to change anything. Start from there. Tell yourself that's important to you for your future, for your betterment. If you can't, if you just say 'oh, it's Father,' it just sounds so cliché-ish and like lip service. You then tempt people to think of that brainwashed stuff.

But I tell you as it is, as you would like to hear it, the way you would understand. There's nothing wrong with that. But keep it to yourself. You know what to me a humble man is? Nothing other a man who keeps his arrogance to himself, you understand me? Everybody's arrogant. Everybody's self-glorifying, or can be. You are so yourself, right? Just try to work with what you got. Don't mind if you just recognize it and sometimes say it—hey, if it's true, it's true. I don't want somebody telling me it's not true when I know it's true. Anyway, something like that. If we can start like that I think we can do something about it. We'll start to feel this kind of stuff in our lives. Then that's something. That is a new beginning. Because you feel it. It's not someone telling you. You feel it. You see it. You can see it in your mind. Even if you don't see it right now—you feel it, at the same time you can see it. That's something. That something is change.

Anyway, I'll be away for a month. I have something to take care of, so I'll see you in May. Sorry, but I have to take care of something. Take care of yourself, okay? See you later.

[*Note: what Hyo Jin Nim so humbly referred to as "something to take care of" was his forthcoming concert tour in Japan.*]

Convincing People That Father is the Messiah
May 14, 2006

There are a lot of young people here this morning. Okay, what is your greatest difficulty when you go out there and try to convince other people who we are? What is the most difficult thing that you face? I guess it is trying to prove "Father is the messiah," right? Let's talk about antichrist. What is the antichrist? Can anybody tell me what antichrist means? Can you define to me what that is? You have to if you are going to tell somebody else the opposite. *(Somebody who thinks that he has all the answers, but he doesn't have it in reality.)* The antichrist has all the answers? *(No, somebody who thinks that he has all the answers.)* Oh, okay. I'm sorry. I got a lot of wax in my ear. Okay. So, what else? What else is the definition of the antichrist? *(Someone who prevents people from coming to the Christ.) O*kay. Somebody who has all the answers, somebody who prevents somebody from coming to the Christ. What else? *(Communism.)* Communism? Okay. What else? Just knock yourself out. We have to talk about this stuff. The more we have the better. *(Someone who is against human welfare.)* Okay. What else?

Let's talk about this stuff. Let's talk about the antichrist before we talk about the messiah. Please enlighten me, and enlighten yourself in the process. Because this is the opportunity. Come on. I am all ears and everybody is listening. And you can say whatever you want. *(Obstacles to coming to God.)* Obstacles to coming to God. Just whatever. More, I want more. Please give me more. *(Fallen culture.)* Fallen culture, yeah. Give me more. *(Influenced by Satan.)* Input by Satan. Give me more. *(Anti-God.)* Anti-God. Give me more. *(Anybody without mind and body unity.)* Anybody without mind and body unity. Give me more. Come on, give me more. *(Someone who thinks he is the savior of mankind but he is not.)* Okay. Give me more. Come on, give me more. *(What Satan is trying through the wrong religion, for himself, for glory, not taking God's perspective.)* Okay. Give me more. Give me more. Let's go, let's go. Let's just try to reach the end of what we have, in and out of desire to understand what the answer is. If you want to start from something, if you expect something from me because of something, because of status, at least give me that benefit of the doubt. So give me more. *(Someone who denies that Christ is born in the flesh.)* I can't hear out of this ear. *(Someone who denies that Christ is born as a man.)* Okay. What else? One day, this earwax will fall out. I believe that stuff. *(Any person or experience or thought that keeps us from fully accepting True Parents.)* Okay. Whatever he said, you heard it and I didn't, and that's about it. Anyway, so what else? Come on, let's go. We want to go out there and try to convince people. Come on. Give me your best shot. *(Satan.)* You are calling me Satan? Okay, I'll see you later. Okay. You know Satan that closely, huh? Does he look like me? *(Someone who doesn't believe we are fallen so they don't need the messiah.)* Okay.

I believe the best definition, when you come to that kind of quest and that kind of questioning, when you have to, is to define individualism as a concept, a raw concept. The antichrist in itself is the concept of individualism. Now that is very, very important. You have to look at it as a concept, not as a single individual. You are not looking for the devil here. It's a concept. It is a concept called individualism. That is what antichrist is. Even old people talk about that stuff. You have to understand that there is the possibility of the antichrist in you. Unless you address that antichrist stuff, you can't fulfill your duty correctly as a Moonie.

You have to get that out of the picture. You have to nullify the nonsense. Because they will get you if you don't do it right, if you do not answer the question correctly. Do you know what I am saying? *(Yes.)* It is a concept. Antichrist is a concept, not an individual. Trust me on this. This issue will live for a long time. That is a good gig. Trust me. Now from here, you build. Do you understand? I will show you something, something you can do something with. I don't know you that well, but this is important. You have to look at it that way. It is a concept that describes what is wrong, and it is not an individual. Why? Because remember the Fall itself in the Garden of Eden, that kind of mythological stuff? This is the opposite of that. Do you know what I am saying? *(Yes.)* Individualism became a concept. Do you understand? Trust me on this. Do you want to fix it? Go back to what went wrong. What went wrong, as you and I know, is that reality changed in concept. It's a changed concept. If you can change that concept, you can change the essence. Okay?

So, I am sure you have a lot to say about why you don't want to be selfish, right? Or, about how you want to suffer for the sake of the greater good, and even be willing to die. Look. Okay, so be it. Life is short. You know, life is short. Life is short. Put it into perspective on your own. Somebody will tell you how to do it, and that's about it. If somebody does not, you can do it on your own, eventually. That's it. God will win. Do not take yourself that seriously. You will die. What do you think this whole stuff is about? In some ways, it is kind of like predestination. Isn't it? Everything is about predestination. And if it is about that, in the end if God wins, it is about predestination. Trust me. Are you stupid? If somebody wins ultimately no matter what you do, that is called predestination, isn't it? You have nothing to say. So, what does that mean? How do we understand the concept of predestination? Excuse my illiteracy and my stupidity and my vulgarity and my life. Look. Let me tell you my opinion. Whether you like it or not, I showed up. It is all about give and take. You are learning about give and take with God. If God is the almighty, that's it. It is learning about the true process of ontology. That's about it. And why do we need good examples? Why? We need good examples to tell us what good actions are. I know you think that. You think that you can do all this. You think this, you think that. That is why we look for good models. Because without even trying, the least we can do is think. That's about it. It's pathetic, but it's true. It is absolutely true. And what do you do when you are thinking? How do you make things go forward? What do you believe? If you want to make money, go make money. I do not care. Have something. I do not care what you believe. Do something with it. Do something beyond just thinking. Be a man. Be a woman. Be human. The funny thing is that animals act just to survive. We think, and we can get away with a whole lot of stuff that if we did the same thing in the animal kingdom there'd be no way you could survive. So, do something. Do something! Say something! If you want to think something, think something! And make that thinking into something that affects someone next to you! Now that is very difficult. Try it. That's difficult. That is very difficult. You think you got something— you can do that to the next person who is already in your possession, in your control, in your dominion. Amen. You do? You are good. Then you are set. You have no problems. All you have to do is improve and increase that stuff. Whatever that is, make it bigger. Whatever that is, make it bigger. I don't know what it is. I don't know you.

Do you want to die for something? You have to die for something. If you want to live, you have to think about dying. Otherwise you are not serious, right? Truly. if you want to be in control of your life, you better know how you are going to die. Trust me. If you don't understand that stuff, you are not going to make it. Trust me. Anyway, if you want to live, you better know how you are going to die. Why? Because you want to be an individual. You want to be American. Okay. No problem. Be a great American. But you have to be in control— nobody else.

You know what it is, you know why you are living, you know why you are dying. And you are going to do your best. Do as much as you can to be the best you can be for whatever is important to you. That's about it. In my eyes, that is the basic premise on which you believe in God. And if you don't, I don't care. I don't care what you think. I really don't care. Because I will live with that till the day that I die. What do you say? That's about it. And you will die.

But it's a pain in the butt, trying to do the best you can every year, whatever the gig, every cycle. Trying to outdo yourself. Do you know what I am saying? It's a pain in the butt. And that never ends. It never ends. How is that? You are going to live for somebody else? That's it. No bluff. That is the truth. That is just the way it is. There is no other way. If you have a better idea, you do it then. Tell me something. Tell somebody. Tell them the easier way. There is no easy way when it comes to really doing something. Do you know why? If you believe in something to be absolute, there is some wall in the end. There are a whole lot of stories about that in life. It's like some kind of monkey in

"Kubla Khan." If you have something better, you do it and make it on your own. Take care of yourself in the end. That's about it.

So, what can we do for each other? I hope that we have good people here to do the things that we need to do. That's about it. That is all I hope for. And I don't know anything else. Know one thing. It's important. There are many ways. In the end, it's about communication, it is all about communication. You know that, right? You know that's important to you young people. It is all about that stuff. It doesn't matter how it is approached, delivered, or presented, it doesn't matter as long as the communication factor in essence is in the message. It's a process.

So how do you go about communicating the message? Look, personally, I go out and I do stuff. I blah, blah, blah, and people say, "Oh!" People who left the church come to listen to the concert. Young people are just part of it. Old people think like they are listening to a principle lecture. And new people, they want to know more. That is a good thing. That is a good platform. I don't care what it is. We need to have Air Force, and Navy, and Army. If you want to put it into that context, let's just do it. I don't care. Knock yourself out. This is 21st century. You have to take initiative. You understand the direction and you are willing to do something for it, amen, you should. And inspire others who are doing the same thing like you. That's about it. I don't want to be reminded of the same old song and dance routine forever till the day that I die. Give me something that even I can be inspired by. Something so I can take one more step, work a little harder, because of you. I know I'm dead, I know I'm dying. Let me die faster, how is that? Or let me die harder, how is that? Let me die while relevant, how is that? You can inspire me to do that; that is a good thing for you. If you help somebody, if you help some pathetic fool, that is a good thing.

Why did these young people come all of a sudden? I was comfortable hanging around with these old people who are dying. Now I have to think differently! This stuff is important. Every day, give and take. That kind of thing is important. Preaching is important. Regimen is important. You can do crazy stuff, but the regimen is a very important tool. You have to know how to balance polar opposites. That is the only way realistically you are going to control reality, if you think you can. Time will tell. So be it.

Basically that is how you are going to go about it—trying to prove that stuff. Why? Because you are doing this for somebody else, not for you, right? Trust me, that's important. When you think that, this is important. Standing here and talking this nonsense to you is important. This is a pain in the butt. You have to live it. It is important. Trust me. This is very important. It does not matter what you get out of it. For yourself, if you are going to do this, you have to do this for your own sanity and your own reality in balance. If you don't do this, you will get corrupted. Trust me. There are other ways people think, but it does not matter. But in general that is about it. Okay? Your life is short. Make sure you can look yourself in the mirror when you say, "I lived for the sake of others." Do you understand me? It is true. Trust me.

So, that is why you have to know how to plan your life and know how to die well. You want to be smart. That is smart. And if you can do that, you will be a free man. Remember, antichrist is not an individual. It is a concept. Trust me on this. This gig will last a long time. We will see. In my mind, it will. It is a good gig. Anyway, nice to see you. *(Nice to see you, too.)*

I will see you next week, okay? I will see you later.

Dealing With Fallen Nature
May 21, 2006

Thank you.

Please sit down. We are still here. Today, I want to share with you about dealing with fallen nature.

Where does God lie? Father talks about vertical and horizontal stuff. So based on principle lecture, where does God lie? On a vertical top, top or bottom, left or right, where? In extremes? Where does He exist? *(In the middle.)* Yeah, okay, so the center. I guess you can say. If you want to cut a three-dimensional sphere you need seven points, right? So, you have to have a center in order to create a sphere, right? You have to have some kind of center.

So, you have the horizontal and the vertical and center. So be it. What is center? That is where the fun begins. Because you have to talk about the extremes. You have to talk about all the extremes—left and right, up and down, based on center—from all different perspectives.
You might have a vertical left and right, up and down stuff at certain point of the angle but as it shifts, stuff changes to that person. Based on that perspective, what is that individual person, as this changes. We've got to change, even when keeping that system or that concept which in the end makes the sphere.

Look, I am trying to keep time with Korea because I have to go there soon. That is about it. Its night and day are the opposite. If it's day here, it's night over there. Literally, it's like that. And there is the degree of difference in that.

So, how do you determine the extremes? What do you think is the difference between, let's say something you fear, and something that gets you inspired? What does that teach you in the end? You think there is some kind of simulation from something, things that are seemingly opposite based on definitions as we know it, in reality or in causality, or casualness?

There is a difference. But within that difference, there is something that brings that stuff together as opposites. Anytime you have an opposite, you will find a center. Trust me. That's the rule. You cannot have opposites without the center. Otherwise, there is no concept such as opposites. Right? *(Yes.)*

So, in order to even understand what the opposite means, you have to understand why the center exists and know the definition. Even just on that particular issue there are many angles, just on that particular thing alone. That's it.

Now don't tell me you can do everything. Let's start from there. Just that particular. You have to find what that general definition is. That thing that is zero that represents God, that brings opposites together, that holds the opposites together. What is that definition?

To me, when I fear something, when I'm inspired by something, just simply put, it gives me a certain kind of literal definition. It gives me certain direction, it gives me discipline, it gives me destination. Why? Because I fear something, I'm inspired. Same thing. Talk about love and hate. When you love something, when you hate something, obviously it gives me some kind of passion for something. It gives me that possessiveness. At the same time, it gives me some solution, an absolute something.

How do I define it? It's up to me. Why? You answer that stuff. I'm not going to answer it. No, you answer it. Because even if I'm not standing here, if I'm gone, you will be answering it, whether you like it or not. And you are not going to blame it on me. You can divorce me, but in the end, you still have to face your Maker on your own, right? Just like me. You can—shoot, look, it's up to you. In the end, ultimately, what you choose to think—because based on it, you are going to act. Right?

If I'm pissed off at something, I might just lose it sometimes. Hey, I'm only human. So what? Take it or leave it. What you see is what you get. I know what the purpose of stuff is. There is a purpose in everything. Do you know the difference between—let me put it this way—there is a similarity between vacationing and preaching. What do you want when you go on a vacation? What do you expect? You want to relax, you want to rejuvenate, see some new things and learn something or get into the old stuff that you liked, indulge in stuff a little.

What do you expect from a preacher in today's world? And who in their right mind would want to do this stuff forever? You go out and try to make something out of your experiences. I'm not a TV preacher. It's not about building my empire. In building anything, money is important. Trust me. That's not my scenario, all right? Even when somebody comes and blows their stuff out at you and given that, you just sit back and you get something out of it. At least in your decency, you should at least be able to protect the one that you love, right?

Anyway, it doesn't matter. I know reality. I've seen worse than this many times over. It's not, look, things happen, okay? I think I went off on this guy. Some things I shouldn't say, but just keep it to myself, you know? Do you know what I'm saying? Do you understand that?

Can I be honest with you? Yeah, sometimes you can lose it. Yeah, sure. So be it. Hey, but I still show up, don't I? Because I really don't care what you think. I'm trying to do my best, okay? If you have problems, some things you just have to keep to yourself. Okay?

I'm not just talking about the archangel. Antichrist, yes, it is selfish. Look, 'the dead will rise' and all that stuff, you see that stuff all over the place. False prophets, people who don't believe in God, because of the time, what is the platform that they are using? Multimedia. Okay? Look, they don't believe in God, they have the opportunity to say all sorts of stuff.

Selfish individualism is wrong. There is individualism and there is selfish individualism. Selfish individualism, individualism. Okay?

Before you talk, even when you talk about the extreme, even before you get into selfish and unselfish stuff, you have to talk about the extremes first. You have to define that first. That's why I'm doing that, that's my point today. Okay?

Before you try—that's the next step—you have to define that extreme first, that place centered on God, that is real. Stuff happens later. That's a different problem. That's a next level problem. Okay? And to find that, you will always find a definition in every extreme when you just look at it as the opposite, polar opposites. Do you understand me? You understand that, and you control it. You move it into the direction you want to move. That is how you control yourself. And screw everything else. If you're doing the right thing, God will bless you.

I guess you are here because you love me, right? Okay, so be it. I'm not a politician. I'm not here for a popularity contest. I couldn't care less whether you like me or not. Okay? But don't judge me. Judge me when I'm dead. Because I won't judge you.

There's many, in certain situations, it seems so easy, many things. But that's just a moment. I know how it's going to end. But they seem, I even know some kids close to me, some people close to me, they are just throwing their life away. Do you know what I'm saying?
They are doing stupid stuff, they are making stupid decisions, and they are going to burn in the end. That's possible, and it will happen. Many things will happen. Things like that will happen all over the place. But that's not your problem, right?

Why? Because if you are going to help somebody else, you are going to start from you. Do you know what I'm saying? It doesn't matter how big or small you are if you can't control yourself, right? That's what you blame me for. I'm such a goof up all the time. I'm so obvious and I actually advertise it. It is not going to work. Okay? Think about that.

Anyway, you can bring children. I won't curse anymore. Hey, I'm trying to explain to you okay, I'm sorry. Okay? I'm trying to make a point. You talk about eternity and you can't even wait for a week for a comeback? Come on. I deserve that, right? Come on white people. Give me a break here.

If it's going to happen, it's going to happen. That's about it. Do or die. That's about it. That's it. This is about talking about a point, okay?

And I'll see you next week.

Take care of yourself and don't worry about me. I'm not that crazy.

Take care.

The Dragon
May 28, 2006

Please sit.

Some people have been commenting that sometimes my talks are a little too short and I kind of run out of stuff to say. So, from now on, at the end I will give a moment to answer questions if I can. If I can't give you something on the spur of the moment, I'll catch you next week. Okay? *(Thank you.)* All right.

Anyway, it's supposedly something—how should I put it—it's a gift. When you have to talk about stuff, there is so much chatter going on out there in the world. You have to try to be almost like a dragon slayer. And you have to know what "The Dragon" is. Because everywhere you look, you are threatened.

In a free society where freedom of expression is guaranteed, the dragon or the monster is pretty much nothing other than multimedia. That's about it. Why? Because it gives you both medicine and disease.

Under the banner of free expression and freedom of speech, whether you like it or not, they can get away with almost anything unless they frequently disobey the law or break the law. Because in the end they can say, "Hey, that's not my problem. People can turn it off, but the problem is that some people don't." And guess what? Guess who those people are? And that's why it is never ending stuff unless you address the dragon in a free society.

There is nothing that free society or capitalism produces that actually affects people to the extent that multimedia can. Why? Because it doesn't sell refrigerators, it doesn't sell cars, it doesn't sell airplanes, and it doesn't sell bombs and gadgets that give you convenience. It basically sells people. It sells people.

However degenerate, however great they are, they sell it for the buck. Period. There is no discrepancy. As long as they can get away with it, they will do it. Somebody is going to do it.

So that's the dragon. That's the monster that we face. That's obvious. It has always been that way. What do you think I was influenced by when I was young, by all these Western influences and culture? Especially through multimedia. Because it's dangerous, it's powerful.

When you have no direction, it doesn't matter whether you have no original sin. Obviously in the Garden of Eden, somebody fell. You can make choice to be evil. But when there are a lot of opportunities out there, for children, regardless of who you are, you are going to make mistakes. Absolutely. Because if it can happen in a primal sense, it can happen in reality. Your reality. That's about it.

Okay, having said that, so how are we going to deal with that monster? How can you stop that monster? I think the best way to approach that question is to start from yourself, start from you. You have to define what you got, the best you got. You have to know what that is. Otherwise, you can't be a warrior even if you wish that. Everybody wants to be a superman, a superhero. You can't be one if you don't even know who you are, what your limitations are, how you take, what you are capable of, on and on. The reality. Your reality. No nonsense reality.

What can you can do to change something? If you are so desperate to change it that you are willing to give your life away. That something— what is that in you? Simply, even when you are listening to a Disney movie, people say, 'follow your conscience.' What is that? What is your conscience? What does your conscience tell you? Does your conscience tell you to be arrogant? Does your conscience tell you to be rich, famous, and live for yourself?

No, the conscience tells you the basic stuff. Basic stuff that affords you the chance to be objective. That's about it. Basically it reminds you of what your least is, not your greatest. That's where you start. And the opposite that conscience tells you is what you're bequeathing, what your inheritance is. Inheritance. What do you think is the greatest inheritance? You think inheritance is money, power? I don't think so. I see that stuff come and go away. I really don't care. It's something that is eternal, something that teaches you, reminds you things go on forever. And that's what you need to inherit whether you call it a heart or whatever. It doesn't matter.

Inheritance of eternity is important. And the basic premises in which you can start to regain that understanding is starting to have some kind of faith that you are a little more than what you have in your pocket, or your reality—or what you can consume, what you can possess, what you can conquer, what you can take. If you are truly selfish. You have to go beyond that. That's about it.

Having said that, what does conscience truly teach you in the end? If you try to listen to your conscience, no matter what, it allows you to appreciate another something in front of you that supposedly is like you. You might not like the way I put it, but to me, it doesn't matter. It comes in all sizes, all different things. I've seen it all.

You have to try, you have to try. That struggle will never end. It will never end. Not as long as I live. That's for sure. And I'm not going to tell you it's going to end with me. No, no, no, no. That's not true. It's going to take a long time.

We really have to address the issue of the essence of stuff. The original sin and fallen nature. I talked about fallen nature. I just kind of tapped into that stuff.

In order to deal with the fallen nature stuff, you basically have look at things in every situation. You have to know how to separate the extreme first. It doesn't matter. Before you get into your selfishness or selflessness, before you get morally involved, you literally have to separate it.

For instance like man and woman. You have to try to define what brings that absolute together because God somehow exists in the center. We don't know how to define the neutron but every living element doesn't have a form without it. That's about it. It's based on difference of the plus and minus numbers in it.

Obviously our limitation is such that we don't know at this point in time how to define that center properly yet. Because there is so much to learn and we are just beginning the basics, scratching the elementary surface of it. We all know that.

It doesn't matter how arrogant you try to project yourself, such as claiming that you have all the answers. It's okay. That's about it. Everybody has all the answers. That's called a free world, isn't it?

Then what? In the end, you have to come to something. Even when you talk about man and woman, there is something that brings man and woman together regardless of your selfishness or your unselfishness, there is something that is inherent.

There is conjugation and appropriation. Something like that. You have to define those kinds of elements and factors in the picture. Before you get into your selfishness and unselfishness, getting on your moral high hat. There is always something like that.

And that has to be clearly defined and recognized if you are going to attack it. Otherwise, you have no strategy. It doesn't matter what you think. You have no strategy—you have nothing to deal with the problem with. That's a problem.

You have to know how to contain yourself. You have to know your limit. Conscience tells you your least. Why do you need to know your least? Because it's very favorable for your situation when you start to be objective, in certain situations. Whether you like it or not, if you believe there are powers that be that are higher than you, you have to understand that concept of objectivity. Obviously if you don't, even in the social world, you are a criminal, right? Well, anyway, it's like that. That stuff exists.

Now, knowing that, know your limitations. Know your absolute limit. And try to understand it. That's the kind of guessing game everybody has to go through. Whether my maximum and minimum somehow ranges within the universal normality, some constant, some zero.

Some might go up and some might go down. Do you know what I'm saying? Some might be literally above something, that maximum and lowest point, and literally above the universal zero. Somebody might be literally under it. And somebody weighing in somewhere in the middle. Plus or minus stuff for maximum and less.

You have to figure that out. That's your problem. How can that be anybody else's problem other than yours? Who knows you better than you? No one. It should be you. Do you get pissed off all the time? I do. Because somebody thinks on my behalf about what my limitations are. I don't care. So be it. I really don't care. Because in the end, I still know it, not you. That's about it. I believe in this stuff. When you accept also the other aspect of that conscience, which is inheritance, you have to have faith. You know what's good. And that's what you want. You want something that lasts forever.

I'm going to keep somebody anonymous. But they have something, and they get used to a certain kind of lifestyle, lifestyle of certain things, luxury. And they change. They move with that kind of people and they change. They like that kind of lifestyle. They like how they are treated because they have all sorts of money. They can have four of this and four of that, and they change. One of the greatest addictions in my eyes is power and money. More than anything else. The other stuff is poor man's stuff. But even that, you can conquer it. But some people just don't want to conquer it. That's why problems happen to the world.

When people of certain significance hold on to something, without knowing that they have problems, it causes a problem. It trickles down whether you like it or not. It's hierarchical whether you like it or not.

It's a free world, and that happens even in the so called free world. Trust me. Then what happens? Same problems happen over and over again. The struggle. No matter how much we can try to give each other basic stuff, the obvious stuff.

One hundred years ago, people used to wipe their butt with straw-weaved rope. They literally used to hang strings from the main-house to the outhouse [motioning a string with his hands]. And they literally go like this [motioning to walk over the string] and walk and wipe their behinds. So, obviously a lot of things have changed. But that's not the end, is it? Just because we have more convenience in comparison to whatever. Everybody in culture can always go back. There might be years of differences. But you go back, that's about it.

And what have we accomplished? Did we get rid of all that stuff? No, we didn't. Then how are we going to do that? We have to compete with the rest, who are morally righteous. So be it.

We have some concept, and yes, it's a good concept. I believe it can happen in 10 generations. It will take time. Trust me. Because I have to let go of a lot just to say this to you. What you see is what you get. It's my struggle, not yours. Trust me. But it's okay. We don't live that long. Life is short. You make your peace and that's about it.

Because it never ends. You give, you give, you forget, you give the more. Nobody counts how much you give. It's between you and your God in the end. That's about it. Worst case scenario. You always have to think about that stuff. And you die. But I control it. Nobody else.

Any questions? Knock yourself out. You have a question?

(Hyo Jin Nim, when you came last week and spoke, you spoke about fallen nature. We all go through so much pain on different levels. But I always think that's Adam and Eve and always have this anger towards Adam and Eve. Last week, I wanted to ask you about that. But that's not what I want to ask you this time. I want to know if there is somebody who is contemporary or already passed on who you really

look up to and inspires you. Not just Adam and Eve who takes everybody to hell, but someone who is really inspiring and you look forwards.)

You inspire me. That's why I'm here. People tell me that people love me and that's why they come and you would not come here for another reason. And I'm the kind of guy who thinks based on what I see normally and initially. And I was really pissed off at a lot of things. I really didn't care. I really didn't care. Okay, you do it then. And that's about it.

The only reason that I started to do this is—I'm sorry for saying this, it might sound selfish but—because I lost my son. And yes, I was blessed with a new family, and I started a new family. That helped me a lot. This is my life and that's about it.

And people started to respond. And they always try to encourage and try to say, don't lose hope. Sometimes I'm a stubborn-headed guy. I only brought this because like I said, from now on, I'll take your questions. If I can help you, give a little more if I can. That's about it. That's it.

Yeah. *(You mentioned conscience and inheritance. Could you explain a little more?)* Why do you want to make money—if you do make money as a family man? You obviously want something for your children. You want something better for your children. Inheritance is a very important concept of God's. Why? Because God is love. He is the absolute entity when it comes to His discipline and His force and His essence absence. So, obviously, when it comes to His inheritance, He has to absolutely mean it. It has to be absolute.

And what is absolute? It has to reflect the entity. What is the ultimate greatness of God? It's His eternal capacity. Capacity of what? Omnipotence, omnipresence? More than that, we believe in religious community, love, eternal love. Something like that.

So, that's what we are trying to inherit from almighty God. Why? Because if God is that kind of God, and He better be, that's about it, isn't it? There is nothing else greater. Because He is already omnipresent and omnipotent. He is the creator of everything. Why does He need you?

What is the difference between a man and an animal? You can inherit God. That's about it. An animal at best, maybe, I don't know, let's say they can inherit you. But I don't think they can inherit God. Okay? That's about it. To me, that's how I look at God's inheritance.

And everything else, we try to take into our own people's stupid stuff. Who cares? For me personally, I don't like to travel because if I go there, I get disappointed. Because it doesn't look like the postcard. That's why I don't like traveling. It's a waste of my time. Maybe I go to see some people, but that's about it. Not for sightseeing. America has so many beautiful places, the most beautiful places in the world. America hogs it all, in my eyes. So, something like that. To me, that's the kind of inheritance.

Conscience? Okay, how many times do you have problems with your conscience? When do you have the most problem with your conscience? Well, knock yourself out. Fill in that blank. It's like I say, when it teaches you, you should be humble. Think about your least. You are not that great. Be practical. I'm trying to tell you, trying to ground you, trying to make you more objective, more like a son, not like a father.

When your head is going all over the place, you will want to conquer your own folks and even God. Trying to bring you down a little bit. You know you don't need to do that. Settle down a little bit. And that's the time when you learn from your conscience. Because it tells you how to be objective. If God didn't love you, He would not have given you conscience. Think about it. What is the difference between original mind and conscience? It's similar in my mind, the same thing. We just call it differently because we associate Fall with restoring lineage. That's a very unique concept, tremendous concept. That's what you guys believe. In the end, we can win. I believe this stuff.

I might think of a lot of fantasy. Many times, at times I think irrational fantasies as well. I wish I wasn't born into this or that, that's absolutely irrational. You are just blowing off steam, that's about it. Sometimes your mind allows you to go into that moment of psychological babbling or rambling just to blow off steam. Otherwise you are literally going to kill people. The difference between a murderer and sane people is only a paper thin difference.

Just like people say the difference between love and hate is that shallow, that thin. It's the same thing. You just have to know how to deal with your reality. That happens. It's okay. Just know how to deal with it. Know when it's coming. Okay, okay. I'm going to use the best I have. Let's just do something a little more creative and creatively stupid. But it's only in fantasyland. Do you know what I'm saying?

Of course it's irrational. Of course it's fantasy. It's only thought. You're not going to actually go out and carry out it into action. Because you are not that stupid. Why? Because you don't want to be locked up forever. Just know how to take care of it. Just walk away from it. Stuff happens. All those little tools there, just a little jam there. You just have to know how to tinker with it and know how to manage it.

First thing is to recognize it—it exists for you. Know how to use it for your benefit. But know what is right. What is right? Guess what? You have to do this forever. Whether I like it or not, for me.

Do you like to be appreciated? So does everybody else under the sun. Anyway, do you have any more questions? Can I go now? May I be excused? Okay, I will see you next week.

Loyalty
June 4, 2006

How are you doing? I'll be away for a few weeks. I'm leaving today. The reason I'm going to be away for a few weeks is that I'd like to go to China and Japan. Something starting in China. I hope that you can have something in your prayers for its success. It's kind of exciting, but you never know.

Today I would like to talk about, "Loyalty." I hear so often, "I'm loyal only to myself." That kind of statement from—how should I put it in the best way—the "enlightened" world. So, when you are enlightened and when you are free, that's what you have to be, I guess. You have to find whatever is out there that the enlightened world and the free world offers, and then get the most out of it.

Having said that, let's get into the boring stuff. Why do you want to be loyal to something? Can you help me out on this stuff? Why would you want to feel loyal? Why would you need loyalty? What is the concept of loyalty? To me, first of all, loyalty, right off the bat, is a concept that exists. And it's necessary for certain things, for instance like forgiveness, eternity, paternity, and stuff that we believe is important, and makes us bigger than ourselves, our individual selves.

Why? Think about it. If you don't have it, what is the opposite of being loyal to something? Selfishness. There has to be some kind of program, some kind of system, some kind of concept that no matter how stupid you are, in the end it will guarantee you some kind of right passage. Not just symbolically, but literally right! Not r-i-t-e, but right. Something that guarantees that for you. Because you can see it all around you if you are looking for it. Many times, it's just right there. There's a Korean saying '등잔밑이어둡다.' "Underneath the lamp is the darkest place." That kind of stuff. That kind of saying.

Many things that are true, are so simple we forget to see the truth in it. We forgo it just because it's so near and so simple. We just don't care to pay attention to it. How can this something be true? How can it be that simple and that idiotic? It has to be more complicated than that if it's going to be truly true. What does that mean? Who determines how smart you are then?

Loyalty gives you a sense of something wholesome, a sense of objectivity. It's a proclamation of receiving a subject into your life. That's about it. That's what it means. I'm loyal to not just myself but to something greater than myself. I'm willing to have that kind of relationship. I'm ready.

If I'm going learn about something that is almighty and comes from the almighty, you have to understand why God is willing to forgo everything just to rely on His concept of love even if He has to suffer because of it. And He has been suffering. Why? Because we're still trying to restore the world. The world is not correct. Even based on the way we think of what an ideal should be, never mind what He thinks.

Do you ever wonder what goes through the mind of God, the almighty God, the creator, the omnipotent God, the omni person. Everything you can possibly think, and you can possibly think about joy and all that stuff that is ideal. Endlessly. All the potential that gives you joy just because you live, you have the presence in your life, you have that opportunity. Because of that you have that experience to learn all sorts of infinite stuff. And it can give you joy just by understanding it. That's nasty, that's powerful.

Why would anybody want to suffer? Many times. To understand love, you have to remember the concept of the wave stuff, ups and down stuff. To me, that kind of phenomenon gives you the understanding of life. Anything that gives, has some kind of benefit to physical existence. It has to have some kind of form. Whether it is light, literally waves, or whatever, any kind of energy. It undulates. It goes on. It has to. Why? Because in the end, everything depends on that phenomenon in the end. That is the way in which all the selfishness, if it exists, will neutralize itself. How can you be arrogant when you go through that kind of cycle?

When there is that kind of cycle that gives you right, literally, in your life you go through that cycle of ups and downs, how can you be selfish and how can you be arrogant? You can't. It's impossible. To me, the greatest addiction is power and money. That is the nastiest addiction. That stuff really does not really end.

You might not be addicted to drugs that might literally kill your body or eat your body, but it will eat your life eventually, that stuff. And you wouldn't know it. It will never end. Because you go into that kind of cycle. You literally get stuck into that cycle of lifestyle, and it's going to get worse and worse and worse. In other words, you are going to measure yourself to something greater and greater. And what is the greater? If you are a millionaire, you want to be a 10-millionaire, 100-millionaire, billionaire, 10-billionaire.

Look. And you are going to measure yourself up to that stuff. Okay? And you are going to get locked into that for the rest of your life. That's it. And power is the same thing. How much is enough for yourself to have the kind of joy and gratification and pleasure that you desire? Then what about the next thing?

What about love then? Love has nothing to do with loving yourself only. That's not true love. Is it? You can try to make it, you can make up anything you want. You can say, "From now on I'm going to call this [holding up a rolled up towel] a stick." But saying it looks like a stick to you doesn't mean it's a stick. "I'm only going to drink wine and whiskey." No, you should drink water, too. Okay?

It doesn't matter how you try to form your life just because you think you have control over it, or because you think you are better than somebody else. It really doesn't matter. Because in the end, those kinds of people are only loyal to themselves. That's about it. And their addiction. That's it.

You worry about people who are screwed up. Because you see right through them in the end. That's what they are loyal to: themselves and their problems, their limitations of selfishness, and their intelligence. Trust me. It's worse than being addicted to anything else.

I have been accused of being addicted to many things, trust me. That stuff is nasty. No good for you. It will ruin your life and it will ruin every opportunity that you might have to be good in the end. And you will lose it all. It's not going to help you. It can't.

Why? It doesn't have life sustaining power. Because in the end, understanding greater the level is going beyond self-love right? That's where the key lies. That's where true happiness lies when you understand something and learn about something true and meaningful.

Who cares about learning new things when you know you are going down this pathway of self-destruction that leads you nowhere? You know that has obvious limitations? But if you are willing to do that, then you have to have a good reason. You better be willing to die for that stuff then. And you better have a good reason for it. Beyond that, why? Why would you want to? You are not going to find something greater. Not down that lane.

Look, I'm trying to get back into the groove of preaching. Please bear with me. Sometimes for me, I step back and say, "What do I need that stuff for?" But because of my kind of experience in life, I know how things that I love come and go. And at times, I see it just go poof and go away. Many things. It's important. What's important to me is that sense of belonging. I need to belong. I need to love something. I need to belong to something. Whatever you can say, personally, I'm sure it makes sense.

But to me, what is most important is that stuff. That sense of belonging. I need that stuff. I don't want to be alone. I don't want to wake up one day and have nothing. I don't want that. That's bad. Not good! You expect a dog to be loyal obviously, but as a master, you should be loyal to your dog, too. But hey, something that you love, it's just no, no, no. That's the worst thing that you can feel. That's terrible.

I need that sense of belonging. Because I am human. I know you feel that too, one way or the other. You need that stuff in your life. You can't live without it. If you try, you are going to miss it one day. No matter how tough you try to make yourself be to go against it, it's not going to work. You're not that strong. Everybody will crack under torture. I don't care how tough you are. You will crack.

And why do you think that exists, that kind of stuff exists? Because God has chosen love. And you, under that light are His reflection and shadow. That's why the evil stuff tries to go into the darkness where there is no reflection and shadow, stuff like that.

And think about it, you have to make that choice. You have to make the choice to become like that. That's why it's always a constant struggle, a constant trial until the day you understand what your responsibility is.

It is a struggle even if you know it. But at least till the day you know it, you are going to struggle, period. But even if you do understand what it is, you are going to struggle. You will struggle till the day you die.

Why? God is not that happy a God. How can you be a happy camper when you see all this crap in the world? Why do we see all this crap in the world? Because people are still struggling to find themselves and trying to figure out who God is and what His true reflection is, what is true being an object to Him, His shadow under the light. The light that guides Him, love. Blah, blah, blah.

You will struggle until you die. Because He wants everybody to understand that. He wants everybody to make that decision. Like God in His darkness, thinking about this, the light of love. Because it came from Him, right? The cockamamie idea. The ultimate idea, right? That stuff that makes us all miserable.

You have to do that. You have to pay your dues. That's about it. It's not going to be a free ride. You want your perfection. I know you do. I know you want to be the best that you can possibly be. I know you want to find your light. I know you want to be perfect in your idiosyncratic ways. And more power to you. But look, that's what we have to go through. Everybody. No exception. And we should be loyal to that. Because that's what Father teaches, and that's where we belong. It's difficult. But we're crazy, right? Don't want to be normal, that's for sure. Anyway, take care of yourselves.

I'll see you in about three weeks.

Leadership
June 25, 2006

How are you doing? Nice to see you again. Today, I would like to talk about something called, "Leadership." Leadership, leadership. Let me just start with a little opening from what I experienced during my absence the last few weeks.

It was interesting. But I did go beyond because of the premise with which I started this, on my own. I did share it with people I normally do not talk in front of. A personal coming together. Because I want to know, I need to know. If you are going to make something right, I guess that is the first response you have to get.

So I did, unlike the way I lived before for a decade. I did go out of my way to try to understand what is going on. I do not know about you, but all I can say is what I feel in front of you, because that's our occasion. That is the nature of it. And somehow after my experience to make that connection with you, that is the only offering I can give. And that's about it. That's the end of it. I know.

Okay, I didn't expect Michael [Jenkins] to be here today because I was going to talk about him. It makes me feel very uncomfortable to talk about somebody when he is sitting in front of your face. [Michael Jenkins, *"Should I go back?"*] No, no, anyway. You know, he took on a mission to be the president of the Unification Church in America. Prior to that, he had his own business and stuff. He had his own ups and downs, and his own turmoil that he had to endure and conquer and ultimately, transcend.

When he became president, he gave it all up. Whether it is technical, it does not matter. But that is important. That attitude is important. That kind of sincerity is important. That kind of willingness to show that occasion is important. Commitment. Basic virtues are important because what we are dealing in today's world, is starting to define ourselves and find ourselves, so we can do something great based on common sense. We are not stupid anymore.

We understand, regardless of what you are, across boundaries, culture, and borders, we understand there is some form of universality. And that common sense, the notion of common sense is getting thicker and thicker and deeper and deeper. That's about it.

And that is enviable. That is admirable. You can admire it. You can respect it. That action, that willingness to separate myself from private life because of the responsibility at hand, now that is good. That is good. It is not extraordinary. But that is good because that is our standard. If you want to do that, if you want to live a public life, if you want to lead it, then that is what you have to do.

You look at the world, especially when you focus on a monotheistic religion, they do have certain absolute kind of ways of looking at the world, looking at the street, and looking at themselves in relation to God. Of course, Muslims, Jews, and Christians have used holy wars in history and carried their banners to conquer.

However, when you look at it at this present time, Muslims are basically still into that stuff. Jews are a little bit too, even at this present time, they have the policy of revenge. And when you look at Christians, of course, it is little milder version than the Jews and the idea of revenge, right off the bat. They will retaliate against what's antichrist. In other words, they do have that sanctimonious something about them, some special prerogative they feel because they think they understand the absolute God, one God. That is about it.

When you understand the absolute God, religion as we know it represents monotheism, it can act in certain ways, in ways to further itself. Because of that, it can never end that kind of strife, struggle, and conflict that we face today. Because I am a violent person, I know violence will not solve every problem. I do not think much about violence.

I have been violent all my life trying to fight my way through school, just to be somebody, and just to hold on to my name. If I have to strike you down, just to hold onto my name, when you do not know me, I will do it. Why? I have no choice. Because there is no hope in sight. Nobody is going to kill my hope. And I have to live with this stuff.

What to do, you live with it. It doesn't matter what. If you want to be the best, you have to make it on your own, right? That is the American way, right? So, having said that, what does that prove? How can we communicate with these people who still hold that kind of concept? Ultimately, in the end that is doable. When you allow that stuff, when you open the floodgate, it is like opening the mythical Pandora's Box. Anything is doable then.

Because apparently, based on violence, that apparent no-no and extreme measure, anything less becomes questionable then. Then it's open to description and interpretation, personal description, interpretation and practice. That is nasty stuff.

You try to do good. And even when you say to yourself, "Oh, I haven't done anything wrong. I have followed Father all my life. I gave everything." And when you start to take on certain things because you feel that you can and you start to do things, you have to realize you are responsible, not Father. You cannot just say in the end, "I messed up. I'm sorry. Forgive me."

And it's not going to go away. You can cry all you want. You can cry a river. It is not going to remedy the problem that you have created. Based on your holiness, your sanctimoniousness, and based on your sanctimonious perception of your reality, what you have done—it is not sanctimonious. And tears alone will not just wash it away.

And if you believe it works like that, you got another thing coming. Do you know why? Because I always call on myself. People like me, like me, have no choice. Accepting the fact that I have no choice—that choice gives me freedom. That is about it. That is ironic. It is paradox in itself. I mean, think about it. God says, "Do not take the fruit." That is a loaded question, isn't it? And you do it, and you can get away with it? Obviously not, right? You can't blame anybody else.

Even from the very beginning, the nature of responsibility goes beyond your individual absolute, and how you describe your perfection, or even how you describe your obedience for that matter. How do you, as an object, define obedience and make that to be absolute regardless of what is in the air to be true that is grander than you? How does that work? Nobody has that kind of prerogative. Nobody has that kind of prestige. It doesn't matter if you are a king.

Look, nobody wants to be a king. If somebody thinks they do, they are crazy. I know my father suffered. He lives a miserable life in my eyes. He lives in a fishbowl that is the size of a molecule. That is about it. How big the neutron is that is about it. That is where he dwells. Try to be king in this world!

But there are all sorts of crazy people with charges, plus and minus, floating around his reality, creating stuff. Becoming this one day, becoming that one day. Because that determines it, you know what I am saying? And that is a miserable life.

And in the end, he is going to be shafted for it. He is going to be responsible for that stuff. All of it, absolutely, as an absolute king should. That's it. And he knows, I know he knows. And people who know him to a point, in basic sense, try to help that poor miserable man. Well, hey, that's about it. Life is short. Trust me.

So having said that, let's talk about leadership. What is a good leader? What do you expect from a leader? You want a leader to be responsible. You want leader to lead the way, to show you the vision, right? The vision. Okay. Now, he is not going to sit back and tell you what to do. No, no. Going to lead the way, going to be responsible. Stand in front, do or die. It's important. If it is that important, that is what you are going to do. Nothing less. That's what you expect from a leader.

Any monkey can tell people to do stuff that is seemingly right, right? Given the authority, position, and power. But are you willing to be responsible? Do you lead through your leadership that you put so many people in misery that you will show them the way, in the end, that their misery is not forsaken?

You want people to be sincere, don't you? You want me to mean what I say to you, don't you? You want me to be responsible for what I say to you. If I say that stuff, okay and you blame me, then I say I am sorry, I will take what is coming. That's about it. But that is being sincere, you know what I'm saying? That is sincerity.

I know what I am. I know what you are. And if I am in a position of leadership, I am going to do that first. If for whatever reason, if I failed, well, guess what? Then the next time it all comes around it's little heavier than last time. Then deal with it. Deal with your object, how's that?

Dedication. What do you believe in? Stupid stuff in the stupid world. The whole country goes crazy just to hear that stuff. You have to have some kind of dedication. Otherwise, you are not sincere. See? If you have no dedication, you have no sincerity. And in the end, you are not going to be responsible. I know you. Because you are that kind of people. Because you really do not care about anything else but yourself. That's about it. Only then can you start to see compassion.

I know what I'm going for. I'm not as lost as that guy. Maybe you and I can help that person. Might as well, right? You only live once. You are going to die for something. Why not? Hey, do a good deed a day. You live 100 years old and do 5,000 deeds or something like that. I would do a week, 5,000, but if you do one every day, 36,500. Hey, you get my point. That is not important. You get my drift.

But you have to count up that stuff because that is what remains. Sure. It is like you going to school and you are getting graded so you can get a better job for yourself. That's about it, kids. You understand me? No, no, no, there are kids here. I'm not talking to old folks here.

That is how I really cursed it out anyway. I am trying to make up. Because every time I go away, I get loaded with stuff that just boggles my mind. If you want to do it right, you have to do it right. That is you. You deal with yourself. It's you, you see this problem and you are supposed to look at it not just based on your reality but blah, blah. Crazy world, eh? Hey, that is just crazy stuff. That's wonderful.

I know you want to be my brother. And that is where it should start. And screw everything else. Let somebody else count the clock and measure the points and measure the crap and whatnot. I do not care. Fellowship. That's important. Cannot do it alone. Too big of a problem that we have to handle, that we have to tackle. And when we know we cannot handle it, propriety to me is just superficiality. Who understands propriety? It is not present. And I do not like to be played. I do not like to be mocked. Do not make me look like an idiot by my desire because of formality.

Look, I understand the necessity of formality. It is absolutely important. Why? Because it creates a shell, boundaries. Sure. But you can't, just because we choose whether we choose the shell or what is real inside, I'm thinking how I should choose in that kind of scenario? You have to understand your limit, you have to understand who you are and try to work within, and then from there work out towards the shell so you don't become wrinkled.

You know, you have to have a simple illustration. Let's split [draws a horizontal line] that pie, with the vertical [draws a vertical line that crosses the horizontal line]. You know, God lives there [draws a horizontal line with his hands] and this is some kind of a wave [draws a wave].

If you can understand the misery of God, in a wave form, you will be a great man and a woman. I'm telling you. But let me just for the sake of this argument let's just use the vertical stuff [draws a vertical line] as an indicator for the sake of our, this little story. This is a sphere. [draws a circle with his hands] But if you are up there [pointing to the top point of the circle], that thing is very small. These ups and downs are very, very small. It's too insignificant to understand God's reality of up and down. Do you understand me?

It is not going to happen. Trust me. That is too unreal. It will not last and I just hope because of, let me just put it this way, I do not want anybody to get hurt. I do not want anybody to be made. I do not want anybody to be going to jail for stupid things, other than that, you do what you do.

If you know what you are doing and you know what you did is stupid and you go to jail, all right, that's what happens in the real world, right? You get over it, right? You do your time and you move on, you get over it and try to make the better of it, right? But when you do not know it, it can really, really hurt you. You know what I'm saying?

How long can you persevere? Perseverance. We are talking about common sense here. Universal values that we all understand regardless of crap, you understand me? We have to be somebody and be right, not in your choosing, but in judgment.

Do you fear the judgment? I do. That is why I'm trying to live the best I can so I do not fear it. I know it is coming. Take it or leave it. What you see is what you get. And if I deserve it, well, I deserve it. That's about it. I can accept that. How long will it take? As long as it takes. But I know it's going to end one day.

But that is the worst case scenario. We all have a best case scenario, too. But I am a kind of guy who kind of – I think I was a very optimistic kid, child, but I became a very, well the kind of guy you see now. I don't know what that is. Your definition is good. That's about it. I will accept it, no matter what.

Judge me all you want. Define it. I will take it. And then you? That's what I am. And I'm going to try to be better. That is all I can do, right? If I am going to do this, folks, then be here, and fill the shoes on this platform, that is what I am going to do. That's about it.

I really don't give a damn what you think about me today. Let's see what I can give you tomorrow when you allow me that chance. That's about it. So be it. If something moves me, I will do it for the rest of my life. How is that? I do not think I can live tomorrow. Whatever it takes, I know I want to make the best of it. I know I want to give the best of me. That's about it. Do you have any idea how difficult being a leader is? Anyway.

Lastly, I want to say you, you have to be honest. These days, people say empty crap trying to get ahead. What you see is what you get. That's how you learn. I'll see you next week.

Love
July 2, 2006

This week's topic is, "Love." I picked this topic because during the week some old member came to ask me for some counsel and I had to talk about marriage and stuff because he was struggling with that, the blessing he received and that kind of stuff.

I guess, generally speaking, anytime you go to church, you should talk somehow about love because everything else sucks. That's about it, I guess. Okay. To people with that need I'm going to try my best to talk about something, about love in a way that I can somehow relate to you and you can relate to me.

Individually speaking, we realize that we have within ourselves three different parts to our reality, we have three different propensities. There is physical, intellectual, and spiritual. And there is the ultimate quest, I guess, in individual lives, which is very short to begin with. It isn't that long. You have to figure out somehow how you can manage to control your body, mind, and spirit because each one has very unique properties. Each has its own very individualistic propensity. Because it does, it can act on its own regardless of the three propensities I talk about.

So, many problems that we face come up because that's the problem. That's the main cause of every problem that we face in our life. Starting with ourselves and because we are in that situation, when we start dealing with others we obviously exacerbate the situation. That's a given. How do you go about dealing with your basic self? You know, even to me perfection is a number. It's number 10. Number 10 is the perfection number, individual perfection.

But it happens on a physical level. If you break down the physicals into formation, growth, and perfection, you do get nine and finally the completion and management of rule??? All?? will give you one additional number; therefore perfection, completion number or management number, if you call it controlling your, I guess your maturation number. It doesn't matter how you call it. It's about controlling that phase. There is growth, there is formation phase, there is going to be a growth phase, there is going to be a perfection phase and every phase can to be chopped up into 10 in completing each one.

If completion is the end, which is the final number? You need to pause, right? To deem such that you have a world at all to have to manage already. Is this for others? Oh, no, you start with yourself. You expand out. You just have to prove it, right? But it starts with something of that nature. That's the standard. There is always a standard in everything.

So there is a spiritual and a physical level. You can look at it, on a formation level, you can break it down to three different manifestations of yourself in terms of your propensity, physical, mind, and spirit. You can chop it up into three. Body into physical-physical, physical-intellectual, physical-spiritual. The next level will be intellectual-physical, intellectual-intellectual, intellectual-spiritual, and finally there's spiritual-physical, you know, spiritual-intellectual, spiritual-spiritual. That's how it goes.

That is a basic platform because it will basically break down from the basic block of individual self into just diversity, that's about it, to create that number. And you look at that 10, body, then mind, then spirit. So, you pretty much have to kind of go through 30 hoops. Only then, because even when you go through the first 10 steps, all you are ready is to just receive nothing else other than, this; just formation, physical phases, completed formation, physical formation. You're basically ready to receive something that has to do with something related in nature to the conjugal. You're in puberty.

You know, for instance, if some families have some kind of situation where they can actually have give and take with children, just do physical things and everything. There is a saying, "If you play together, you stay together." Okay, that's physical stuff. Next you go beyond that, beyond being just physical playing and excitement and whatever pleasure you gain from life experience in gregariousness. Beyond that, go do something a little more intelligence involved. You start to create.

I mean start with cooking. Let's say that you have a situation where your children grow up to a point they start to actually help you and try to, you know, and you talk and you give and take, try to make the stupid food that you make every day whether you are going to eat this everyday but you are going to somehow turn it into something better. And you are going to give something into that dish.

And that stuff is a very, very important tool to your kids because they are going beyond just physical, physical-intellectual whatever that comes from this idea of speaking. They want more. And it's intellectual. And of course, beyond that is spiritual. And that, even in a formative phase, every phase has formation, growth, and perfection.

Formation, growth, and perfection is nothing other than body, mind, and spirit in that order. You need that stuff. It happens whether you like it or not. It's there. But it's important to recognize as such and teach the child as such because if you don't, it can be anything. It can be whatever it can be out there.

Once you don't define it correctly, under your own auspices, when you go out into the public in a multimedia setting as we know it today, free society it can be jumbled into anything. That whoever is in control can gain whatever the heck their agenda might be. That's the problem. People have an agenda. That's why they become famous and they become powerful and rich.

And then it's, I mean, there aren't that many Bill Gates. Even Bill Gates, he has acquired enough. Now he wants to be charitable. Okay? So, that's pretty much the highest standard in the secular world.

So, how do you go about controlling what affects your children? In these times when people are out there in the secular world who have way more control than you to oversee the airwaves through multimedia, to bombard you with stuff that in turn will benefit one person, themselves, and later on down the line, once they have accumulated enough say, "I'm going to be charitable."

Well, do you think you should be at the mercy of those kinds of people? Because they have done their game at your expense. They are not going to make their billions without you. I mean, it's illegal to print money. You have to somehow legally take it out of your ass. How do you control it? Do you leave it up to the people who ultimately in the end, because you believe in almighty God and think in the end everything will just flatten out, are going to be charitable? Well, you are going to be waiting for a long time.

Now who's the next in line after Bill Gates? I mean even Oprah, and she says lots of things. She is a very, very rich woman. She's doing a lot of good things. That's what she thinks. She has an agenda, too. And until she is ready because she's dying, she has reached her end, because if you are intelligent you have to know your end, you have got to know your limit. Otherwise, you'll be a stupid monkey. Whatever is coming, I might have the ability to control whatever the hell it was in the past and present, but what's coming I can't control. Smart people, normally, that's when they retire, they start to become charitable. That's about it.

In almighty America, the most powerful nation, still when a woman is powerful, this raises an issue because that still can have a biting force, right? So, that's some teeth. It hurts when you chew, when you start chomping. Sure, then what? What are you trying to get to? What? I'm not going to try to discredit somebody today. I'm just going to talk about the basic stuff, the physical stuff at this point in time right now.

Even the physical stuff has that kind of level. You go through that phase. When you look at your children, you see them struggling with physical-physical and physical-intellectual, physical-spiritual. That's formation right there. Then they go to the next level. Then, instead of physical, they put intellectual. Then they go intellectual-physical, intellectual-intellectual, intellectual-spiritual. They try. They actually try to control it. You start to see that stuff.

Then after that phase comes the spiritual phase. It's the spiritual-physical. You know when they are actually going into that final phase. It's not final phase but in that phase, it's final. And that spiritual stuff, when they are struggling with physical stuff they are actually trying very hard to include you into that picture.

On their own they are thinking about you. They are thinking about what you think is important. What you told them all those years. if you had them doing what you did, or were supposed to be doing, they're actually thinking about that stuff.

Physically, even the physical stuff that they do, they try to correct themselves—or try to at least kind of manage themselves to the point where you can kind of accept them. Yeah, okay, you're thinking. Then comes to the point when they're actually intellectual, they are rationalizing. And ultimately in the end, they really want to do it simply because they believe it's right.

See, the only way you can feel, and you can determine spirit, is when you know what is right and wrong. It doesn't matter whether you think like a bug. Well, if you think like a bug and you know what's right and wrong like a bug, you know what's right and wrong like a bug, in a spiritual way. And everybody has a place. Everybody has a place to begin. You know what I'm saying? And I don't mean it's in our place to make that judgment call. How does one start to realize what right and wrong is?

It doesn't matter. It can be in the death of an era. It doesn't always have to be on a plateau of glory and all that. It doesn't have to be on a pedestal. It can be in the bottom of hell. Because God exists everywhere. Because if you can remember, God knew about good and evil right from the start, didn't He? It's the choice that He asked you to make. That's the irony.

God says, "You have no choice, but you choose to accept the choice that I don't have because I want to be part of your head, part of you." And you say, "Because you are the almighty, you are the life-giving, omnipotent, omnipresent God that I need to learn a whole lot of stuff from, I will follow you, I will learn from you. I will do my best to be your mirror-like person, to be your ultimate counterpart."

And you measure yourself by that. Nobody set that standard. It's up to you. How hard do you want to go? How far do you want to go? Nobody tells you that you are going to do this, you are going to be born doing that. When are you going to do right, and that's the problem.

That is why we have to think about the basic stuff always. That's why it is important to remind ourselves of a basic right and wrong because we can get ahead of ourselves sometimes trying to do things without knowing who we are. And we have done that many times. That's the problem. It doesn't matter that you think in your head, 'I'm the greatest.' Are you really? Based on whose standard? Supposing you win American Idol? You become a star. Whoop-de-doo. Oh yeah.

It doesn't matter what you look like. You just sing well because that's a program, it's that kind of era. Because people are willing to do what the big boys do because they know. Oh, they can make tons of money just showing it and then after that what, make a movie. And those people are going to be instant stars.

Every criteria prior to this kind of reality goes off. I mean just think about it. The era of just radio waves stuff, you got to sound good. If you sound good, you can make it, right? Somehow. But you got to be lucky because not many people, only a selected few are controlling these kinds of airwaves. And they have all sorts of agendas. Self-interest, obviously. For some other business.

And they do all sorts of stuff and in the end obviously, they can't really become responsible because it was just a kind of passing thing. It's not like multimedia as we know it today, all encompassing. It's just in your face. It seems like it's up for grabs for all. Earlier, it wasn't like that. So, there's a whole lot of politics. All sorts of different strata, you know, strata that causes bifurcation in all that exists, and in all sorts of different ways, even in multimedia. It all becomes separated.

It wasn't unified like this. So, all sorts of stuff, all sorts of odd roles will crossover somehow into the general population. And you know, it will just mess up the rest of it here and there. That's why it was so difficult to control. But today, it's very easy to control if you play the game like the big boys. Yes, I think we can do it. It takes investment. But I think we have a real chance, tangibly speaking. And just go down the list of how body and mind and spirit works in formation, growth, and perfection. If you can set the pace, and having people who know what they are doing, just like the other guy, that's all you need to do. Let the best man win, right?

How did Fox Network become so big? They started with the stupidest stuff. You know, "Married with Children," and what is it, "The Simpsons" and all those crazy stuff. Then they start branching out into Cable and then News Network and boom. It only took them 10 years to become what they are today. Yes, they put in a lot of money. Look. We already put two billion dollars into print media. Any monkey can do this stuff. When you got to act to resolve things – got to deal with the a-holes that you got to—you have to lead. That's about it. They can lead, no problem. If they can do it, we can do it.

Look, it's not about me being a star here, right? It's about us winning as a greater family, right? Unification Church, right? Right? *(Yes.)* Yeah. I know what a lot of people think about me. I must have been stupid for reasons I don't talk about, because it's my problem and I bear the burden. That's about it. Right? I pay my dues. I do the time, not you. And I don't believe there is anybody who knows me that accuses me of this stuff.

Anyway, so what, who cares? What's in the past is in the past, right? You move on. But wouldn't it be great if every step we take is right in the eyes of God? Every choice we make will turn out to be the greatest? You know, wouldn't that be nice. It can be done. And that's what we need to strive for. Hey, take it or leave it. That's the privilege that I have. I can do it for free. That is not to say that I don't know how to build myself from scratch.

Anyway, just want to fix this, just getting to know each other. Anyway, what you see is what you get. I'll do my best not to lie to you. You want more? Well, we'll see what more can happen.

Take care of yourself. See you next week.

Compassion
July 9, 2006

How are you doing? Good morning. *(Good morning.)* Today I want to talk about, "Compassion." What is compassion? I feel it is very important for us to think about that and live with stuff like that on a daily basis. We need it to realize what is greater. True love, that's very difficult. I don't want to just talk about it. One way or the other if you want it you have to get it.

So, let's talk about something we can understand. Talk about compassion. Latin stuff, com- together in passion means to suffer, to suffer together. That's what compassion is. You have this kind of sorrow for other people who are suffering, who have problems. And you want to do something about it. If you want to go by the dictionary, that's what it says. You want to help somebody, you want to do something to reach out to somebody because you know they're in a funk.

Okay, now, before we get to compassion, let's talk about our basic subject, our individual selves. What is generosity? How do people become generous? Many times, you really don't think about it. It just happens. Generosity happens because you think you have something more than you need and in a moment's thought you just do something for somebody else. Sharing whatever you've got. That's about it, isn't it?

And please, [Note: Someone's cell phone in the audience rings.]— Hello?

Basically that's what it is. That's what generosity is. You do it at the spur of the moment because you think you have something to give. If I have more money than I normally use I can do that kind of stuff. People become generous because they have something to begin with and people act on generously because they have something. They have more than what they need. So, yeah, okay.

Compassion is different. Compassion says you need to feel something. You have to feel sorrow for somebody. You have to feel something for the plight of others first. You don't just automatically go into your good intention or give because you are made that way, or because you have something. There is thought involved. That addition of a kind of thinking process, that is the kind of growth stage. You can call generous a formation stage, then obviously when something provokes you to think and reach far beyond, that is a growth stage. It's on an intellectual plane.

To feel compassion is very, very important for you to understand about love. If love is perfection, compassion is the way that you can understand how love works—because you are going to think a whole lot about it. You are going to struggle with it.

For example, I try to make documentaries and try to find all these people who are supposedly giving something to others. But it's not really the case, you know. Even this kind of thing becomes based on the dollar, there aren't that many charity organization based that give 80 percent of the dollar. Eighty cents to a dollar, 70 cents to a dollar. It is most likely 50 cents on the dollar. What's that?

Having said that, now how do you believe what's happening when you are given to those charities. The little dollar that you give because you care. That's why it's important that you show what compassion is, how to think about giving. How to be generous by giving. You have to know why you want give.

For crying out loud, are you Bill Gates, I mean, or whoever, what's his name, second richest guy, Warren Buffett, he gave 31 billion dollars to the Bill Gates Foundation. I mean, you know, if you're over 50. Anyway, he's the second guy. Hey, look, if you have a few billion dollars, you are going to be well off. It doesn't matter how old you are. With that money, you can go do a whole lot of stuff, sure. You just go and literally tackle whatever that is poignant and feasible. Most likely you will do it in medicine.

When you have that kind of money, let's say you got 80 billion dollars. When you have that kind of money, you can literally take on many, many operations. That means 200 million dollars or whatever, 300 million dollars, let say just 200 million. You can literally pour 30, 40, 50 operations just on the 200 million dollar level. That's the kind of money we are talking about. Okay, but they're doing a lot of this. They can actually make a difference because they're investing in something.

Because in the end, it comes down to creativity. We need to be involved in creativity. We need to be involved in things like the arts. Simply put, art is very, very cryptic and it changes too fast and it is pain in the neck. I don't encourage people to be in it unless you are willing to die for it. There are things that are more safe and still allow you to be in creativity. Whether it's engineering or structural or architectural design. It doesn't matter. Something like that or medicine or what else is there? Anyway.

For medicine, you get into medicine, engineering, or be a scientist getting into crazy stuff, in the end, something that's more secure. You need to have some definition. You need this every single second of your life. If you do this, you'll have a better chance. But I believe that's what we need to do. Our children need to do. That's practice. Why? Because it matters in the end. Because I'm, you know, for me personally, I do have a good accountant, very good. Not a church member. I used him for all sorts of different stuff, corporations and stuff. He's a good guy. He knows his stuff. But he needs to believe in something. And in the end, I have to be responsible for that guy. Why? Because he's my guy.

What does that have to do with compassion? Well, let's think about yourself and see where you are at. When you teach your children about giving something. When you are teaching your children how to behave. What kind of an experience would put a smile on your face, and on the face of your children, you know what I mean. What did you do to teach them about generosity per se. Say you have something, then the little brothers and sisters know that you got something and they want a piece of it. And why not. Now, that's the drama, isn't it? That's where drama begins.

What happens to the kid who holds that something that the other little monkeys want? What does that little kid do? Now, you are in control, you people. You know how that story should end because you know all those comic superhero stories. You know how the heroic stories should end, right? Anyway, you are going to somehow divert your children to that story. And it's only that. Dot, dot, dot. It is not difficult.

You have to try to teach them how to be generous. And we're not talking about compassion here. It's just one tenth of the goal for something, right? How can you guys—you can't give something unless you got something, right? Now, what to do? That's what you are trying to teach your children. You give what you got. Why do you give it?

Now, if you give that kind of thing, you have something to work with, something to move it to the next level, right? You can talk about the next step. Compassion kind of stuff. Because, you give because you feel something. Before true love, you better think about what giving is. You know what I'm saying? You don't just do it, you better think it. You better know what you are thinking about when you are giving and you better know what that reason is and it better not be self-centered, you guys. All right?

Now, doing that is a process of becoming compassionate. No, I didn't make this rule. That's the way it is. You can't think about yourself when you think about being generous to other people. Just to be defined as compassionate, that's what you got to do. And that's the rule. You understand? Otherwise, it is not action based on compassion. I don't care if you're uncomfortable. That's about it. So, you better give, do you understand young kids? You better give your up your stuff.

I want to reach out to those little monkeys and I'm going to give it out. No, no, no, no. That's not compassion. I think that is called desperation. You want something in-between your legs and you are just being stupid. Okay? You will never make that into compassion no matter what. I don't care if the world stands up upside down tomorrow.

Please don't take certain things just based on convenience. Look, in the end you have to die for something. Please, think about dying. Okay? Don't make it that simple. You make it that simple, and you are not going to die for it. That's about it. That's about it. You are not going to die for it.

It doesn't matter what other people think, what the world thinks, even what you think. If you can't say that to yourself, don't even talk about it. Please don't. Because it's stupid. It will never last. It will never work. It will never happen. Whatever you believe in, no matter who you think you are, it will never happen. You want love? You've got to go beyond this stuff. Now you're thinking about something. How, with all this crap and beyond, do you really make the people you say you love become a part of you. And look, otherwise, don't say that because it is a lie. It is not true. You don't mean it.

You have to understand compassion to understand love. I am telling you. It is not that easy to understand love. Yes, you can be generous. You better be willing to die for something. That's about it. Otherwise, don't even talk about it. You can never leave anything behind; you can never do anything if you are not willing. Trust me. You have to grow whatever works. Hey man, that's what it is. Let's not talk about that crap. That's about it. You know, screw everything else. Who gives a flying hoot? You have to deal with the situation as it is, realistically. Let's not talk this stuff unless you can die for it. You know what I'm saying?

When you talk about that stuff, you better mean it. And it's not that simple. And that is the truth. In the end, remember, when you have to fight, you got to compete and win. Everybody believes in God. Oh my goodness. Hey, let the best man win? Do you have any idea how difficult that is? Okay, simply put formation generosity, growth compassion, and perfection love. Now love is very difficult you guys. Okay? Very, very difficult. I have to talk about this stuff. You need to learn about compassion. You need to teach that stuff. Why? Because it is better than playing a video game with your kids. If you live, then you have no excuse. You better tell your kids and others what that stuff is, otherwise you have no excuse.

Everybody wants to be good. Hey, everybody can be happy, too, in the end. Because of simple stuff. So, it's not about taking more and more. In the end, if you have the basic stuff, you can be happy. As long as you have a purpose. I believe in that stuff. You want to marry a handsome looking actor and get divorced a few years later? Hey, remember that the highlight of it all is for the children's sake. Excuse me, old people. I'm just going to talk to young kids here.

You know, in high school, it's most likely physical, jocks or just a little better make star stuff, pretty boys, and nerds. And everything else is boring. It's not important to you. The nerds are important because they actually excel in something whether you like it or not. You get an F and you are a great jock. Somebody got an A plus and you aren't a great jock but you are a nerd. And obviously, that is some kind of stigma.

Okay, that's about it. Look. Till the day you die, you better learn something. If you live from birth to death you create something, one thing every day, best you can do, I guess, is 36,500 things. That is not much. Or you can learn 36,500 things. You can speed up that process. It is up to you. Creating something every day is very difficult. If you can, knock yourself out. Nobody is going to stop you. Because this is America, nobody can stop you. You can sue your own parents, if they try to mess with you. So, hey, that's about it. Knock yourself out.

So, create something of that nature, to that extent in terms of some amount. Or you learn something to build up that amount. It's up to you. Well, do something! Make something up or learn, take something. Give something or take something, I don't care what you do with your stupid life. But that's about it if you look at it that simply. If you want to make it complicated, then you are going to be responsible for more than what is ordinary. That's about it. Trust me. It is not that simple. Any case, do you understand that? And you better understand that. That's about it. You got me? You better follow.

[*Note: someone coughs/chokes.*] You are going to be fine.

So, you want to talk about love? Let's not talk about love unless we talk about something a little lesser than love. I believe it's more realistic. You are going to help each other, talk about this stuff that is less than something ultimate. And anybody who says otherwise, they have nothing coming. That's about it. You are going to die. You are going to leave me hanging. That's about it. You know what I'm saying?

Look, I understand. But it can be done. Why? Because this is a great time. So much information can go so quickly. If you do the basics, literally go to the basics, within stuff and build up uniformity, you can make changes that can make that kind of difference, the kind of difference that means something to people who can see afar, and see that what you're doing has something to do with how we live. That's the way it is. It can be done.

It's all perception in the end because information is already there. And that work is already there. Whether you like it or not, right or wrong, you are going to get it. You know what I'm saying? You can't stop it. It's already there. You can't change it. You just have to accept it and accept yourself to make it better.

That's about it. There is no other way. I'm telling you there is no other way. Start with compassion. Try to think about other people's problems and other people's suffering and try to help out. Find your own, not by someone else's design.

Think what makes you better. You have to practice this stuff. Practice makes perfect. You don't just become something. There is no such thing under heaven. If you want to be good at it, don't think you can just go easy, you have to suffer. You have to put your behind into it. You know what I'm saying? Look man, that's about it. And I don't care what other people say—it doesn't work. It's not true. It's not going to happen. Because you want to do this stuff and as we grow, we can help each other to be better. That is why community exists. You understand? Right?

So, be generous. Be compassionate. It is better when you give something when you have nothing. Now that is something. God bless you if you do.

I'm going to be away for a while. I'll miss you, okay? Anyway, I'll see you later. Okay? Take care of yourself.

To Die For
July 16, 2006

I thought I was going to leave earlier [*to accompany True Mother in Africa*] but the schedule changed so I am here. [*Note: Hyo Jin Nim will be leaving later today.*]

My topic today is, "To Die For."

When somebody says they would die for something it seems to sound so terrible and tragic.

But it's kind of like the saying about the glass being 'either half empty or half full.' It all depends on how you look at it." To die for" sounds terrible, but to have nothing worthy of dying for is worse. We feel that achieving perfection is very difficult and not many people are successful at achieving it, so we focus on living. You will die anyway.

Yesterday I drove past a cemetery with my son. He asked me, "Daddy what is that?" I told him it was a cemetery where they bury you when you die. He asked me "Why do we die?"

Many times it is difficult to face what we are doing wrong. Even with someone else that you know you don't want to deal with the things that are wrong with them so you don't face up to them and just hope that these issues will just go away. It's not easy caring for someone's limitations. You want to be optimistic, to reach up to the stars, to become stars. You want to get your small time of exposure to become a star. Your 15 minutes of fame. What do you live for?

In a free society the thing that sticks out—and I believe that America is freer than any other nation that I've been to—the thing that sticks out is that you have the freedom to fail. How many people try to think freely about every question that comes into their life? What is the result of free and deep thinking? When you go to college, you are kind of forced to go to college. That is the only place that you are really encouraged to think freely and deeply. So, you get a degree and then you get a job and go to work and come home tired and turn on the television and let somebody else do your thinking for you. Where is your deep thinking?

That is your reality. So, how many people in a free society really speak out and make their voices heard? How do you think deeply and really have your own thoughts? What do you have that is worth dying for? You need to think freely and deeply about what that is.

You need an opportunity. How can you say that I live for my family, my society, my nation, and for God? What degree of greatness are you willing to live and die for? So, what is the greatest purpose that you can live and die for? Which is harder or more difficult receiving or giving to others? Giving is harder so it must have more value. Every free moment you have to think about this. I struggle about this as much as you. Because of the position and duty that I have, I can only help you here in this moment. You have to think for yourself. I hope that everyone can make it to the ultimate goal. Some people give up.

Change is inevitable, everybody changes. Possessing something that is unchanging is the most valuable thing. Unchanging love is the most precious thing. I can't tell you about that because I'm not there yet. If I get there I'll tell you, but most likely I'll be dead. *(Big laugh.)*

So, this is something that you have to do for yourself that nobody else can take responsibility for. You have to figure this out for yourself. I wish for all of us to be successful.

I'll see you in a few weeks.

Bye!

My Story
August 6, 2006

Every time I do this kind of stuff I have to learn a lesson. [*Note: HJN is likely referring to his recent tour in Africa with his mother.*] I have to do some soul searching.

I want to share with you, "My Story." What became really apparent to me is that Father really cares about Cain's children. You may not feel it, but …

There is formation, growth, and perfection. That is the way things are done. The manifestation of some new foundation, that is the proper way to actualize it. Anytime you have an ideal based on a vision, you have to have a plan, and that plan has to be meticulous. It has to be absolute. Whether you like it or not, because of the circumstances of the situation that we're faced with, if we're really going to try to make it work it has to be based on something that will last beyond ourselves. You and me, we'll die in 100 years, to say it nicely. So, based on that kind of cursory observation something is done—the ideal is done. Of course, that is why you wait for the test of time. What we can see is, what we can see as we struggle to influence it.

You have to do some soul searching. When you really want to understand ideal stuff. It's not just about you. You're not that important, you're not the subject of the matter. That's the first thing one has to recognize before you try to understand what the ideal is. Then how would you understand if someone tells you, hypothetically that you only have 10 years left and that the ideal will not be realized by then. Does that truth become non-truth just because you don't feel it. Just because of whatever you feel at that moment can the truth no longer be the truth? You really have to think about that. And what gives you that right to evaluate the truth based on your viewpoint and decide which way to go in your life? What gives you the right to make the right or wrong decision? That choice will define whether you are false or you are true, whether you have failed or you have succeeded.

Remember success is relative as well as is failure. It will depend on you and what you recognize. Success is making it to the next level. A lot of people just want to get out of the neighborhood that they're in. I just want to get out of my neighborhood or out of my country. But just because you made that escape it doesn't automatically give you the right to say that you have the right to be in possession of eternal wisdom.

What you make of what goes out into the world and how do you put yourself in a position where you can actually make a difference? Forget about somebody else. Just think about you and me. To believe in the ideal, you actually have to be in the position to stand in the ideal. There will be a process, there will be a point of growth into perfection. You have to know how to expand this process on your own. Otherwise, you can say you're the child of God but it doesn't mean anything.

Do you understand how we want to be in formation. We want the ideal—that's a process. How can we overcome the challenge—the challenge of our goals? Whether you like it or not, you will face it one way or another. It depends on what you're chasing, what your vision is. What you're going to make your life to be. What YOU make it. I'm going to die for this. That's what you're going to die for. Trust me. I'm going to die for something that you're not. You make a determination based on your will as to what you are, and you cannot blame anyone else. You can't blame anyone for what you don't like in me. That's just the way it is.

Unlike any other time some people, the 'Cain-type elders,' say that my folks love them more than me. When you talk in terms of subject and object and you put the emphasis on eldersonship, Father and Mother are subject. That's about it. Blood lineage is continuity. Blood lineage is never ending. The reason that you get into this stupidity is because of a disconnect. That's why you get into, "I'm the eldest something, I'm the subject." You have to follow whether man or woman, even your mother. The basic concept of family that is broken is that you literally separate what is the family. Why do you want to be subjective? Why do you want to take over a title? What is the point? What can you actually put into the picture?

In Central Africa on Mount Kilimanjaro it is absolutely fertile. It was incredible. We think about inches of top soil, there they talk about meters. If you practice basic cultivation and farming techniques you can grow crops forever. Any time you want to create something, you can't just jump to high tech—you have to master the basics—food, clothing, and shelter, that kind of basic stuff. You don't want to aggrandize yourself—you have to find something that is usable, what is actually applicable to your circumstances. Go for quantity, quality, and numbers.

If raising pigs works, then raise pigs. Every time they give birth they have nearly a dozen and they do this two or three times a year. They are omnivorous and you can make an organic garden using their waste as compost.

Look, if you have the will you can do it. The reason or kind of excuse that I got from the people that I met there is that even though the land is so fertile yet they are not farming is that they have resentment to the colonialism of the past, that this and that happened in the past.

That's BS. I don't care what color you are. Anybody that wants to make it better for themselves better go ahead and do it. For $100 you can buy a pig and you can buy a sow and there will be exponential growth year after year. In terms of basic knowledge all information required to be successful in farming is available.

We need basic stuff. *The Washington Times* and Father's rallies bring results. That's pretty much it. You gather politicians—so who cares, they come for a reason. I realize more through my soul searching that the essence of what Father is saying will really work in the end.

Look! People are killing each other. We have one Bible and out of it came three religions and they are fighting a holy war each in the name of God for whatever reason. America always provides a reason. The freedom country allows freedom as long as you don't directly hurt someone. It is okay to do things that are detrimental in the long run, like pornography. Unless America restructures its constitutional thinking, it will fuel the fire of hatred from Muslim nations forever. We know that pornography is not good for our children and as long as you protect it based on the guise of freedom, somebody is going to hate you based on their religion and they will attack you in the name of God. Any Christian Church condemns pornography.

Militarily the United States cannot completely defeat militants unless they are willing to use nuclear weapons and kill millions of people. There is no way this will happen. It's not possible. The terrorists will play the game of war by different rules than ours. If you feel like someone is sitting in an ivory tower telling you what to do then you'll take your chances won't you?

Christianity has something that has stood the test of time and that has meaning for humanity.

The last time I was in Zambia where Milingo is from—if the religions are trying to kill each other, then is married priests really an important issue? These three religions believe in one God, so I guess we all believe in one God. Those who wage holy wars ultimately do so for revenge, an eye for an eye, a tooth for a tooth. They can't forgive so they have to kill. You can't do that stuff, you have to overcome that kind of feeling. You have to understand why things are this way until it gets better somehow.

The ideal is very simple if you are an ideal person. Who are you going to blame if you are not an ideal person? My father and mother? My sisters and brothers? My dog? I realized. I had to do some soul searching. My father always puts me into a narrow lesson. I had to figure it out. Finally, it's just people there and we have just to reach out to them and change them.

I'm just sharing my feelings with you. If it helps you, so be it. I can see the possibilities. I believe it can be done.

Hey. Take care of yourself. [*Starts to leave and pauses.*]

Hey! It can be better.

I saw people starving in Africa and I can't believe why. Ask yourself, "What can I do?"

Finally, we have to find the way.

Bye. See you next week.

Family Values
August 13, 2006

Please sit down.

Good morning. *(Good morning.)* The world is kind of chaotic. I don't think there is any overnight solution. So, let's just try to talk about something that we can focus on at our level.

Why do you think democracy is popular? Because I guess it guarantees you more options, choices that you can make. And at same time, it guarantees you the least amount of obtrusion from authority, right? That's pretty much the attraction. That's the value when it comes to the democratic situation. But I think the main problem in dealing with the democratic society many times, is that we fail to recognize certain realities. That's the case, not just with democracy, but with any kind of society whether it's a theocracy or even a dictatorship, there is a certain structure that is real. And so basically all this just grows out of the fact that individuals can't live alone. No man is an island, right?

So, you group together in certain packs; in other words, loosely based tribes based on their occupation. Something like that. You can break it down into say just interest in general. But most likely, it's going to be some kind of occupation-based circumstance that attracts people together. Especially when you look at democratic society, it's more apparent. You will belong to some form of tribe one way or another. Whether you are involved with the people in your same occupation or your job is with a certain institution or with some company, you are going to have something like a tribe. Even within a company, for instance like in America, there is management and there is also a union. Even within a so-called corporate kind of family setting, there is still a division of tribal reality.

So, we're all involved in that kind of reality, even just for our livelihood sake. We're involved in this whether we like it or not. That's reality.

And many times there's conflict because of self-interest. Sometimes you have a hostile rivalry, but even a normal situation can be extremely competitive, right? This happens everywhere. You know, you get a job somewhere making some house appliance and you are competing with other companies who do the same thing—you're going to have some form of rivalry simply because of normal competitive situations. And rivalry becomes a tribal kind of situation.

Many times it becomes a kind of a pathetic tribal rivalry. That's the problem that creates pretty much all conflict, and any kind of disturbance. If it expands and exists within society it is due to this kind of rivalry that arises within this kind of tribal expectation—or to put it bluntly self-interest.

That is the basic premise of pretty much any kind of conflict. If it exists, it arises from pretty much that kind of reality that exists in democratic situations. In order to restore that kind of democratic reality with conflict in it, and especially because it happens so often and so easily, we have to put in a certain emphasis. We have to shift the emphasis to something else. We have to shift it from individual to family values. I think that's the key to changing or reforming or restoring democracy if that is doable. It has to be done through that theme. It needs that kind of orientation. Only through that, when you set premise on that value, that's the only realistic way in which you can actually transform democracy.

You can start with children, the value of children, the protection of the child. You can start getting more and more people involved, even politicians. We can get politicians involved in protecting that reality which is, for instance, like I just said, protection of a child's situation.

There are so many crazy people out there. There are so many threats that hamper the proper rearing of children. And that is something that everybody can relate to, and that is something that inevitably can move out to greater family values.

But you have to start with something. That approach has to be something practical in nature. And that's something that we can do.

Ultimately we need to have that kind of value system, and that standard has to be rectified clearly. Otherwise, you can't really transform democracy and you can never change the situation of this kind of hostile rivalry. Why is that? It's because if you don't take the focus and the emphasis off the individual, you can never address what creates the conflict to begin with, which is self-interest. That has to be addressed. Only then can we actually expect to do something in this world.

You know Father says—you know, Father wants us to bring this nation from selfishness to unselfishness, right? Well, how are you going to go about achieving that? How is that actually doable? How can we actually do that in our lives? We can try, but we have to have some form of direction and basic strategy. And I feel the best strategy is to put greater emphasis on family values. Start with things that everybody can relate to. There's a tremendous threat out there. If you have a family, your children are under threat, whether kids open up the internet or they literally open the door and walk outside—there's tremendous threat.
Why? Because there is no absolute value put on the family. You do have absolute value given to individual rights, individual existence—to a point, I guess—but there is no absolute value put on, given to, the family.

That's how we can restore democracy. When we can bring that absolute standard, make the society accept it and actually implement it—start practically according to law and move to absolute to family. Then we can start to see many things change. That way we leave no room for those crazy people who use God's name to blow you up.

Their excuse is that America's just an immoral country. It's culture is corrupt and it's destroying the world, the future, our children, and blah, blah. It makes sense to a point. If you think about it, it does make sense in a way. But killing people is not the way to go about changing stuff and making a difference. If you see something wrong, that's not the way to solve the problem. But there are people using God's name doing that every day and that's tragic, and we're going to see this for a while. It's not going to disappear overnight.

So, how can we make things change? I think that's the first step. We need to first recognize that we need to have absolute values and family values. We need to protect the family reality as best we can. We need an absolute standard, but it doesn't have to be maximum. It can start with something minimum, just above individuality, you know what I'm saying?

Take a step at a time. It's going to take some time. You can't really expect a band-aid solution or overnight solution because it doesn't work that way. Society doesn't change in that way. Even you don't change that way. So, it's going to take time. But what's missing is that issue. We have to try, based on understanding that. We have to recognize what's missing and what's important. We have to put an emphasis on that, and of course, putting a fix on it, ultimately in the end. Then perhaps we can do something about changing the world. Then it's possible.

I believe we have to try to put that kind of value system into the book somehow in the end for the sake of America. For the sake of democratic nations all around the world. Because only then you can guarantee the basic microcosmic society in itself. If you are a hypocrite to yourself, then you're a hypocrite. You are not going to have an ideal situation. So, it's necessary to have that kind of focus.

Of course, we also need to address our individual self-interests. And we have to understand what's wrong, what those things are, recognize them and remedy them. One thing at a time. One tribe at a time.

And I want to encourage young people to go into creative stuff. Get into medicine or whatever, engineering, all sorts of engineering. It's your own. Something creative. And be a preacher, too. That's a very creative vocation, you know. A little bit, well, it's difficult. Pain in the butt but as you know. Something, something. Because I feel that natural change can also come based on what Father is teaching, blessing and through children like you, second generation. That's going to bring about the change. When you actually venture into all those different quote-unquote 'tribes,' you are going to make the difference.

And it's not going to be pretentious. You are what you are. That's about it. And you are going to shine because you believe in something, right? I hope so.

Only you know yourself truly. And ultimately, only you can answer to yourself and be responsible for what you turn out to be, right? Can't blame someone else for what you are in the end, right? Whether right or wrong.

So, there you go. It's doable. Because we put emphasis on blessing and we have lot of children like you. And that's the key. And we are going to create a great model in every which way and in every which 'tribal reality' that is out there in democratic society. And you are going to become a living model. That's the way to do it. That's the only way to do it, realistically speaking. So, it's going to take some time. It's not going to happen overnight. And the key is you, especially young people.

If your parents have sacrificed to be here, to rear you as best they can, and send you off to the upper society to have an understanding, a greater understanding, to become what you want to be—find your true calling. Well, that's about it. You are going to make the difference later through your own hands, that's about it. And that's the future. That's the key. You can come up with all sorts of strategy but you have to have some sense of permanence. And that's within that situation. Okay? *(Yes.)* All right, it's short. That's it. That's all I have to say today.

I'll see you two weeks from now. Okay? Not next week but a week after, okay? Okay.

Salvation and Growth Through Experience
August 27, 2006

Please sit down.

Good morning!

There are a lot of young people here. [*Note: members of a second generation workshop being held at Camp Sunrise were in attendance.*]

Salvation is a concept of the Divine. That's where we can understand salvation—that's where it comes from. It's not mankind's concept unless you are in connection with God. It's not mankind's concept alone, so if you think, look around the world, and see that things need saving, the answer will lie not in your own heart. Only if you are connected to God ultimately will you find the answer.

How do we learn? You are forced to go to school, and I guess you learn something even when you're forced. (*laughter*) Some kids do like studying and reading, but most kids, especially boys like to be active, and they don't come around to see the importance of studying until it's too little, too late. Most likely when they're a little older than you gals.

In America it's kind of unique that you encourage your children to be independent, and to be equal, almost to the point of fault. They're a lot of tomboys out there among the girls you know. You have to be competitive, and you're kind of encouraged to do so, even on a social level.

That's kind of an American phenomena and it does get spread around the world because of the influence America has through Pop culture. Because Pop culture is powerful you see it everywhere. Nowadays you can't stop it because all the kids have to have a computer just to do their homework and they're connected to the world-wide web. So, it's very difficult to take care of kids in that situation, you have to monitor them constantly. But you can't. It's impossible. Who knows what kind of—

what kind of information your kids are soaking up whenever you are not vigilant?

We learn things through experience. Experience is very important. For instance, when I was growing up all I can remember is persecution and just fighting, fighting, fighting. Someone would try to steal something or put you down because of who you are. Sometimes they'd literally threaten my life.

In every phase of my life that's all I can remember, just fighting, fighting, fighting, fighting; One conflict after another. For me living well, it doesn't matter. Life is short.

Life is very short. You come to realize how short life is when you have to constantly fight all the time whether you like it or not. Nobody likes to fight but you are forced to by being in that circumstance because of your uniqueness. I certainly didn't choose to give myself this position or this circumstance.

So, you are kind of a product of your experience. It could be said that— that having to deal with that kind of stuff ended a long time ago. But I still do kind of have a kind of morbid way of looking at things. I do talk about dying a lot because it's important to me. Your life is short. You never know when you turn the corner what kind of other struggle is waiting for your sorry butt. (*laughter*)

The end is coming, one way or the other, it will always be there for me. It will never change. Some things will never change for you and for me. It might be different in your case. I don't know, because I don't know you that well. Everybody has some kind of experience that molds them into something. There is a kind of cycle, stages of life; a 10 year cycle, 20 year cycle, 30 year cycle, 40 year cycle. For members the 40 year cycle is mid-life crisis. What the heck am I doing? Who am I? Where am I? (*laughter*) The 30 year cycle normally happens in the family setting, on the family level, in the conjugal or married situation. For example, a woman starts to think that her biological clock is ticking.

At 20 your cycle peaks in terms of finding your limits. When you're 20 you challenge yourself in all sorts of areas. You think that you can do anything. That's when you're invincible, you're superman and you go out for the biggest thing possible that you can tackle. But as you get older in the valley of the cycle you start valuing simpler things, right? Simple things matter to you.

The 10 year cycle is like an individual growth pattern. You go through the individual, family tribe, society, nation, and world, levels because you feel those things. You think about those things. Those things become important to you. There is always this kind of basic pattern for us to measure ourselves based on what we learned, and what we learn through experience.

So God gave you a certain kind of system or pattern so that you can always check and balance yourself. You just have to understand how to adapt yourself to the plan. Something like that is always there because God is loving. Whether you understand that or not it's up to you.

You have to figure that out. You have to experience that. Otherwise it's not going to be yours. You can't be taught something that will last forever. You have to experience it. It has to become part of you. The things that you experience, that literally become part of you, are the things that you are going to die with.

You can experience something just for fun and say that I did that. I'm not talking about that kind of experience. That kind of thing just comes and goes. It's not important because it won't stay. You have to try really hard to recall that experience for it to matter to your life.

But if something became part of you, literally became part of you through experiencing it, that's the stuff that you take to the final resting place, or final dwelling place or whatever. That's why you look forward to that stuff in the spirit world. But I'm not about to strap a bomb on myself and blow myself up (*laughter*).

I'll pay my dues. I'll pay the price. And when I'm gone, I'm gone. Bye-bye. I won't look back. And hopefully everything is taken care of. My kids will take care of themselves and take care of their children. Hopefully, I will get to see my grandchildren. I sent my wife to attend the wedding of Father's grandchildren. They're getting married. Father is going to be a great-grandfather soon. I don't know if I'm looking for that kind of opportunity. (*laughter*) A short and sweet lifetime is better for me (*laughter from Hyo Jin Nim and the audience*).

If you want to connect with God, you have to really know how to live your experiences, because in the end you're in control. You're the captain of your own ship. You have to steer it to the kinds of experiences you choose to have.

Balance your cycles according to the system that is out there. It's made by God to protect you and give you wisdom and natural guidance. Hear that, look for it, find it, and make it yours. That's the way of learning because it is literally yours. That is the creative process. You take a certain concept and apply, and you kind of make it yours. People consider that the creative process. You can literally become a product of your own creativity.

When you experience this it really lasts. You can literally take that home.

This was simple, short, bang!

That's how I like it.

See you next week. Okay?

Awe
September 10, 2006

Good morning.

Please sit down.

Do you feel awe when you see Parents? *(Yes.)*

When do you feel awe? Some young people are in awe if they are face-to-face with movie stars or something, a rich man, Bill Gates or somebody. Let's say even if you walk into a palace. Let's say it's your own palace and you walk into it for the first time and you're awed by the magnitude, everything to the extreme, great dining halls, great gathering halls, everything great-great, grand-grand, magnificent, and you're awed by it because of that presence and that ambiance, everything grand. But let's say you live in it. How long do you think that awe will last?

Let's look at the opposite side. Let's say that you go to prison. You're awed by that uncertainty, that fear. But let's say that you have to live there and you have to survive in that opposite environment of living in a palace, by living in a hell hole for however long that you're sentenced. And what you have to face initially is that awe, that awe of uncertainty and then you transcend that. Eventually what happens is just plain life. From that moment what's important to you is life itself. So for instance, say we believe in religion, in your case you believe in True Parents. You know sometimes I feel awed by it. Even though they're my folks I don't know them as deeply as they know themselves.

So, in that sense, I am awed by them. Of course, through more interaction, if we could actually live together like ordinary folks, then I'm sure through normal life we would get to appreciate each other in life and understand the basic human experiences that we all go through in an ordinary setting.

But in some kind of extraordinary situation the awe can really get you. If you get addicted to that kind of stuff it can really mess you up whether you're living in a palace or living in a jail somewhere in a hell hole, or wherever you might be.

So, in essence, in order for us to understand what's important in life you have to remember life is more than, "Boy, I'm just trying to have fun." Of course that's important to young people because they want to experience life to the fullest. It is part of human maturation that you go through many extreme experiences so that you can understand your potential range. A lot of young people take risks while they're young and some people never grow out of it. That's a problem.

Of course, there's the obvious process of trying to discover yourself through experimentation. Because you have to, and you will, because in the end that's what stays with you till your dying day. That's what you take with you to the grave. But beyond that, the experiences that actually mold you and give you some kind of enlightenment as to how you should live and how you should control your lives comes from living with other people, because you don't want to live alone.

Many times you take extreme experiences not just to understand your boundaries, but you take other extreme measures to understand how to live as a human being in a gregarious setting. That social experience sometimes makes you push yourself a bit. Why? Because you need to understand your boundaries, your limitations and you do take chances at times. Some people mess up and break the law. There are obviously consequences to every individual action.

Even when we think about True Parents—Parents to me do not just symbolize parents and the ancestry of humankind and restoration. They also embody or symbolize law, right? The American government has three branches executive, legislative and judicial. My view of True Parents as the incarnation of law embodies pretty much that aspect of it.

So, when you talk about Parents as that kind of symbolic figure, that is what a King is. And the reason that you don't trust kings is that historically kings have abused their powers. But that's what True Parents represent, technically, theoretically, and in every aspect. It doesn't matter what kind of historical tribe you come from, what kind of heritage or background you have, you pretty much follow that route. Many times you don't trust those kinds of circumstances because of historical experience. Then eventually we don't trust at all.

With True Parents, however, when they talk about individual responsibility, to me that is the way to be free from judgment. If you're individually responsible then you're free from judgment from God, from history, and from posterity. That's freedom. We're not talking about freedom in the sense that there is no law, no boundaries. That obviously would be nihilism, anarchy.

Responsibility is in freedom. That's what equalizes things. And even if you fail, in God everybody has the opportunity to be God's child, to feel God's love. Why? Because even if you fail your responsibility, there is a course you can take. You suffer the consequences and pay indemnity. With restoration through indemnity everything can be restored.

That is the greatest freedom, in a sense. We all can achieve that in the end. Sometime when you are in the middle of going through paying the consequences it becomes very difficult, but you just have to live through it. It's not somebody else, it's you. You have to live through that stuff, and that's nasty. Sometimes it's painful, sometimes it's hopeless, helpless, powerless, and it's bad.

Your whole perspective on life changes sometimes when you're going through some kind of serious situation and paying those dues. It's bad, nasty, but it will end some time, it won't go on forever. That's about it. That's what you have to walk through. You try to tough it out and try to reason with yourself, "There is a purpose for this and I accept it. I know this will end one day. It will not last forever."

In that sense when we're awed by things in life, whether it is positive or negative, it has to do with life itself. We have to understand the basic premise of life and see the value in it. We need to appreciate that value of the plus or minus experiences we might have. If you can try to understand the essence of why they exist, and how they affect you and why they should be relevant to you and you accept it, you have taken one step closer to understanding and mastering your life. Ultimately, you can help other people, if you can help yourself.

Yesterday some second generation came and I showed them some videos because they were wondering about Archbishop Milingo working on the issue of married priests. Actually these are productions from a company that I created several years back, and since last year we have been working on this kind of partial format stuff. I was going to report to you when we had over 100 interviews, but now we have a little over 20 interviews on these kinds of topics in that same spirit. They're inspiring and I want to use them.

You also can access them at http://definingmoment.tv because they will benefit you.

My plan is to create shows like these. The host is Bret Moss. He's been around for a long time. If we have more of these we can put them together and make an internet broadcasting company. It's a cheaper version of cable TV, but you have to start somewhere. It can be done— it can be done.

The reason that we want to pursue this is because it's for the purpose of immunization, detoxification, and straight-forward education. A lot of people to this day still have a kind of negative notion about the Unification Church "Moonies" that they still hold on to. Something that was influenced by broadcasters in the beginning of our ministry in the early 70s.

We still hold that stigma, and that is something that we need to detoxify. We need to provide our people with information. People aren't out there just to be our enemies. We can bridge the gap through this kind of understanding, and build on the similarities that we have with others to create a positive outcome. We can grow into something more constructive. Because it is doable when you do things in a practical way.

You can always attack. There are times when you have to attack. Most likely you defend yourself first. We should always try to educate people and if it works, that's great isn't it? That's the way it should be. I think it can be done that way. Because it is just about detoxifying people's hearts and strengthening people's minds, by sharing and educating about what is right and wrong.

There are some crazy people that we may have to fight, but in general, in essence living in a civil world, I think we can do it through education. Basically, that's the first step we can take on the 21st century platform. The fastest way we can achieve this is through the field of multimedia. That's why I've always pushed this kind of work.

We have several other production companies because we have to be self-sufficient. Some things are non profit, just for education, others produce income. You can't do anything without money. The more money we have the better will be the quality. This is low budget, but the content is okay. We try the best we can and we'll do other stuff to support the growing community that we have.

The executive producer of DefiningMoment.TV is in the back. Please raise your hand. These projects will give us more tools to communicate better. This is our strength. You need to network. The more networking you have even in your personal things the more you will improve your personal life. I don't know how precisely, because I don't know your exact talents or what you do for a living, but I am sure it can help you in many, many ways. Of course I'm not asking you to be a self-centered fool.

See. I'm getting better with the language, huh? *(Laughter.)*

Check out DefiningMoment.tv, and help yourself with it. I'm sure that it will be helpful to you. And we are going to produce more and more content and add it to the site. The more the better.

Anyway we're trying.

Take care of yourself.

See you next week.

It Doesn't Matter How Old You Are
September 17, 2006

Did you check it out Defining Moment TV?
[http://definingmoment.tv/web site]

Is it Okay? We'll just keep it coming.

Well, it's got a format so it can grow as much as we can keep inviting people to do interviews. You can e-mail suggestions about what you're interested in, what you want to see, anything, information that you think would be useful to you. Let us know. We can do it.

At the same time we can develop new characters too.

These days more than any other time in history it doesn't matter how old you are. Obviously young people live under pressure to become something great, something that can put you in the limelight as quick as possible if it is doable. They need to really prove themselves, because there are so many ways to put a spotlight on an individual. You can do it to yourself deliberately, or you can end up in the spotlight because of circumstances, because of whatever occupation you choose, and suddenly an inquisition is on your tail.

People want to know what the best trend is. They want to know what, whatever it is at all times. In order to actually find some kind of success in today's world you have to go through scrutiny. That's the kind of reality that my children will face, and that young people are facing now. Today's people, in whatever profession that you're involved in, have to contend with this kind of pressure just to further your careers.

Having said that, how do you go about achieving a reality where you can actually do something that you can compete and win with? Obviously, with something like this—http://definingmoment.tv/—the more we have of it the better.

For our church we can provide incentive for people to seek out and further individual aspirations and understanding. With that you ultimately can get control over your destiny and take care of whatever responsibility you might have. Ultimately in order for you to be successful, you have to put aside big dreams for a while and just deliver what's expected from you. Do your responsibility and be up to whatever standard is expected of you in the present. These expectations dictate what you have to deliver in the end. It doesn't matter what other people tell you. That's about it.

You can't change that reality. It would be nice if we could just go out and witness to several politicians and through some kind of miraculous inspiration convert them into our way of thinking. That's not going to change how America will be the day afterwards. America is a very different place. The 400 and some odd people in the House of Representatives) who make the laws get elected every two years. To pass a law or make an amendment to a law and put it in the law books, people from both sides have to agree. In America, people then went out of their way to avoid the kind of king and feudalism system that they ran away from.

It's a very difficult place and even the person who is in the position of management doesn't have absolute power. Yes, the president gets presidential treatment to a point, and within the context of the law he does have absolute power, but his power is limited by the law and by term limits.

Ultimately in the end in order to change America, you can't do it with judges. You can't do it with politicians. You have to convince the people, people like us have to be well informed as to what America stands for and how it work—even just basic nitty gritty stuff from the bottom up that's the essential point, no nonsense just the facts.

In America there so many ethnic and religious groups in this land of opportunity, this land of immigrants. So many groups hold on to their own traditions and their own cultural identity. Never mind their religion.

In religion too, it depends on what part of the world you came from. So, you have to understand all those facts. It's not a silly thing. It's crucial information if you want to believe that you have the potential to change these people. You have to know these things whether you like it or not. Otherwise you can't communicate. You are speaking in a different tongue, speaking a different language.

It would be like me talking to you in Korean. You could understand my gestures to a point but even that's limited to how universally we understand body language. So, as long as we clearly do not have a universal language to present a universal culture, then it's very important we stay informed about these variations of human history. Why? Just to communicate, just to say hello in the right way. If we don't have those basic fundamental facts we get nowhere.

We can dream all sorts of dreams and anything is possible—I believe that. But I also believe that certain things will take time. I believe that certain things can be done relatively faster than others. However, you have to dream the dream in a realistic way. And the way to dream of changing the world, the universal idealism, the ultimate stuff, regardless of who you are means that whoever does the basic homework first has a better chance of scoring than somebody who is not doing it.

Eventually everybody, every organization, every religion that wants to realize the dream will put greater and greater emphasis on that fact of knowing because that is the only way. There is no other way.

We can talk about stuff we understand and we can inspire each other because we want to hear things that make us feel good, and because it distinguishes us from some other groups of people. We think our beliefs are greater than the other guy. So be it! That's beside the point in changing the world. I don't think that religion should be something that just caters to holding on to and managing someone's personal view of reality or frame of mind. I think it should be more than that.

For us to increase who we are it is important that we use formats like this that are so readily available. Of course, it isn't cheap, obviously it's cheaper than network, but it's global and we should use it to the hilt. We should use it as much as we can. Why? Because ultimately, if you are better informed, and you can deal with basic facts more than the other person then you will have a better chance of reaching out and connecting. It's very important.

You can't do it alone. We need more and more people like you, not less. Just even for your children's sake, just imagine. Let's get to the point on every issue, how the government works on every different level. If we can have something that you and I can feel comfortable with and give them the facts on how things work, starting with the government, wouldn't you feel better?

For example, what is the extent of the power of the president, and what is the extent of the power of the legislature, and so on and so forth. If you know these things, wouldn't you feel better? And if that information came from somebody like you and me who are committed, then that's important. We should have more of this, and it's never too late. I try to do more— more—as much as possible, but it's limited. I don't want to sound cheesy, but stuff costs and you can only do so much. But you want to do more. Okay, all right. That's your limitation but you try to do something more. It's easier said than done, right? Always, right? Let's make a greater commitment and take a greater risk and all that troublesome stuff, that pain and heartache. There is no guarantee. But that's what needs to be done!

Somebody has to do it, right? Somebody will always say that. I hate that term. But that's true though. Somebody will say that and somebody will have to do it.

I want to dream what Father dreams. It's very difficult, but I want to dream what Father dreams. I want to believe it too. But my inner mind says that it is going to take some time. I've got to be patient. It'll take time. It's going to take time to convince Americans. It's going to take time to convince the rest of the world. It's going to take time even in our own situation, just to get all the generations motivated together.

Starting with ourselves, I don't think it's that difficult—if there's a will, if there is some kind of uniform will. I feel there's a problem though, because so many people still want to insert their way of trying to proselytize. Their way of evangelism still has a certain validity even to this day and that's the tragedy. What's important for us is that from Father's blessing we go out to the world using whatever means necessary that gives us the ability to spread the news as fast as we can—clear, concise, and to the point. There is no other way to do that. We must use multi-media. There is no other way because multi-media is so flexible.

It is through communication that we can succeed. It's not just through showing how great we are. We can also educate ourselves about what kind of similarities we have with others. For so long we thought that we were different. But the more that we have in terms of building strength between human relationships, the greater our opportunity, the greater our chance to make something good come out of it. I know that everybody wants to be good in the end.

We should do away with the idea of just saying something to people on the street because in America the time of the 60s is over where you can just talk to some hippie on the street and they'll say, "Okay, I'll come over." That kind of time is gone. That might have been a unique experience in America, but that's not going to happen anymore. I'm sure a lot of you joined that way. *(Laughter.)* A lot of the late baby boomers are still into the hippie way of thinking. Okay, more power to you, but that's only an American experience. You don't find that anywhere else.

People know that life is short and that we'll do the best we can. They know that there is law and that law should be absolute. People say that death and taxes are absolute. Yes, the IRS will come after you and the government can harass you down to the letter of every law on the books. Within the bounds of the law the government might be lenient or they can enforce it to the max. That's absolute. If you disobey the law you could be in flight for the rest of your life.

It's like that in America too. There are things that are absolute, but a lot of people don't know that because they live a kind of routine life where they just wake up and go to work and come home and enjoy the weekend. They take off one or two week's vacation. That's just how they live. They don't know anything else. Even in America you have to obey the laws. If you vote, your vote gives absolute power to the people you elect to public office. These people make laws that they feel are right for you and that will get them reelected. Then they can boast that they did something to help humanity.

That is real. It's absolute. How can we better reach out to people who are important, somebody who has something to give? I wish it could just come naturally. You have to know yourself, and I have to know my limitations, but if it has to be done, you have to do it right? You have to do as much as you can. People that share our beliefs are some dedicated people and I will invest more with bigger stuff.

That's going to take some time. If something can be done like Father says, "Hey do it!" that maybe it can be done in a month, on my own maybe it will take a few years. That's my limitation, even if we dedicate every resource that I have into it.

I know it's important. I know that's how you're going to change the world. Let's start for real. I don't care what other people say. What better way is there than to hear it from the horse's mouth? You say, "Okay, talk about yourself. Let's talk about our problems. Let's talk about your problems." That's powerful stuff, first-hand information. Having that footage is powerful in a world where you have to compete with communication.

If you become more able and therefore feel more confident, we all benefit. That strength is in us. And if every individual that's dependent on basic information received firsthand accounts, then that would benefit us all. It will help us further our cause, and to make the dream come a little closer to reality. That is the only way where you're going to succeed in America and elsewhere in the world. There is, in my view, no other way.

Anyway here's another speech and I'm saying the same things over and over again. [*Hyo Jin Nim laughs.*] I say you can never change certain main things. I'm just giving you what I feel from the bottom of my heart. You know that when it comes to that question, I don't see any other way. I just don't see it. They can try that hocus-pocus stuff on me but I'm not going to change. I can't because I'm a product of it. That's reality, my reality, our reality. That's the bloody reality. Do I like it? Does the stuff that I am constantly bombarded with inspire my spirit? Enlarge my spirit? Mature my spirit? Heck no!

There are many things about it that infuriate me. Does it titillate my intellect? Some of it does. Some of it doesn't. With much of it I get offended and I get concerned because I have young kids growing up. I have to accept it because it is reality. That's about it. It is that important. It affects me that much I know. And I know that it affects you too, just as much. We have to live with that. Let's keep on doing it!

Okay? *(Yes.)*

We need hosts for different age groups and for different specialties. We have to make these things ours. We have to get people involved and bring it to our community so it's not foreign to us. Whether it is science or medicine it doesn't matter. The things that are relevant to your civilization—well, we're going to become familiar with it. It's necessary. I'm not saying we have to be like that. We just have to know what we're dealing with.

Just because you study something doesn't mean that you are it? I live in America. I am accustomed to American culture but I'm not American. Why? Because I choose not to be in many ways. And I'm still a legal alien. I never had a desire to become an American citizen. That's about it. I look at it that way. Not because I hate Americans, I just don't feel the need personally.

I know America is important. I know we have to win here. Why the heck do I need to be American when I have a lot of Americans like you, right Joe? *(Laughter.)*

Something like that. It's that kind of attitude—go boldly and be brave. Within us everything can grow. Everything can happen. Everything can exist. "Everything has a purpose," God said. That's the attitude that we must have. You have to think big, but be practical. This, I think is the best approach. Please become effective and become more confident. Also be more loving. You can feel more love when you are a little strong and confident than when you're the opposite. You know what I'm saying. *(Yes.)* Something like that. [*Laughing.*]

See you next week. Okay. Take care.

Dream
September 24, 2006

Please be seated.

Good morning. *(Good morning.)*

Let's talk about "Dream." *(laughter)* I'm not talking about fantasies or nightmares but about our dream. I guess that everybody knows about Martin Luther King's "I Have a Dream" speech.

So, when you talk about dream, you're talking about a vision, and when you talk about a vision, obviously you're talking about something greater than yourself beyond your personal individual desires or reality, something grander than that. Hopefully if you believe in God it has some kind of religious tone to it.

It is a kind of mission statement. When you talk about a dream, ultimately it becomes a mission statement. I believe. I dream about something. We like to talk in general about world peace. Everybody does whether you believe in God or not. We don't want people killing each other. We want harmony. We want peace, prosperity. So, that is basically what it is in the end when you talk about a dream—something beyond yourself, something greater that involves a higher power.

How one interprets what is a higher power obviously can vary. Communism had its own ideology that lasted about 70 years, and pretty much conquered the world—almost conquered the world but they failed. It lived about the average life span of an individual human being and disappeared. Nobody will believe in it again.

It's something like that. A dream is something grander because it's vision oriented. And when you think about a vision obviously it's beyond what you are immediately pursuing and need. So, how do you go about achieving something that you immediately need and can achieve?

Whatever the circumstances might be, if you make a mission statement, obviously you have to prove it. You're committed. You're basically telling everybody this is what I am. And you create expectation in other people, a third party. That's what you're doing. You set this up in the end for your own sanity's sake, your survival's sake—your dream then becomes a need-to-do responsibility. If you don't do this kind of thing, you will fail.

When you fail after saying all those big things it's miserable. You're asking for it. That's why we have to think hard before we make that kind of mission statement.

Why do we do it—for what reason are we doing it? Are we doing it for ourselves or are we truly pushed because of some kind of circumstances that make you genuinely feel that you have to do that. And if you fail with that honesty at least you'll find you have some dignity in it.

Even if you fail, start over. If you don't you're in trouble. Why? Otherwise all that bluster was just arrogance. Keeping your word is very difficult. Being humble is keeping your word. Avoiding arrogance is trying to be humble. What being humble is—is keeping your word.

It's very difficult. You can be a humble guy and try to keep your word and fail miserably. But in the end, the good people, the ones who observe a higher power, can forgive you. If you don't have that, it is very difficult.

It is easy when you look at this world and decide to self-promote. You think, "I'll become a star." But becoming a star has nothing to do with becoming something relevant to changing the world. Especially in relationship to God, it's going to have a negative connotation. It's all about megalomania stuff.

Most stars you see, they put on a front. They're different, but it's difficult to find the definition to describe those kinds of people. They definitely have a certain kind of mental state, whether you describe it as a disorder or not that's relative, but something like this hounds people who are in it. Obvious they do have a sense of self-grandeur through power and money, or whatever.

What does that have to do with a vision? What does that have to do with a dream we seek?

There are examples out there all over the place. The problem is that this stuff comes into our sanctuary. Our individual home is, in a way, our individual Garden of Eden. Do you know that? You as a parent who have children, you're basically going through the process of building the kingdom of heaven on earth starting with your family. As the story goes, the person whose job it was to give proper guidance to Adam and Eve, was corrupted and because of that things were tainted and the Fall occurred.

Do you think that you're absolutely in control of your Garden of Eden? You're not! You have so much corruption coming in whether you like it or not. Unless you make your house a prison, you literally can't stop it. You can't stop those influences. It's corrupt. It's decadent. And sometimes it's outright criminal. Just because it's available and just because you can do it, not everything is good for your Garden of Eden.

The problem is that you can't control it. You might make your house into a prison, but the children have to walk out to go to school. They're going to spend at least 60 percent of the time out of the prison, even if you did build your house into a prison. How are you going to control that? I can only control the Garden of Eden, but not the other stuff.

You have to start from somewhere, the individual level and the individual family situation. From that multiplying and through connecting you build the ideal Kingdom. Now put aside the connection for a while. Can you protect your own Garden of Eden? And if all sorts of stuff is coming in that can contaminate it and corrupt it, then what are you doing to replace it. Do you have something or a system to replace the corrupt influences?

You can't stop the mind, or the hunger of the belly or the mind or the spirit. It wants to grow and it's going to take in stuff one way or the other. When you're thirsty in the desert you're going to drink piss water. If you're adrift on the sea and you've got no water, you are going to start drinking seawater and kill yourself. It's that kind of stuff. It's the nature of survival. So, you have to deal with the basic element of what it is. It makes us who we are.

We cannot avoid what we are as a human beings, physical human beings, intellectual human beings, spiritual human beings. You can't just emphasize one. You have to align that stuff in the proper way and that's the difficulty. And you have to keep it coming.

Wouldn't you like to know how people think in politics and religion and business and what makes them tick? With any age group, young people, middle aged people, old people, the more stats you have the better chance you have in dealing with the physical world right? Wouldn't you like to have that kind of information? Wouldn't you like to know how your children think? You might think that you know how your children think, but what about their peers?

It's not just your children who are living on this planet. There are hundreds of millions of 15 year olds and 14 year olds, 13 year olds. Wouldn't you like to know the answer to the basic question of how they think? Wouldn't that give you a better understanding as to how you go about dealing with your own children? It's better to take the guesswork out of dealing with the problem.

If we can do that we will be a better organization. That is the kind of empowering attribute that can change, not just the world, but you, your family, and can make a difference in your family. That's the kind of stuff that can stick—the kind of stuff that can take root, and from that you can build. So, you don't have to fight when you come across these crazy kinds of people who get into your world just because they have something like political ambition, maybe oil-rich people like Venezuela or Iraq pursuing their own agenda and have some kind of hoopla in the moment. In the end because these types are pursuing something personal it's not going to make anything better. Real change for good has to be fundamental. If you really want to change—if you really want to really make a change that matters in building an ideal world you have to include everyone. And how is it possible to do that? By knowing what they're dealing with in life, what kind of people they're dealing with, what kind of world that they're dealing with. The more information you have the better.

I know that you're not going to go and betray somebody—you're not going to backstab somebody, if that information is given. You are not going to use it for your selfish abuse, your gain, your greed. That's important.

That gives you the power, if we have to survive on our own. We can survive because we understand how the world works, how people think, and every aspect of life. The more you have it, the more detail you have, the better for you. Then it can really build the strong root. Screw the flower. The strong root is what is important. The flower will blossom one day. The whole point is to be the best, to be the knight in shining armor stuff. Right? To be the vanguard of humanity.

We're competing with every other religion in the world. I know that in the end we don't need religion. What is your dream? The people who precede you should try to give you as much information as possible.

Go ahead and learn your skill. Learn something, learn your skill, find your calling. I don't know what your calling is. Wouldn't it be great if we were in a certain position where we could take care of all those things and reward those who actually sacrificed for something because everything is managed properly? Even if it isn't. I still believe that's right. If you do sacrifice, so too then I will try to do whatever I can in my little power. Let me just put it this way—I will be there for you.

With Father every time is always an emergency. The reason is that he has to love you right? And he has to love a certain tradition. We all have to have that. It can be done right and it can be done wrong.

If you go into the game of criticizing—I can do that really better than you. [*Laughing.*] I went out of my way not to do that for a long time. I made myself not speak and taught myself how to shut up. I'm just picking it up again.

To be honest with you, I'm feeling something. I started this speaking at Belvedere on Sunday mornings as a condition. Something changed in me. I said that I felt that I need to do this, but it's a little more because time has passed and I see certain faces and when you have that kind of human relationship and human interaction, things do change.

That's personal and I don't want to get into that. This is something that is mine—you try because you have that kind of stuff. You don't always find hope at the top of the mountain. You don't always get inspired by the biggest things that you see. Sometimes it can be big and other times it can be invisible.

It's up to you. What are your dreams? There is a way to make that dream come true. You can do it. You always have to know where you stand before you die. When you die everybody knows that you're going to be judged by God and history and posterity, if you believe in the spirit world. Before you die, the greatest judge is the judgment that you give to yourself. I want to be proud. I want to have no regrets. I did everything that I could, the best that I could. Regardless, I did it the best that I could.

Okay?

Dream the dream. I hope that we can meet each other in the end.

All right—take care of yourself. We'll see you next week.

Propaganda
October 1, 2006

Be seated.

How are you doing? Good to see you.

Today's topic is "Propaganda."

Is it necessary? Propaganda has been around ever since people started to group together. Leaders and kings have abused it throughout history including for the sake of organized religion—it's very useful for them. Also, it's necessary at the same time as something they need to promote their faith.

Pretty much that is the pattern of what we know today, and what we see all the time on television. You can see infomercials and commercials. The need comes because we do need to propagate the message, whether it's to sell cereal or a message from God.

Having said that, the first thing we have to think about is how we go about applying the concept of propaganda for commercialization or to the purpose of propagating the faith. There are many countries in the world, first of all, right? Every country has a distinction that they try to put forth. They do that based on their law and on the unique way they proscribe and actually implement the law. The way that they accept that is how they are as a nation.

When you talk about law you have to go to the beginning and ask God, "Did You need law?" Did God need law when He was by Himself? He was almighty. So, going back to the pre-creation period when God was still God. He was almighty and omnipotent and omnipresent, you have to ask Him, "Did You need law?" I'm sure that He didn't.

Why would you need law when you're by yourself, especially when you're almighty, omnipotent and omnipresent? Was it necessary? So, I guess the answer can only be that in the purpose of creation as we know it and explain it, the law exists because God wanted an object. The law exists for the sake of the object, not for one's self.

Of course, you know God was almighty and he wanted to create something. Being a creator is the ultimate that the creator can be. That's the miracle I guess. That's why we exist. Unfortunately, we had a difficult time understanding the value of the law, but that is the essence.

So, when you talk about the concept of law which defines us as a group, a nation, or a world, or even a universe, ultimately you have to accept that concept of what God intended. God's intention ultimately by having law is to create a family, something that reflects Him and that has volition, consciousness and can reflect what He is. That is the essence.

From that we have to start trying actually to create something, something that we can showcase to the world, because ultimately we have to compete and win, and that won't be automatic. Even if we have our own laws by having them and being who we are, we have to reveal ourselves to the world and through that revelation people must choose what we show. That is restoration. Something that is greater and has greater promise, greater than yesterday, greater than today.

Making that kind of statement is very challenging. How do you go about doing that? Do you think it would be easier to just shine the limelight on a few individuals? I don't think that will work. Not today.

Throughout history propaganda has been abused in so many ways. Mostly it's a kind of psychological warfare tactic. Propaganda really doesn't have a positive impact. It has a kind of negative connotation. We have to try to spread positive propaganda about our movement systematically.

You have to constantly prove something in today's world—a world where there are so many issues and so many questions. If you can't handle the volume of all the stuff people put out, stuff that literally can go around the world in a few seconds, it's going to be very difficult.

What's the best way if you're going to use that concept? We have to use it somehow too, because others use it, even to sell cereal? It's better that we increase the standing of everybody in the group. That's the challenge. You can invite people from third-world countries who want to live better. There are still a lot of people out there. I don't like traveling, but if you do travel there are a lot of places where the people live miserably. In certain places, because of physical hardship and the challenges these people have to face, it's easy to bring them to a workshop and convert them to our movement. Why, because they have nothing to lose.

I know that feeling. If you have nothing to lose then you'll do anything. Are we ready to prepare them, take care of them step-by-step, to raise them to the position where we can say, "Hey! These are the kind of guys we've got. Look at their quality. They're better than you."

How do you go from there to there? Does it happen automatically? You pray a lot and things change? It doesn't work that way. As much as we need to disseminate the faith, disseminate properly the information, we have to increase the quality of the faithful. That is the most important thing, if you are going to use propaganda. In the end that is the only way it will work in today's world. There is no other way.

I wish that I could believe that by going to Father's speeches, and I do go to those, it could change people's lives. But usually it doesn't happen. It is just a condition. I'm trying to be honest with you. There is only one True Father. It's not going to happen, but he is going to do what he is going to do. So be it. Make that commitment. More power to you. That's his prerogative, and there is only one man like him. Right?

When others start to do that, that's a problem. That's a serious problem. Why the hell do you want to be that famous? Why the hell do you want to be the focal point? Why? Why do you want to be that important? Why the hell do you use propaganda? This is not the 1920s. You must be crazy. You have to be beyond stupid using imagery, stupid sentiments, and crazy stuff. It's ridiculous. Even a teenager will laugh at that in today's society, never mind grown-up people who have been through that nonsense all throughout their lives.

Everybody sitting here, you know in today's world and in today's media-driven world, we are a victim of that stuff one way or the other. We can't even use what is obvious for education. Sometimes we blatantly just use it for ourselves. That's ridiculous. It makes us look so stupid. That's shocking. That's shocking to me. That has to go away because it's just absolutely humiliating. I believe it's better to inspire and uplift. Make other people the star, not yourself.

If you have that capacity—if you have that realization or enlightened heart, you should do that because that is better, and I have something to give that is also great, much better than just a commercial. Even if you approach the whole thing cynically and still want self-promotion—that's still an even better way to self-promote.

There are certain things that are basic, that are fundamentally basic and if we don't practice it, well nothing is going to change.

What you see is what you get.

Have you ever thought of the relationship between desires and self-control? You think about your desire a lot, right? Sometimes it can be a problem. If we have a problem dealing with our desires then what good is freedom? Freedom can be a problem if you have uncontrollable desires. What good is freedom if people living "in freedom" can't control their lives?

If it's uncontrollable, they'll probably kill each other in the end. What good is freedom? Why do you need freedom for the people when they can't control their desires?

It's that kind of basic stuff. Unless we can address those kinds of basic questions, all the ideal stuff we think and talk about really doesn't mean anything. You can talk about it 'til the cows come home I guess. It isn't going to happen till until you have all sorts of stuff in your head that you want. You have to know how to control stuff—you had better know why you want that stuff. Think about this week, okay?

You're free to do so in America. That's why it's silly in the end. I live here, I have freedom, but you have no absolutes. Of course you have a lot of laws and regulations, a lot of secondary absolutes. I call man-made laws secondary absolutes. God-made laws like simple
physics are primary absolutes. We make our laws because we need to live gregariously. If we didn't have any laws we would probably kill each other or something. There are layers and layers of complicated laws. They will absolutely go after you if you break one of them. It's absolute—trust me! They'll penalize you in an absolute manner. When they come after you it's absolute.

Think about what you want to be and how we want to present ourselves to the world and try to do something to help each other. [*Hyo Jin Nim is in tears.*] Do something meaningful, something from the heart. Don't do it because someone is watching you or because of your pride. Do it because you are made of something and it's just the right thing to do .... [*Hyo Jin Nim's words become hard to understand because he is in tears.*]

Do you know the story of Sun Wukong, the Monkey in Buddha's hand? That's how you feel. That's what you are in the end and you know it.

You will die. You want to leave a lasting propaganda? Die well and let somebody else say, "He died well." That's the way to do it. Anyway, something like that.

Take care. I'll see you.

Giving Thanks
October 8, 2006

Sorry I'm a little late.

Just a few days ago we passed Korean Thanksgiving, Chu'sok.

What are we thankful for?

I don't know if a baby can realize the status of their own being at the moment of inception or when they emerge from the womb venturing into something that is absolutely foreign to them.

That's a different state. I don't know whether the newborn coming out of the womb can actually feel that stuff or anything for that matter. This is something that I wish that I could understand. Does the infant coming right out of the womb feel anything, and if it feels anything what does it feel? That's pretty much where you have to start.

For anything that is going to be anything—that is the start. Do you see God? And that kind of stuff. Do you know God personally? Do you have His cell phone number? *(Laughter.)* That kind of stuff. We believe in something because we want to, because of our intellectual capacity to look at the past. And the past doesn't really look pretty in terms of building what we want in the ideal sense.

That's why religion is a powerful force in history. Because we want to know—what did I think when I first came out of the womb? Think? If I did then, what did I think? Was I happy to be here or not happy? We could start with that.

Do you remember what you thought when you were first born? Can you honestly say to somebody else, yourself even, that you know absolutely, for sure, that I know the answer, "I was happy. I was not happy." Or whatever in between, I don't care. Do you have that answer?

Pretty much, basically that's where we start from, our individual self. Everything else is influenced. If you are not sure of yourself, if you don't know who you are, if you don't know your limit, then you're pretty much the product of influences around you, your reality.

Go back and think about your situation. Think about your reality. How far can I go back? To my beginning, my beginning. Now just put aside somebody else for now, okay? Your beginning. How far can I go back and start to fundamentally ask myself and give myself fundamental answers?

What am I thankful for? If you want to change the world you'd better answer that question. As far as you can go back, teenage years, whatever. Middle class parents want to do their best to put their children through school and a good school is all the better, Ivy League even better right? Because they will get preferential treatment and go on to the next level.

You start off with an annual salary of $70,000 or $80,000 up to $120,000 with a law degree from an Ivy League school, an MBA or whatever. The more the better. Actually, just for fun because this information is so easy to get these days I found that from established schools like Harvard, Yale, etc., about 25,000 to 30,000 kids come out every year. Obviously, there are more prominent schools out there in America. Every state has state universities from grade "A" to whatever and it's like that everywhere in the world.

Then what? Other issues? What is free in America? It's a land of opportunity, sure. You know mind and body stuff to me is sometimes very simple. I look at it sometimes as life and death, life and sense, and life and love. You kind of have to measure people based on that kind of stuff. When you look at civilizations what are they chasing?

Of course, even in spirit it can be good and bad. Even in intelligence there is good and bad. Even in body there is good and bad. Right? Just because in comparison to some spiritual dumb ass on a physical level you might be better off than that because you seem opposite it doesn't make it right forever. It is very temporal.

Father has invested in the second generation. I know for sure two kids that have gotten a Ph.D. in economics. They're doing well on their own, but that's about it. I could go into detail, but it's not necessary.

There is a lot of stuff that it is not necessary to talk about. You just have to understand the essence of stuff. You have to ask yourself, "Why do I want to give thanks for something? Do I mean it?" When you are thankful for something what happens? Most likely you're thankful for some kind of personal reasons, that some kind of personal benefit might happen to you. If you're someone who is thankful—what happens to you if you're normal? You make some kind of offering right? You don't make an offering unless you feel something like that. Obviously unless you have something to be grateful for or thankful for it isn't going to last long. That's reality right?

That's why you reached some kind of understanding. In spirit there is an end to reality as we understand it. Because of that basic reality—our ability to understand stuff, God doesn't want to be alone. God is almighty by Himself He doesn't need law, but because of His counterpart He has to have law. Law exists for the sake of the counterpart, that's it.

When you have that reality obviously there is a give-and-take principle that's the basic law to bring about that happening, to bring about somebody wanting to give something because they are genuinely thankful.

That's why there is a funny phenomenon in America where you always try to look for bigger gurus. In this wealthy country you have time and money and I guess you have nothing better to do. Find the greater defining meaning of being truly thankful. That's what we have to compete against. Do you actually believe that stuff? I've tried it all—there are so many ways in which you can abuse things. There are so many ways in which you can do right, but you have to make that choice.

When you try to do right you will suffer. You will suffer, suffer, suffer. If you take, take, take or you try to do the opposite, you'll suffer, suffer, suffer. It's up to you. It never ends.

What's the difference between Mother Teresa and the Bill Gates' of the world? Both started with nothing, seemingly. They're self-made people. That's the commonality between Bill Gates and Mother Teresa. That's why people respect them whether they like them or not. For whatever reason it doesn't matter. You respect them to the core, to a point—they started from nothing, in general.

They've gotten somewhere based pretty much on the traditional kind of sacrifice—based on religious direction regardless of what religion. A self-made man is a good opportunist that comes along at the right time and meets up with something that was there beyond themselves. They were in the right place at the right time. Their contribution will stand and they will be given credit at least for discovery, application, and implementation. To what degree? It doesn't matter. They did something and we accept that. It seems like some sort of offering.

We have to try to teach ourselves to be thankful on a daily basis. Remember your life is an offering in the end. Right? The way I look at it, and I'm a simple and morbid kind of guy, even if you die it's not important. It's about an offering.

There is a connection between freedom and desire. If you have uncontrollable desire what good is freedom? How did the Fall occur? Because desires couldn't be controlled. Why? Because of individual responsibility. Even if you're given the freedom to make the choices — freedom means we have the ability to make choices, unlike dumb animals that act on instincts and impulses.

We have the faculty of higher, developed intellectual processing, to actually go further than the desire, to determine beyond the fate of simple impulse and instinct. It is constantly expanding and seemingly infinite. What the heck is freedom then? It has no meaning in the end. We have to live by the law of God in the end, right, whether you like it or not. Why? Because God says, "When I made you I had to obey the law. Because of you law has to exist. Otherwise, I'll kill you. The law exists so that I won't kill you." I don't feel that way all the time, maybe everyday once, but what if God is more extreme than me? *(Laughter.)* How the heck do you know?

Some second generation ask me, should I go to school, what should I do? What should I major in? I tell them that in your life you have to make choices and in the end it's about making an offering, whether you make your livelihood out of it or from the body you make something greater and greater. Pretty much it's about that.

What are you good at? What do you like? Start from there. Don't ask me! How the heck do I know? I have a hard time keeping myself on track sometimes. There are so many things that can distract you in a tick-tock moment. Just be sure whatever you learn, that you apply it. Sometimes you can really logically process everything till it makes sense to you.

How many of those Thanksgivings that we talked about do you think I will see? How many will you see? It happens once a year, how many times? How many times did you see Thanksgiving? Most of you maybe 40 or 50 times, maybe some of the young kids here 10 or 20. Will you see three digits? Good for you. That's reality. You can't deny that.

You have problems. I have problems. Why because stuff happens. The thing is, what can you do about it. What am I willing to do about it? I can blame stuff 'til kingdom come or till hell freezes over. I'm just doing my part here. What you take from it doesn't really matter. You really don't have to own the world to change the world. What we do with our lives and the choices we make can make a difference and we can inspire each other. What kind of choices do you want to make?

You don't need a billion dollars to change the world as long as your intention is correct. I know about self-promotion and I really don't do it. I go out of my way not to do it. I know it better than you. Trust me. It's not about that. Why do you want to promote yourself?

You see this terrible situation in the Amish community where those children were shot?

[*Hyo Jin Nim broke into tears over the killing.*]

We aren't always good and great all the time, but you don't want to be foolish and judgmental. If you think that you can judge someone, then prepare to explain yourself according to what standard you live.

We all want to receive love from God equally and we should all try to do that. That is the only definition of the ideal world that really matters.

Our life is an offering—correct? Yours too. It depends on the choices you make and history will judge you by it.

Include God and you won't die.

See you later.

Entitlement
October 15, 2006

Please sit.

Good morning. Today's topic is "Entitlement." This world is crazy. Let's go to the story telling phase. Let's go back to the beginning of how we build our understanding as to what is right and what is wrong. What are we inheriting? That is the question, right?

In democracy and free society we talk about entitlement, and that is about basic freedom and human rights. It is a fundamental thing that makes you who you are in relation to God. It is the case that there are many people who see things otherwise. It is basically where we stem from. That is where we start. That is the conflict. If there is any conflict in a fundamental sense, that is where it comes from - entitlement issues. Why? Because children of God have a certain promise based on religious doctrine and traditions that are inherently yours because God exists. That is it.

When you take God out of the picture, the entitlement issue disappears. It is every man for himself. If you do not have parents you do not inherit anything. You do not even exist to begin with. That is the fundamental stuff.

When you are dealing with people who do not believe in God, that is when anything is open to every kind of crazy stuff that comes down the pike based on conflict or whatever situation that exists based on voluntary issues. Ultimately things get crazier because they do not have any root. There is no connection. It is very difficult when you have to prove yourself and how great you are on a moment to moment basis, why you are better than the next person - if you do not have some kind of connection that allows you to speak representing good. It does not work.

The only reason that good is accepted in the world is that we believe in God. I know you never saw God. You do not call Him on a red phone or something. I know that does not exist. The only reason that we try to take the moral higher ground is because we believe that we have some kind of relationship with God. Whether we understand it clearly and whether it is real to us, and to what degree that is true is an individual case thing because there will be many variations of it. That ultimately becomes the focal point no matter how you address it. That will pretty much determine the outcome.

When it comes to dealing with what we have to face in reality, there are people who do not believe in God. Another unfortunate fact is that it does not end beyond that reality. There are many groups of people who say "My God is better that your God." I am not talking about polytheism here. I am talking about one single God. "But my belief is better than your belief, my faith is better than yours."

It all comes from the concept of entitlement. I deserve something because of a religious teaching. God promised. God exists. God created everything. God gave me the opportunity to be something. Based on that, people try to translate whatever and however they want to translate entitlement issues. That is it.

Let's go back to the Christian stories. We kind of get along. It does not matter how strange the stuff we do is, still we seem to get along because of the Christian concept. You have to promise something. What is the entitlement? If you go to the mythological story of Adam and Eve in the Garden of Eden, the Fall occurred because the entity who was delegated to raise up the primary ancestors of the human race, Adam and Eve, had a falling out with that particular entity God based on entitlement issues.

On a hierarchy level, jealously normally comes from the bottom up. It does not come from top to bottom. Top to bottom you will have contempt. "That is contemptuous. I am disgusted with that person's actions." It will not be out of jealously or envy. Jealously and envy are due to things that you see and feel, tactile things, things you need to feel and you need to have. This application will trigger jealously. If something is just out there in theory, you cannot be jealous. How can you be jealous of something that you cannot measure? Jealously and envy exist because something is measurable.

You want something. You want to take something. "Oh, he has more power." That is measurable. Based on that kind of thought provoking emotions you act upon it and try to claim it for yourself. This causes all sorts of problems.

When you talk about entitlement, what is the essence of entitlement? As the human race if we believe in God and God is the Almighty, the Creator, we have to accept the will of God. What are we ultimately inheriting? Do you think it is something that will trigger jealously and envy? I do not think so. It has to be something better. Why?

Because you have to ask the question: What do you say when somebody says, "I'm perfect?" What does that mean? Perfect in what? Am I perfect in suffering like God? Am I perfect in forgiving like God? Am I perfect in sacrificing? What kind of perfection are you talking about? That has to be clear. And why do you want to be in that position? Why do you want to emulate God? Why do you want to assume God? What is your intent? Do you really know what God's perfection is?

Or is your perfection or your desire just a product of human history in the general sense? It is not religious or secular. It is just filled with all kinds of things from all over the place. Why do you want to assume that position? Why is it important to you, and if you are a representation of God then what can you do with that stuff? What is the thing that makes a difference ultimately, not just in the present, but in the future?

You cannot judge somebody until they are dead, right? So I will leave it at that. You will be judged by your children and by God. You cannot just think about yourself, my children, my posterity, my people. There is no such a thing!

We are obviously going through religious strife in the most appalling way possible dealing with racial differences and all sorts of issues. That is why you have to talk in general when you try to understand God because no matter how we try to understand in detail it will take time. It is not going to happen like that. Why? Think about yourself. Know your limits. You do not live that long. History did not start from you.

There are many things you can be addicted to. I have seen all sorts of addictions, but the most devastating is power and money. That will make you think all sorts of stupid things. If you are high on drugs you do crazy things and it is not you making the decision. It is the drug making you do things that you will regret. Ultimately you are responsible for it whether you like it or not.

It has to be that way if everybody is going to achieve perfection in the eyes of God. "I did not do anything wrong" In whose eyes? To what standard? The world will change. No matter how crazy it is, it will change. In the past it was crazier. We know a lot. That is why we struggle in our discretionary measures. We do have a greater understanding of how history works, of how human beings work in a basic sense, physical, emotional, psychological. So basically it is mind and body, body and mind. People 2000, 4000, 5000 years ago they were trying to have a relationship with God. We are still going through that phase and we still struggle to this day to have a spiritual relationship with God, a God that we all see, that we all talk to every day.

Obviously something has improved. We understand that but we still struggle. Why? Because it is real! Because we cannot control what the spirituality is to the level of our understanding even on the individual level. Remember that reality is various. It is not uniform. It is different in all sorts of strange ways. But that is what it is about, nothing else.

When you talk about your entitlement, what if you are a prince? What kind of entitlement do you allow yourself that this is legitimate, this is justifiable, and what gives you the right to do that? Because I am a prince? What if you are not? What if you are the lower rung of the ladder? Does individual responsibility differ from the people at the bottom to the people at the top?

Even society, secular, democratic society does not allow that. Do you really think God's ideal society will allow that? Just because it is based on voluntary participation that does not mean that individual responsibility does not exist. It might not be coerced and enforced by punitive measures at every turn that you take, every little step that you take, but it exists. There is nothing different in the end because it cannot be.

Who cares? Why do you want to be that important? You have no idea how miserable that is based on how Father prescribed it. Based on His pathways. it is miserable. It is not fun. It is not glorious. It is not easy. It will be miserable and you are willing to do that? That is something that I still have problems with.

I will tell it to you like it is. A lot of people think that they are more effective, more able, smarter, but they all want something, the thing that I have been burdened with. Take it! I could care less because that was the source of my misery all my life. Take it! I wish I could be like the other guy and just kick you out and say "I am better than you," live like that. I take care of myself and do good in my own way and let God sort it out.

But I still care. No matter how selfish you want to be because of climate or whatever you care because of your blood, of your lineage. Sometimes I get a call, "I'm your brother, I'm your sister, help me!" I need help, too. What can you say? Can you turn them down? That's part of your family.

When you have nothing to look up to, when you are hopeless because you are sitting in a hole somewhere and you feel that pressure, the enormous shame and uselessness, and hopelessness. It bothers you. It eats you up. What are you going to do? Kill everybody?

In some ways when you talk about this kind of human stuff, the most fundamentally important stuff is that entitlement stuff that created all this other stuff. When you open up to the spirit world it is a two-edged sword, too.

I do preach a lot about dying. Life is short. Do the best you can. Give the best you got. In this short span of life you do not want to put your nasty things first. Try to build something that will be lasting like the spirit that is given to you, which is entitled to you at birth. You have to acquire and earn that stuff and make it matter because in the end you will be judged. How do you think you will be judged? You will be judged by the standard of what the spirit is. What is that? You are going to answer that on your own.

Am I helping you? If I am helping you with something so be it. I am going to talk about God and I am going to talk about myself. If I am making a difference, that is all I can do for you. That is all that matters. Stick to your role. Stick to your purpose. I started this for a reason and it is personal and I admit it and you know it. Take it or leave it. It does not matter to me what you do in the end. I will not be your judge.

The fact of the matter is I do not even know many of you. It just happens that I am in the position where I can make myself useful if I choose to be. If I did that it hurts and you get disappointed, too. I do not want to be hurt again. But that does not mean something stops. You know it is right, and ultimately the practical defensive approach that I have at this point, I know that can change.

I want to do the stuff that we need to fight and win. At the same time I am disgusted that I have to be defensive about myself in my own world. It is just for now. I know it will change. You cannot be that selfish forever. You cannot be that self-righteous. Try to control your angers because anger in certain cases lead to jealously and envy. It can lead to self-righteousness and superiority stuff. Just be grateful that you wake up in the morning and say "What am I going to do today?" Count your days and be grateful that you can.

There is a world that is difficult to understand with all kinds of content that is hard to understand. There are all kinds of crazy people out there who are influenced by the strange spiritual world doing crazy things. It is a sad reality. Is it not? It is depressing. There are many people who estrange themselves and live in a small hole they made. Basically, they are trying to decipher codes that have come down for tens, hundreds, and thousands of years.

We have to become realistic. We can deal with these contents. We can deal with Christian stuff and with other stuff, too. I am trying to do more. I have another audition (for a production on http://definingmoment.tv/). You just invite all sorts of people and just let them talk about themselves, all different Christian denominations. We have access to their heads thanks to modern technology. The more we understand the better. That is the basic essence of communications. We are just going to do it because we have a purpose as a church and something has to be done in fundamental ways. That is essential for our success and the future.

The more we understand, the more information we have the better. Not guessing, we know exactly what you are. The difficulty is that we are guessing half the time, more than half, 95 percent. We can be clear in dealing with humanity because we are clearer when we practice that stuff. Practice what we learn from these interviews and that is good schooling, is it not? It is not just because you have a Harvard degree you might have a lot of learning, but learning does not stop there.

I do not think you can change the world with physical things or intellectual things. The world will be changed when we understand God. Spirit, mind and body all that has to be proper, not the other way around. Any other mixture, variation, or alternative will fail. Either you do that stuff or get out because you are going to lose in the end.

No matter how secular you are, the world will teach you. You have to know your limit. No matter how gangsterous you think you are, other men are tougher and stronger and bigger than you. There is no doubt that America could nuke North Korea and pulverize it theoretically, but they cannot do it because of radiation fallout will contaminate Russia, China. Let them compete and see who comes out stronger. Let them do that stuff.

Let us get our act together and make a difference. In our lives, as individuals, that is something of a good legacy. If there is any value in anything, it has to happen with a purpose, intent, and action. That is how we will be judged in the end. So please, the more you do that and make a difference, not just to yourself but to others, the whole hell, the human race all too can change somehow.

Anyway how are you going to inherit something? Become a king and control everything? What does that mean? That is the curse. That is why God suffers. Do you understand me? Do not like that stuff too much. It does not work like that. Take care.

Building the Kingdom of Heaven
October 22, 2006

Good morning. *(Good morning.)*

I don't see many youngsters here. I guess the parents didn't bring the kids today.

Today's topic is, "Building the Kingdom of Heaven." If there are children here, I can ask some questions. Do you have rules at home, house rules? That's where it starts when it comes to having anything. That's where civility starts, right or wrong it starts from home.

You should ask your children. The best way to understand the family situation is to ask the children a general question about what is right and what is wrong. If somebody doesn't know you they can take that and they can run with that till the end because that's how serious the family situation is.

In a difficult world we have to deal with many issues in a less-than-ideal setting. If it was ideal obviously you could literally understand the status of a family by asking questions to the children about what is right and what is wrong. You get a better answer, a more truthful answer, a more direct answer, not contrived answer, than you would by asking you.

So, even on a family level you have stuff that governs your household, your county, your state, and at the federal level in America. Most countries stop at the level of state. Now the Europeans are trying to federalize themselves because of competition with America, which is the greatest nation on earth in terms of power and wealth.

We're a church. Our foundation is built upon Christianity. I did a video in the early 1990s called, "A Portrait of Jesus." Still to this day Koreans carry this portrait of a blond haired, blue-eyed Jesus. Europe carries the tradition of Christianity and has propagated it throughout the world. It takes pride in that.

There is a pride factor when it comes to European Christians. When it comes to Korean Christians, it's tradition. They are indoctrinated into a certain way of thinking because they are a very receptive people when it comes to religion. Because of that tradition and because of who they are as a race those things come into play. They take certain things certain ways. They are very dogmatic about it. It's very difficult to introduce new interpretations into their way of thinking whether its tradition or pride, it's a very difficult thing.

You literally have to start from scratch going back to wherever they are and trying to build something from that, just purely out of logic alone and create some kind of explanation that dates back thousands of years which you cannot possibly find factual stuff that they will demand. It is very difficult.

On the other hand America, yes it's a European white people's land, is a relatively new country, but they still pay attention to equality. They don't care too much about the pride, they don't care too much about the tradition, because you're relatively young and you have this idealism. That's the key in my mind. America is important.

If we're going to keep on trying to convince the world of what we believe, I think America is the only place that will allow what we have to actually see the light of day. For the Korean people it has to be something special like white people with golden hair and blue eyes. It's mysterious—it's mystical to them. That's absolutely true.

If you're bombarded by a certain way of thinking, that in itself is a daunting challenge, because it's impossible for you to change no matter how much plastic surgery you have you can't look like a blond haired, blue-eyed white person.

They believe that it can't be them. It has to be something else. Isn't that the picture in the end? Isn't that why we struggle with the concept of the messiah? Because he can't be something like us. He's got to be something different. He can't defecate, he can't fart, he can't even piss because he is the messiah. Some people just require something mysterious.

What is the mystery? You can ask yourself what is the mystery of becoming a good parent? In America 50 percent of marriages fail. When a marriage fails the father and mother decide to separate. Obviously the children will suffer. The family will break up. It will be separated and destroy the essence, the value of the union that brought forth the family to begin with.

You face that kind of constant challenge pretty much on a daily basis. It's almost a routine. It's almost something you expect. It's like hit-or-miss. That's the tragedy. It's not something certain. It doesn't have that kind of certainty and security that we deserve, if we think about the ideal.

Before we talk about idealism we have to pull ourselves back and think practically. In reality, that's the case. How do you talk about idealism even if America is prepared as the setting in which Father can be what he claims to be? He will die soon. He's not going to live too long. He is an old man. That is a fact. He is not going to live a thousand years.

There is some kid that I know that goes around meeting with big shots and rich people, saying that if we eat certain stuff we can live 700 years. Maybe it's possible in theory. He thinks like that because he has money. He has access to stuff before it's available to everybody else. Good luck.

People like to think about all sorts of things that give them some kind of comfort. I guess living long is a comfort to them. "That's the purpose of living—living long and I do what I do and somehow the world is working in my favor when I do what I do and I have what I have and get what I want." What's that kind of stuff? It's not life. Then what? What if it doesn't happen? Well, too bad kid. It's about that person only.

It has nothing to do with anybody else. Nobody will think that kind of stuff in general. No ordinary people will think that. That is just so beyond their reality. There are people who literally think like that. They're not stupid. They're smart people. They believe all sorts of stupid things.

What does that mean? How do you build the Kingdom? Even if you have a great opportunity, in my mind, in America. Why because they are free to listen. In my mind it's ironic. We're equal. That equality thing is actually good for us in the long run, because there's no other way to put that kind of stress on reality to everybody. You have to do it like everybody else.

If we do our part correctly, if we present our self and at the same time we can show that we are who we say we are—in the end that's how you can make a difference. And if you can make a difference in America, if you can stand out, you can stand out everywhere as long as they believe in Christianity.

Muslims and Islam is indigenous to regions where there are tribes that have hatreds that are thousands of years old. They have successfully dominated regions in Africa and South East Asia.

That's why America is important. We can fight fire with fire. Beyond killing each other and knowing who is greater at killing the other guy, we've got to have something more than that. That's why America is necessary before the spirit. The spirit talks about a lot of stuff that is absolute. But you struggle to think about spirit and never experience it. To be honest, I never heard God tell me to do something. What I do is just trying to understand what I am, and what I have to do.

America is a very important place because it will allow us to compete and prove that we can win—to show we're better than the other guy. Through our actions we can do it. The reason we can do it in America is because of the equality stuff. It's not just based on a few people that winning comes. It's about raising the standard of all. That represents who we are. If we have to deal with religion, we should know more about all sorts of different religions even than the followers of any other religion. In general, you should focus on making sure that what you are trying to say becomes real. After that the next thing is controlling material wealth. We need to know whatever ideas that are out there. We should have access to the people who are in charge of doing something for the good of the people in general. Go out and get as many ideas as possible and give them out. How to invest in this, how the stock market that, starting from that, there are so many things that you can do.

Give people understanding of the things we take for granted. Most people don't even care. We should care. We should know about everything whatever is its inner principles. If you have access to that stuff, you can make your own decisions. If they can do it, you can do it, because you understand the basics of their world. Sometimes you're hesitant, kind of shy, whatever. It doesn't matter, stick together. Create a group so you can divide your risk. We have to actually be effective at something so we can take care of ourselves, our physical needs, our intellectual needs. And based on that whatever spirit says that God is willing to offer us, it is going to happen. Only then the meaning will be true. Only then can you really digest and interpret that experience—the ways it will benefit you to take the next step.

You can help others. It's important to know how to take care of yourself regardless of what happens and I think that is the duty of the church to do that. Otherwise, it is just words and nobody likes to listen to empty words.

You have to take responsibility. Even on a secular human level, at least we want justice. But what if we talk beyond that and think about idealism, the original stuff. Would the original stuff deal with right or wrong? If I cause something, if I'm willing to die for an idea I will do my best to make it back to what it was originally supposed to be, no matter how difficult it is.

But if I did something wrong, well then everybody has a responsibility, but because of what I did all my brothers and sisters went their own way—do I want justice or do I want the ideal? If I truly care about the family and my father and mother. What would you do? What is the ideal?

I know what is ideal. Ideal is keeping your family, staying together, no matter how difficult, you have to try, and I'll try at least. Because in the end what you have to try to do is do your best to become what you think God represents, what God is to you. That is the best you can offer. That is the best you can do. That is the greatest control that you can show to God, to the world and to your posterity.

You get a traffic ticket, you have to go to court—you get instant judgment. In the secular world or in a theocracy justice has to be practical. It has to be efficient. It gets served like fast food. There are a lot of people involved, a lot of people who make mistakes. This is part of learning a lesson, because we all have to learn something to become better, but idealism is the ultimate law. That's why it's so difficult. A lot of people have cynicism because of the actual reality of the history of religion. The actions people have committed, the actual trials and tribulations are real and undeniable. Some people feel it more than others, but we all do to some degree, and it's real. That's why this kind of cynicism comes to religious kind— absolute stuff.

Someday, people can change. We all have limitations but ask God, right? That's where idealism comes from, understanding that. That's why we need to learn from our limitations. I don't mind sharing mine with you if it helps you. Why should you hide yours from me when it could help me? So, unless we can give and take in all the Tree of Knowledge of Good and Evil, we'll never be completely liberated— right?

To me that's a kind of mystical story, but in a sense it's true. I can understand what the old folks were saying. The less that you can deal with that in reality, subject and object relationship, because that's how it works to create order. From that you build love. That's how you create an ideal world. You truly care about relationships no matter what. If you can build that, it doesn't matter what kind of misery, what kind of crazy stuff, chaos too, you will never forget you will never let that go. That kind of relationship always has a place and time. It will be timeless. It only takes a thought to get there, and you'll be right back to where you started, back to how it was. You will die someday. Think about what you will leave behind.

I'll try to do as much as we can. I'll just pump it out to you and we'll get into that stuff too, more physical stuff, more realistic material stuff, information, because we've got nothing better to do. [*Laughing*]

Working together means a lot in America. We need to win here or it will be more difficult. Father is preparing for his dying and stuff. He has to do a lot of conditions, but the church is not catching up. That's why it creates distance because people can't understand it. Some of you have a hard time understanding it, then how the heck can outside people who don't know anything about us understand stuff. It's crazy stuff if you believe all that's happening.

It doesn't work like that. To make sense to teenagers you have to have an impact on them, never mind people with accomplishments and pride. To build the kingdom, how are you going to achieve that? We have to raise ourselves. All of us have to know who we are, and know all the other people around you. That's the first step. That's the first right step we should take. We have to know everything about other people's religion. The fastest way to get it out, no matter what it is— that's the way we should do it.

First things first, we're a religious organization. Let's worry about big steps afterwards. Step-by-step.

Any questions that you want to ask me?

I'll take a few questions.

No questions?

Good. (*laughter*) See you later.

Joy
October 29, 2006

Good Morning. How are you feeling today? Are you happy? (*laughter*)
Let's share about, "Joy." When do we feel joyful, happy? May I ask
you a question? When do you feel happy? Anybody want to share their
answer with us? (*lots of different answers from the audience*).

We could go on and on like this, but there is a theme in everything that
we do in life. It's all about lessons, about knowing something. Knowing
something gives you joy—nothing else.

It's up to you. You prefer a certain perspective in a moment in time. If
you try to look at the reality of a dice, it has six sides or six
perspectives to it. In order to understand just the dice reality, you have
to know those six perspectives.

Let's say there's more, a sphere and every perspective is the size of a
pin head. Just to create a sphere the size of a marble you will have
hundreds of perspectives. When you consider a perspective the size of a
pin head, that's reality—that's where you start.

Knowing gives you joy. Oh, I got a raise, I got promoted. It's that thing
that gives you the recognition from others. You don't live alone and
there is some counterpart in terms of your relationships—whether it is
divine or horizontal it doesn't matter. That knowing that somebody
thinks I'm worth something, that gives you joy. I got more money so I
can buy whatever I want. I got a position that I think I deserve, because
someone appreciates you.

Joy comes from knowing that.

Joy is knowing what God intended, religiously speaking, about your
true self, because it's only when you're true to yourself, that you can
truly understand who you are, that you can truly be joyful. You don't

need anything else. That alone will suffice. And you can grow from there.

The way, the speed, the manner, the quality, in which you grow is up to you. It all starts from that because it is all about fulfilling the will of God. What is the will of God, creating an ideal world? How big, how much, it doesn't matter.

Father has many children. I don't think everyone of them wants to be elder son. I don't think that's proper. It would be absolutely chaotic if that happened. I don't think everybody wants to be the younger son either. Even that won't happen because you belong to something and if you do, you do as who you are, not somebody else.

In the beginning Father was accused of all sorts of things. People came because they wanted truth and they were getting fire. They were getting a spiritual experience physically. During that time the wife of the president of Korea was an American citizen, Maria Park. She was a devout Christian that accused us of all sorts of things because a lot of things were happening at that time. Young people from the highest educational institutions were joining in droves.

They accused Father of doing all sorts of crazy things like putting an electrical blanket on the floor to make people think they felt fire. There were a lot of spiritual people joining too, all sorts of crazy people. Some of it was legitimate. How can you know about spirit? Do you know about spirit? You can't really say. Some people might be legitimate.

The final test is the test of time.

There was physical stuff that was alluring—there was spiritual stuff that was alluring—but the most important thing is that the bulk of Father's ministry is about intelligence.

When he goes back to finalize his own mission, his personal mission, whether he goes through spirit world or using his palace, of course, there's a physical ministry. How many people here come from the former Soviet Union? [*Several young people raise their hands.*] I know that you guys come from that area. You need those kinds of places, those great halls to do politics right—to play a role in society right? Not just in this society, global society. Those kinds of things, that's His course.

Put that aside. Let's talk about us. That's not really important to us. That's what he has to do. What's important to us is how we understand, how we adapt and adjust and make our mark in the scheme of things in this providence, in this dispensation in the way he sees it.

Let's pull back and talk about joy. How do we feel joy? Let's talk about sex. It's about the consummation of procreation. When that moment happens the intellect rises up to the spirit. You feel something that is real and from that you recognize something, because it's real you're knowing something—you're recognizing something, something that was meant to be. That gives you joy. You can translate it cheaply into just physical pleasure, but it's more than that because you are more than just a body. It's about knowing your true identity, all about yourself, everything that is about yourself. In the end you have to know about the intent of God. Knowing that is knowing truly how you're designed. Without knowing your design you can never be happy. Let's talk about dying. To me it's just something natural. You don't want to make too much fuss about it. You came from something and you're going back to something. You think dying is bad? You came from something and you're going back to something. That's it. If you know that, dying doesn't look that bad.

Time seems to go by so fast, but what if it never ends? Time will fly, it will go. Time won't exist, but it never ends. You're part of that. Knowing that is something. Why should we fear the eternal time, time that never ends? You fear it because to us this life is important. There are many ways to die, natural causes—you can die of disease, die of accident, die of murder, and by suicide. Natural is the best way.

You will die. That's inevitable. You want to live an eternal life—that you have to know about an eternal life—and if there's a process about which you learn about yourself dying, then that's the process you will inevitably have to go through, whether you like it or not, because you will die.

What's the purpose of putting you through that kind of process? To accept the eternal life that never ends. Time moves forward but it never ends. Yes, there are struggles in life those peaks and valleys, but can you handle it? That's how we struggle practically speaking.

What's the point? Why do you have to face dying? Think about a situation. What would make you feel okay about dying? When you think you know something. Think about that. Little kids become soldiers that defend their country. What kind of knowing keeps them going out knowing that they might not come back from their mission each day? They keep doing it because it is their duty. How does that work? What is that knowing? Do you have that kind of knowing as if you are a kid going into war? That kid might not be as dumb as you. He might be smarter than you, but he's willing to do that. What does he know that I don't know?

What do you know? What do you know about dying? If you want to be truly happy you have to know. Know what—what you are dying for. Dying is the ultimate way to discover why you were born. Only you know why. People die for all sorts of reasons, even patriotic. They do it because they know what birth is all about. That's how they think. That's who they are. They connect themselves from birth to death. That gives them that kind of defining answer, that knowing, that they feel, "Who is me?" Nothing else matters.

What is that? Only you know who the best you is. Only you know the true nature of your spirit, your mind, and your body. Yes, there can be some kind of standard, but it doesn't matter if you have a standard of measurement. In the end it's how you think that matters. What good is a law if no one is willing to accept it? What good is it if you have a government where you make laws superficially but everything else is corrupt? That country will pay for that. What good is a law when we the citizens don't understand the true meaning of it?

It's of no use. It will not work. When one man dies, like Father dies, everything will crumble. There is no guarantee. The only guarantee is what we're willing to die for. If we have more of that we can change the world, because we know clearly who we're dealing with. Knowing is joy. Knowing increases our vulnerability and therefore increases our survivability. Let us survive as a unit—then we'd better know that we're dying for.

I hope everybody in the picture feels the same way. Otherwise, we're no different than anybody else as an organization. You have to get some basic things right or otherwise we're no different. What can we show that we're better at? We know how to squeeze money out of people, especially the Japanese. I don't think that's something we can be so proud of in comparison with other religions. I know they are guilt ridden because they did a lot of bad things, but that is in the past. We want to move forward. Okay. The only people that seem to like me are Japanese. (*Laughter.*)

There a lot of things that we can appreciate—can give us joy. It doesn't always have to be big. It can also be the opposite. Find the meaning in life. Tweak yourself. Find what makes you feel joy in as truthful way as possible. Don't put stupid thoughts in your head that it always has to be big. If small things give you that sense, that's the stuff that is tailor made for you. That's what's necessary for you in the moment in time. That's what you need to focus on.

Always try to think in in terms of duality. That will give you some sense of stability. It's very important when you try to go forward to have that sense of stability that you're going in the right direction for you that might be the way. There are myriads of ways. Just look at it as a spectrum, night and day, that kind of spectrum, big and small, high and low, whatever. Max it out! Put it into the context of extreme. Wherever you understand the sense of joy, that's where it should start. Discover yourself.

I'm not asking you to do crazy stupid things. Don't take my words as an excuse to do all sorts of crazy stuff, okay?

As a church we need to give more information out. We can easily access knowledge, not just about what Father is doing. I don't always need to know exactly what Father is doing, because I know that he will do his course.

Individually, we should try to make a difference. If you're not doing that, shame on you. There is no other way. Otherwise, what is right and what is wrong? It's difficult to admit that you're wrong. It's difficult to be punished. My joy will be to know that Shin-Gil has found his place and that he is okay and moving forward. That will give me joy, personally speaking. I could care less about the rest. Why? Because I'm a human being and I need to grow. I need joy. I need to know.

Did you see the "Extreme Makeover" on television? ABC realized that the cable channels home improvement stuff is gaining momentum so they have "Extreme Home Makeover." People see their house and get excited. I suppose that's joy too. Some people cry their eyeballs out when they win the lottery. That knowing, right—ah! I got a nice house—I got a big bank account. Knowing it gives you joy.

What do you want to know? That's the question. You should ask yourself that every day. I wake up every morning and ask, "What am I dying for?" It's important. If you don't do it nobody is going to do it for you. Certain things you just have to do for yourself. You sit on the toilet—you clean your own butt. Some things you just have to take care of yourself.

Something that is that important you consider it, like cleaning your butt after you go to the bathroom. You can't ask someone to clean it for you.

However, you chop it up between body, mind, and spirit you have to measure it according to yourself. Make sure that you have the standard,

"When I go to the toilet, I clean my own butt." Like cleaning my own butt, only I am responsible for knowing exactly what I'm doing. I'm not going to blame anybody. If you see somebody with a dirty butt, that's their problem, nobody else has to clean it up for them. "It's your problem. It's nobody else's problem—and then you die." *(Laughter.)* It's not that bad. You're going to a place where you will actually feel the time, but it never ends.

One more point. In this lifetime nothing is forever, is automatic. There is manual labor involved, Okay? So, you have to find the joy. I don't know your name. I don't know your idiosyncratic stuff. You've got to find it.

Okay?

Take care. See you next week.

Tradition
November 5, 2006

How are you doing? Today's topic is, "Tradition." We talk about tradition. We all have it, right? Regardless of who you are, we all have it. We inherited something from somewhere. We belonged to something prior to coming here. Everybody has tradition. To people in general, tradition is important because it deals with survivability. Time ticks forward in the timeline of history. In order to be something, in order to have something, in order to hold on to something, secure something, you need to have tradition.

The value of tradition is about that—it is about securing something. It's about prolonging something, defining something, setting some kind of standard that will define you beyond your existence. That's what tradition is. That's why it's important to a lot of people.

Even nationalism goes to tradition to promote itself, to encourage that kind of fervor. You can galvanize and excite people—you can get stimulated because you think you're part of something great, now you live not just based on survival, but something big and enduring.

Just like everybody else in a free democratic society, you want to be something special. What you pursue has to have that kind of essence in the end. That defined essence, if that is true, it should stand the test of time. It should go on and on and on as long as we procreate, as long as we survive on this planet. That's why people think tradition is important—because there is a sense of joy in knowing, right? Yes, when you define joy, it always has to define a certain understanding, a clear understanding, the more clear the better, then the depth of joy will become greater.

How can we position ourselves or present ourselves to the world in terms of a tradition we want to be part of? That's the question everybody asks. If they think they belong to something then that's what we're competing with. Everybody out there who believes in God or who believes in a higher power wants to perpetuate themselves. It might not be a monotheistic value—it might be polytheistic. But still they have their own tradition that they want to present to the world and compete. It's a never ending struggle. Why? Because I think there's only one God, at least that what I have chosen to believe for the rest of my life. That's the challenge. That's where you start. You have to ask yourself—How do I fit into this tradition? In what way can I be the best that I can be to represent the tradition?

How many people here clearly can say that I know my absolute true value? I know what gives me absolute joy till the day that I die? Why, because joy comes from knowing. Divine joy comes from knowing the divine truth and it starts from you. Do I really understand my divine truth about myself? How do I fit in, if I do? What can I do in knowing who I am? The divine truth, how does it configure into the greater picture of creating an ideal world? Everybody, idiosyncratic as they may be, has something that is divine, that is unique to you. You must find that and you must somehow figure out how you can fit it into the greater picture. Achieving that is very difficult. It is easily said, but doing that is very difficult. Why? Because if you're just based on the concept of order, even in a free society like America, you have to play the game by the rules. I guess it's kind of healthy to a point.

Remember, America allows religious freedom. At the same time it separates religion and the state. The state is pretty much secular. Why, just to be fair? That's the basic premise, the basic fundamental argument because historically speaking religion hasn't been that much of a model institution. The cliché people say is, "Absolute power corrupts absolutely." Because of that, because of the disdain the founding fathers of America had towards the British rule by monarchy, they decided on this American system of government.

This is what is so attractive to the world. More and more people starting to empower themselves, and with their empowerment make something, make positions on their own, making their own definition of things, defining themselves on their own, on the world stage.

It's becoming more and more easy. One thing about today's world that is different is that in the past, it was very difficult to understand the omnipresence of God. In today's world ubiquity, a lesser word of omnipresence, is doable. The internet—you can literally transcend time and space. It doesn't matter who you are. If you have something to say you literally can use technology as we know it—you can be in one place and all around the world at the same time. That's the difference. That's why it's not going to be that easy to force upon people just by saying that this is the right way, that this is the right tradition. You really have to literally go by the principle. You can't just have it by faith—you have to have substance. You really need more substance than ever.

If things are complete in terms of restoration conditional-wise—if that era is over—the new era is not going to be automatic. By nature it's going to be more substantial in terms of delivering the ideal. You really have to be careful what you promise. If you don't deliver it, you can't stop people from talking to each other on a global scale at light speed.

When you deal with tradition, what is the essence? What is the essence that brings things into focus toward what is good in us? You have to know your game in any competition. We have to compete with what we know centering on God. If you're in science class get those facts correctly, not history facts right? You have to know what class you belong to. You have to clarify your category. You have to clearly define what you're doing and what kind of class that you're dealing with as a people. Otherwise it's nonsense. It won't work! Why? It's obvious.

If you walk down a New York City street it really kind of boggles your mind if you actually think about, "How the hell do I change that guy?" Every guy, every head you turn—where do you start?

It might be easy if you just came out of jail. You are walking where you want to walk. You don't walk where other people tell you to walk. You want to walk the line that you want to, and so does everybody else in the free world. How do you achieve a tradition?

What's good in religion? Let's talk about what's good in religion. I don't care what kind of religion, what's a good teaching that everybody can agree with? Everybody wants to be special. People want to be the messiah. I don't think that they would want to be the messiah if they really understood how difficult that is.

At least we have to be sure that everything that we do in general is good. At least you have to back it up with your body, your mind, and your spirit and you stand alone in judgment for that if you're in charge, if you're responsible. That's where it should start.

In the basic fundamental stuff, if your children go bad, then in the end, then you're responsible for your children. That kind of sense of social morality, you have to start with that. You have to be comfortable with that. We have to be sure. If you do have something—if you do represent something—the basic fundamental question that you have to face is you're on your own and you'll not blame anybody else. You'll not just shed the tears for forgiveness and beg like a wretched wimp.

You want to go higher? Okay, that's up to you, up to those people. That's the way it should be. Life is short. You have to make those things matter. You have to feel that that matters. That's the only way. In the end it comes to that. The determination has to fit the desire and the dream. Otherwise, you're only kidding yourself.

It shouldn't be that easy—a thing that great shouldn't be that easy, something that awesome, that never-been-done stuff shouldn't be that easy. If you believe that nonsense, well you know how it's going to end.

When you talk about individual people, "This is a rule in my house!" Well, okay, if you have a house. Start with that, some kind of little kingdom. What kind of standard do you have there? And grow. As it becomes bigger it will become difficult. Unless you want something as you see it today to exist forever, you want to make changes. You seriously have to think about how things work.

In America, next Tuesday [*November 7th, 2006*] is Election Day. They are constantly accusing each other of this and that and playing the political game mostly by trying to degrade each other. Wouldn't it be nice if they could find something in common for a change and actually gave credit to each other? The best man win stuff even if it's an adversarial two-party system just for the sake of checks-and-balance, so be it. Wouldn't that be a little different? Maybe people would actually look forward that stuff.

That's the greatest nation on this planet. That's reality. The funny thing is all this freedom is because the government itself has to be secular for the sake of diversity of religion, and protection of it. It allows all sorts of crap as long as long as you say, "Well, I didn't force that guy to do it. It's his volition, her volition. In the end it's up to them. I didn't put a gun to their head to make them do things. I didn't hurt anybody, immediately." You can pretty much get away with a lot of stuff that hurts many, many young people.

The government needs to separate from religious values in order to preserve this system— which makes America unique by separating from religion, in order to give freedom to religion.

There are certain perks to being a religion, like you don't have to pay taxes. There are a lot of things to use as an excuse to justify the way things are. Mostly the justification comes from historical failures of mankind. It has nothing to do with futuristic stuff.

This is based on the past, that we can't trust people in the future or the present. Based on that kind of logic things will pretty much stay the way they are unless a dramatic change happens like a catastrophe or some earthquake and Manhattan sinks into the sea or something. Or like some alien UFO lands on the White House lawn and says we're going to zap your ass and says listen to this and don't listen to that. Unless that kind of stuff happens, America's not going to change anytime soon. Unfortunately that's the case.

They have analyzed every possible marketplace, and in America just teenagers spend about 40 billion dollars a years on crap. It's just escalating every year in terms of the amount of cash that they spend. It's ridiculous. It's a vicious cycle that feeds itself. That's reality. I'm not making this up.

You have to start somewhere—positive re-enforcement, basic understanding in dealing with human relationships. Knowing about who we are, knowing about other religions, other people who are socially active trying to do some good in society. All those things are useful kinds of information. You have to start somewhere and that's where you start.

It's better that your children know more about those things than you do because that's the proper way of growth. That's what's ideal. People in the past, people might have suffered, might not have had all the tools that your children can have. But if your children have the tools, that's called progress right?

You don't always have to make them suffer to make progress. Progress can just happen just by knowing. Knowing who you are and knowing who others are, more clearly than you. They can have a better chance than you out there. Isn't that the whole point? Why do you suffer? Why do you sacrifice? What's the meaning of sacrifice? It's not a sacrifice if it doesn't amount to progress. It's just words. I'd rather do a comedy show and get a good laugh than just hear a bunch of stupid words.

If children could see that, they wouldn't struggle. I believe that. That's a good father's way. There is no other way of being a good father. He has to love everyone. So be it. I know what the essence of a good father's love is. That's what we also have to practice in general in our reality based on our responsibility and our capability. I want to do so. Do it! That's the kind of stuff—that's the only way to start the change.

We have to start changing our environment, even starting with your individual self. You will change if you try. You have to because you want to win! I want to complete this stuff. I don't want to give up. If I say it, I want to do it. For whatever reason, even if you just don't want to be a failure. If you're that primitive then start with that! You have to start somewhere.

Not everybody's motivation is love.

Anyway, take care of yourselves you guys. I'll see you next week.

Success
November 12, 2006

Hello.

We all want to be successful, right?

Let's talk about success.

What is success? What do you consider success?

In America especially, there are a lot of kids who graduate from Ivy League schools—by mid-20s or late 20s a lot of people become millionaires. When you make a lot of money it does give you a lot of opportunity to move into things and do things that you want to do.

In the end success is defined by individuals. It is true because it connotes something that has to do with one's career. Is success just based on your career? A career doesn't have to last until the day you die—you can retire I guess. What's today's average retirement age, 60? It used to be 65 but it's going down right? Now it's going back up again, but anyway it's something like that.

I guess the way that we should look at success—it should be about a lifetime. It's one's lifetime and you should define it as such, because the way that we look at Father is basically that. He's a successful teacher. He's a successful father of mankind, and because of his lifetime work we define his example as something to be revered. That's what we're trying to do—to commit our life to follow that kind of exemplary life. And he's still moving on right? He didn't retire yet. I don't think he's going to retire till the day he ascends to Heaven, when he dies.

So, when I look at my family model pretty much that's how you define success in my family. I don't know about other people, but it's my family tradition, so that's what I have to accept. I could make my own definition of success. I could define it in my own way just like everybody else in a free society. But because of what I choose to accept that's pretty much what defines success in my family. If you can't do that, if you don't have something within you to which you can make that kind of commitment to your definition of success, then you have no goal.

You feel Father is rich and owns a lot of land. "Oh, if I acquire this land and that land, this property and that, and put it all together, then I'll have a billion dollar company." You can think like that statistically. You can think like that as if it's your right. But nobody in the world will recognize that as success. What kind of success is that? That's just privilege gone bad. That would be the reality. You can certainly do that crap if you want, but it's not success.

If I do pray, and I rarely do, but if I do pray, I pray that, "Father, you had a great start! I want your ending to be great as well." That's what I want to see happen to him. I want that to be the legacy. I don't want anything to be changed as far as that is concerned. In order to do that, even in my own family, you really have to understand Father's course. It's not that simple trying to care for other people. That's a very difficult thing, and helping people continue believing as the generations go forward, making that connection is very difficult. Even my father is having a hard time achieving that. That's the reality. It's not that simple.

And how do you even connect to your own generation. Where is your input? Where is your sacrifice? Do you sacrifice truly for the sake of belief or do you show sacrifice for the sake of putting on a show? Which is it?

Then we should have politicians come and preach all the time in churches all around the world. Even in the secular world they try to distinguish between politicians and preachers right? Of course, they both screw up all the time, but still there's a distinction. One has to do with governing a society and one has to do with governing the hearts and minds of people, the soul of humankind. One is about the physicality more so and the other is about spirituality, right? That's the basic difference.

And there's this institution devoted to education that tries to govern, tries to manage the minds of the people, the intelligence of people.

I define success as people who give their lives to God. Wow! That is the ultimate success. There are many degrees of success. People see success in all sorts of ways, but that's how I see it. And how do I go about evaluating that success? How do I give my life to God? How does one give one's life to God? Where does it start from?

Maybe you're lucky if you just get zapped with the Holy Spirit. *(Laughter.)* "I've changed. I just want to dedicate my life to God from now on." You're lucky, but most people don't. They go through all sorts of individual situations to make that determination. A lot of people do it out of desperation as well. They've got nowhere else to turn so, "I've got nothing so what the hell do I have to lose by turning my life over to God? Let him take care of my miserable situation." You can do that.

Most of you made choices, or are trying to make choices in that way, because I see some young people here. People that are at my age and above you have no choice. That's how you made it. Okay? *(Laughter)* That is how you're going to die.

If you can do one thing by yourself and if you have groups of people who can work together for the sake of each other just following all the basic principles of goodness, I think we should try to encompass that first before you try to take it to the next level—talking about messiah stuff, that 'we're a better religion than yours' stuff. I think that's the first step. We should try to do that and help each other physically—then on a larger scale—then we can afford to take care of each other intellectually and expand the mind and then ultimately it's up to you to connect to your spirit.

It takes that kind of formative essence. You need that kind of basic foundation to achieve that kind of spiritual connection. And that's what we lack, I believe. We're too much like "every man for himself, go figure it out on your own." We have all been through workshops and they are very limited. You cycle 40 days, three times for 120 days. What is that? And somehow you can go out and change the world? Well, you try. And then you try to move up the church ladder. What happens? The same bureaucracy—so what's the difference between them and us? Nothing, I don't see anything different.

That's a problem. What can we do? Can we do something about this situation? I think so. It's important to empower individuals within the church. You have to give more and more information that is critical in doing our work. We have to share that information in easier, more acceptable, more efficient, and more effective ways. Let people familiarize themselves with that stuff, because familiarity breeds confidence. When one gets confident, that's something. It gives a willingness to commit to action. That changes people. Just having basic information about the essence of principle is good, but this is society, and society is different than the essence of principle. You have gone down like this [*gesturing to the focal point at the bottom of a "V" shape*] but now you have to go back up.

You might have found the focal point, that's all the workshop does, try to give you a focal point, and this is how Father connects to God. That's it! That's where it ends! Now you're going to go out there and conquer the world? Now you're going to go out and build the kingdom by yourself? Give me a break! That's unreal. Why are you not doing more of that kind of stuff? You have to start somewhere. That's what we can do.

I found another host if you want more of it—it's called http://definingmoment.eu/ to focus more on the European nations. I also found a Spanish-speaking host.

We have to get to know Europeans, we have to get to know Hispanics, we have to get to know how they think. We have to know about their different religions, about their culture, and about themselves. The more we know the better. If you have that information it will give you confidence. That power will transform you into an active person. I believe that. We won't stop at that. We'll branch out into giving more advice on pragmatic things, finances, or whatever.

We can do that, get that kind of network moving and working. Invite hosts, and all sorts of guests, and get that critical, useful, practical information out there, and just delegate it to all of you. That's what the church should be doing.

Father's course is more of overall and centering on him and we are bound by that tradition, but after that we have to be independent. Father's course is a very dependent course. It's a course of dependency. It has to be. But the next phase is more independent. We have to realize our greatness centering on Father's vision and let that proliferate out into the world and make a difference.

Yes, we need a body, we need an organization, sure I understand that concept. But it will have to go toward that direction unlike the structure and organization during Father's lifetime. We're not going to make a dependent structure—it's going to be more independent, but in what way? Bearing the heart and spirit of Father's teaching.

Not just, "You do this and that! I'm in control!" Those idiots! You walk around shit not because you're afraid of it, but because you don't want to get your shoes dirty. Those people make me sick. Hey, it's not my problem right?

You have to love, you can't kill people. *(Laughter.)*

Anyway, wouldn't you like to see that happen? *(Yes.)*

I believe we can literally see change. I believe that we can literally see our progress if that is the basic reality in this church. If we take care of that basic stuff we can literally see our own progress. Collectively, of course, you will see more. That's how you compete with other religions. If you don't have something to show, you can't win. You can't win by bluffing. What if they will fight you? You got to have what it takes to take the blows. Otherwise it is only a bluff.

That is what we need to do. I think we should encourage that kind of stuff, and open up to each other.

I can't be here at the last Sunday [*of this year*] because I have to say hello to my folks, but after this there about six more left. My condition's done.

You like what we got here? *(Yes.)*

You want me to show up for one more year? *(YES!)*

We'll talk about it later. *(Laughter.)*

I know that's doable. I can see it in this very small kind of model.

But it will work. It will work.

I believe in it with all my heart.

It's not just coming from me. It's coming from somewhere else too.

I believe it.

So, I think your success is how you define it, not just with your body or with your head, but with everything that you've got. Right? See you next week.

Repentance
November 19, 2006

Good morning.

Some of you should have stayed home. *(Laughter.)*

Do you want to be happy or do you want to be sad? *(Happy.)*

I'm sorry, but my topic is, "Repentance." Penitence demands repentance, right?

Do you like to see humble people or do you like to see arrogant people? There are so many ways to see people these days because everybody wants to be somebody. They want to prove that they have something to offer, whether it's for money, power— whatever it is in the secular setting. But to really be somebody takes a lifetime to prove.

Why? Perfection is given by God, not you. The ultimate judge is not you. When you even ponder the notion of individual perfection, you're only kidding yourself if you don't understand how things ultimately get judged.

Your parents force you to go to school and in the end the grade matters. It's not you who can dictate that you should graduate with the grade you think that you deserve. This is the same system reflected in the basic outcome of dying. That's the basic premise that you have to accept. What you're actually experiencing is a little taste of that.

You have no control over your perfection. That is the ultimate irony, because you can't judge yourself to be perfect. It doesn't work like that. Basically you're going through a certain conditioning process. It's not easy to get good at anything.

I'm here to talk to my age group or above. That's my forum here. It has nothing to do with what else I can do. Everything has a purpose. It's very specific. You have to target things to the point where it matters, to what you're actually trying to accomplish in that specific event or scenario. If I see little kids I know I'm talking to your parents. I'm not going to talk to you. It's not my focus. I can do that some other time, some other situation, I am here trying to do what I think is appropriate, that can best serve for the greater purpose. You have a whole lot of time ahead of you. I hate to see a lot of young people here. I want to see a lot of old people here. *(Laughter.)* I see young people when I go home.

You don't have to change anything. You have to change what is real. Real is not always you. Real is what is real. That's what we have to understand—real is always beyond you. That's why God is a suffering God, because He has a concept that makes Him a slave for all sorts of miserable things.

Please do not think that everything revolves around you. Repentance is a very necessary tool for conscience because it keeps you motivated. It keeps you moving forward. It causes you to evolve and find your perfection ultimately. Even that is not dictated by you. You don't have absolute control over that end.

You will have to die first to have the finality of that. Do you understand me? That is absolute. No one is an exception. Ultimately, it has to be represented, and the messiah is the representation. How do you go about using the tools we have? Conscience is a tool. Conscience, the device that makes you do something. It's a tool that tries to make us better. It's a blessing. It's a gift from God. A blessing is a tool that comes from God.

It's something that will aid you and support you, to make you into something better than you are. You have to know how to use it properly, because if you don't, you'll mess up. You'll lose the opportunity. You can't blame it on anyone else. In the end it is your responsibility to correct whatever you have to correct, whatever you have to complete, whatever you have to perfect.

When you talk about the concept of perfection, it is all about your idiosyncrasies. "I'm somebody special!" Perfection is just about catering to that nonsense. "I'm special." Special in what? You must prove it in the end. You have to die for it. You have to prove it by dying, and in doing so you'll prove your idiosyncratic, unique greatness, however minute, however miserable it might be. Trying to go beyond that and getting into grandiosity—why do you want to do that? Do you think that you can change the world without going through the basic process of things? I don't think so. If you don't understand what is basic, you can't even find yourself. There's no way you're going to get a grade. That's just the way it is.

Then what the hell are you dying for? That's the problem. There is no one else that's going to answer that question other than you, your individual self.

Why is repentance necessary? Because it keeps you busy, because lazy people get corrupted. When you start to have riches, why do you think people get corrupted? You might have all the good intentions for being a politician, and, of course, in politics you'll be full of ambition. That's what drives politicians to seek the highest office. They believe their ideals are better than the other guy, they imagine that, "If I just get power I will change the world." The problem is that you have an environment that is susceptible to all sorts of stuff that is not right for individual growth, and for finding oneself. Let's say this rich country is more privileged than other countries. You're going to have problems when things start to come easier and easier for you. Obviously you're going to get corrupted. Why? You have less time to repent and repentance at least keeps you busy.

You try to be responsible for your own good, whatever you did, and not blame or worry about everybody else. "I did this and I'm responsible!" Repentance is a tool of conscience— through the evolving process that hopefully can give you that completion you desire. If you hold on to it maybe you have a chance, but if you let it go you have no chance.

Right or wrong, in the end you have to stand, because God will judge you. Even Sun Myung Moon will be judged by God. My father, the messiah will be judged by God. Absolutely!

I believe that. That's what I've learned. That's what I accept. There is no exception to the rule. If anybody says otherwise, [*hits the podium*] Why? Who are you? You have to analyze those little monkeys. You have to find out where that guy's tail lies. Not tale stories, animal tail. Someone will step on it one day. Because it is not that simple. You pay for it. And you are going to live with it. You are going to make it right. Not somebody else. It's not you who suffer, it's I suffer. Do you understand what I am saying? If you do something wrong you are going to suffer one way or the other. It doesn't matter how you excuse yourself. If you're man enough you wouldn't.

Everybody can be broken. In a war situation when someone is a torturer, they're the one who has the self-righteousness on their side. They are the one who is greater and superior. That's what gives them the right to torture their enemy prisoners to make them repent for their sins against you. Everybody can be broken. What does that prove in war? Nothing.

Let's talk about historical indemnity. Let's say that you went through that torture for the sake of humanity, for your lineage. Make it true to that. Don't say anymore beyond that. Let it go. You move on, think about yourself from now on, because nobody is going to take care of you. You have to take care of yourself and each other, if we have a community, if we're building one. I would like to see all sorts of people in my family. I don't want to see just yellow faces in my family.

I don't intend to be something more than what I am. That is the essence of people like me. That means a lot. I don't care what people say. I make my own decisions.

What's important is what is good, and what is basic. Basic ultimately can bring the idealism regardless of who we are. That's the most important thing.

You think you can make a living, yes, but what if everything collapses? If you have a lazy mind it will be absolutely corrupt. And you have an environment that caters to that kind of reality then it will pretty much wipe out the young generation. But we can change that. We have to make a difference.

Define what you get beyond yourself. Try—keep on trying until you see the light on your own way. I don't care how long it takes. I hope you make it before you die. I can't help you beyond that. If you don't take care of your residual stuff it will get passed down and somebody else will bear the greater burden. That's just the way it is. What if an asteroid the size of Jupiter comes from outside our solar system and you get vaporized? You want to know the truth? Start with yourself, and then get into the bigger war, then you and everybody find more truth. Everyday truth is changing. Hey, don't kid yourself.

Everybody has the voice to be heard, but don't kid yourself. Do something before you die. And you will die. You will die of disease, accident, suicide, or natural causes. You will die. Even if you live to your fullest, how long do you think you will live? Do you know how you're going to be judged? Are you working on your grade? Do you really know what you're going to be graded upon? Be real, all right?

Do you think people want to be a prostitute? Do you think people want to be a junkie? Do you think people want to be a criminal? Do you think people want to be a con-artist? No, but they do it for all sorts of reasons.

So, there is nobody like that among the young people in this room, so at least that is a pride you can point out. You have to be real. Balance your reality, your physical self, your mind status, and your spiritual awareness. If you have a family situation where you can exchange with your folks, by all means take that opportunity, because you're lucky if you can have that. I don't think that there are any parents who if they have the ideal scenario like that would let that kind of opportunity go to waste.

[From now until the end of the speech, Hyo Jin Nim was very emotional and often in tears. There were several long emotional pauses.]

Please be aware of your situation. Please be aware of your reality. Know what it offers. Always measure yourself. If you want to grow you have to have balance so you have to know the extremes. As you grow the extremes will only get bigger. It will constantly expand—you have to grow into it. The stupid thing about arrogance is that you think when you reach some kind of level that you're in control. You have some kind of sick sense of superiority. It doesn't work like that.

When you try to think about it, even when you appreciate rock music, you have to get to a point where you really appreciate it. If you just use music as sonic jambalaya that gives you a hoopla for parties sake, that is actually defeating the property of music in itself. Do you know that?

You have to have a different agenda if you are into music. You are just into chattering and socializing, but you want that atmosphere because you are so young and you are so physical, and it's all physical stuff. Because the age factor it is primarily important, blah, blah, blah. You can give that primary excuse that everybody will to point understand and accept because that's the way it is, to a point.

But beyond that, it's nonsense. It is not even music. Any monkey can make that. That's why monkeys do. It's not funny.

Anyway, I'm sorry. The reason why I brought up this is because this is not my audience. That is about it. I don't want to talk about this stuff. It has nothing to do with why I am here. It's for the little kids. Before we talk to our kids we have to question ourselves as parents. You have to be responsible. Yeah, I did wrong. No excuses. Did I love my kids? I'd even go to hell for them. It's easy when I take all the responsibility, blame. I'll pay for it until they come back.

So, in America I have a different kind of justice because I'm Reverend Moon's son. That's absolutely unique. Anyway God will judge. Please,

please, please. You don't know me that well. Since you're in this room and I see a response, I'm just reacting. I react to things to a point. Today just happens to be one of those days. It's okay. I'm just responding to you. You will see who wins in the end. You'd better know what you do. You have to be willing to go a long ways through all sorts of difficult crap and suffering. You can't get away that easy. Some things you just don't want to mess with. Hey, do you think I like living— ... All I'm here for is for sharing. I'll do what I do.

Homogeneity is about the closest thing we have to monarchy, because there is no such thing as a pure monarchy in today's political situation. Conservatism is a little closer than liberalism. America's standing is very young. Liberalism is the opposite because it's an adversarial system. The point is that is something tries to hold on to boundaries, and then something else will try to do away with boundaries. That's the problem. That's what we have to deal with. That's the kind of work that has to be done in Democratic free society, especially in a developed nation.

That's why repentance is very important. You have to make sure that the politicians don't get lazy. It doesn't matter whether you're a Democrat or Republican. In homogenous countries like Korea and Japan there are many political parties, but if you screw up you pay. Everybody is after, you. Why? Because it is a homogenous society.

When you are dealing with all sorts of different races and cultures, it is very difficult. That's why certain basic principles are very important. We have to master those. We have to project those. We have to make that better, not just in terms of presentation, but in reality.

You can't make a living with just words. It's body mind and spirit. You are going to be judged one day. I believe in God. I might not believe in you or I might not believe in anything else—I might not even believe in me, but I believe in God.

Sometimes I don't know how I'm going to do what I have to do, where I have to start. I just have to figure it out. That's how I start.

Nonetheless, in the end you have to prove it. If you expect things to be easy it means you got caught up in this lie. That is why in the end, even in the rich nations, marriages end up divorced. If you think you are the best but you're just lazy then you are corrupted. You don't know your own limitations. You think of awesome things and expect the best in every way—the 'I'm American' crap, and in the end it all comes crashing down.

If you want something to last, you'd better know what you're asking for. Isn't that obvious even when you buy a used car, don't you want to ask basic questions and have knowledge before going ahead with the purchase?

I'm just talking about secular things, but if you think about ideal things then you'd better understand the basic things because the basic things are important. That's reality. How much you want to do is up to you. You can always enjoy the security of your boundaries. Boundaries are secure. If you can protect your boundaries you have security. If you try to expand them you're asking for trouble. There's risk involved, uncertainty. But how far are you willing to go, in what way, for what reason. Because every time you skip a generation you go into that basic premise.

You need to question yourself. I know that's the way—I know that is reality, but how far are the people on top willing to go? If you want to do something there is a basic principle. Just ask yourself, "Am I willing to die for this?" It's nobody else's business but mine.

That's always why I ask you to think about dying more than living. Living is easy because you're already breathing. You're living right now. It's easy for you. Dying is important. Dying well is harder, reaching perfection is much more hard. With living, you take for granted just sitting there while you breathe and eat and think what you want because you are allowed to at this point in time. You get comfortable with this and the same thing happens and you want to take it to the next level and the next level and the next level. What level are we talking about?

You can say that New Yorkers are jaded and sophisticated but they aren't going to change the world. They live in the capitol of capitalism—in the end nobody takes them seriously. They aren't going to change the world. It's just about them. Familiarity gives you some kind of confidence, but you have to understand that confidence can be a double-edged sword. In what way are you confident? Anyway, okay. So, I need to repent. There's always room to repent. I need to repent because I didn't intend to be like this today.

For whatever it's worth, if this helps you, nobody is ever going to do this to you again, maybe your mommy or something. Let's just be happy because I believe that it's doable. I do. I do. It is doable. We just have to do it step-by-step. We've just got to in reality. We have to have it in reality. We need it in reality. We need more of it. Hey! It's not too late right? You don't want to think it's too late right?

Do you want this to go on? Do you want me to come every Sunday? How long? Give me the days. How long do you see that being? You give me a time and I'll do it. Whatever. How long? That's what I'm asking.

(*one sister says, "forever"*) (*laughter*) I'll be here as long as you need me. If you don't need me just tell me so and I'll disappear. I'll be more than happy to disappear. Take care of yourselves. Okay.

Indemnity
November 26, 2006

Did you have a good Thanksgiving?

It's a turkey day right? I don't know if it's purely for being thankful. *(Laughter.)*

When you talk about indemnity that's kind of a heavy topic isn't it? But should it be?

In the beginning God expected us to be something. He had a vision. He had the ultimate divine vision, the purpose of creation, and in that light we had a crucial role to play. Just based on that reality alone, that's something significant. That should be something that we should all celebrate, that possibility in itself. Whether it happened or whether it didn't happen, whether we're still struggling to make it happen—that's an afterthought, because hindsight is always 20/20 right?

It gives us something to try to strive for, to achieve that ultimate, the vision of God. We all have that and we all dream that we'd like to see ourselves living in a world where there are no wars, and you can trust somebody even if you never met them. Somebody in your life, where you can just walk up and shake their hand and somehow that alone can have a lasting relationship.

Because even in a personal relationship, if you try to build or even contemplate about making a true relationship, an ideal relationship, it takes a lifetime. You can't really say to yourself that I can know somebody just because I've been with them a few times. I see him do this. I see him do that. I see him in this extreme state, I saw him in the opposite extreme state. So, therefore I can conclude that I know. But it's not that simple. People can change and there's all sorts of stuff in between that makes us unique.

So, even when you try to understand an individual and try to accept the basic kind of religious teaching about an individual being idiosyncratic—that they're unique, something special in the eyes of God, it takes a lifetime to really understand it.

Because if you don't try to understand people based on that kind of common sense based thinking, it's improper. The conclusion will be false, and you have to bear the responsibility in judgment. Because ultimately in the end what you are doing is judgment. But that should be left up to God. We should try to understand what God has intended and then try to create an ideal world in essence, before we try to be God.

If you don't have the basic understanding as to why you are here and what we're struggling to achieve in creating an ideal world there's no point in trying to say that I'm great, or trying to declare some sort of happiness that's just centered on you. That greatness is just centered on you. That has nothing to do with God. It has nothing to do with anybody else.

So, before we try to define ourselves, including with the most difficult kind of concept such as indemnity, we have to try to understand why such a thing is necessary for us to become what God intended to be.

Talk about indemnity. It's like you're compensating for some kind of stuff right? You cause some kind of loss and damage so you're going to redeem yourself by making compensation. That is the concept so when you think about any kind of situation where a standard is set, and when that standard is breached what has to happen? Because you're going down the path of conflict—to diminish it, what do you have to do?

You've got to do something. You've got to do something to make that conflict into zero. If you don't do that you can't rebuild, because indemnity is about rebuilding. It's about recreating. It's rebuilding, but the process by which you rebuild and you recreate has a standard that you have to earn. It's not automatic. You have a specific responsibility within that kind of give-and-take relationship. You have to earn that to complete that process. And if you don't do that properly, you go into a process of conflict.

You have to pay indemnity. You have to neutralize that. You have to make that into zero first to make it true. That's the standard. Ultimately that's my view or concept of indemnity. The important aspect that we have to achieve first is to have that understanding of earning your way to your expected position, especially in the divine relationship, the relationship between you and God.

Unless you address that clearly, and you do it on your own—unless you earn it, it doesn't work. It's a very important process that you have to understand through action, through your deeds. Earn it. Earn that title. That's the natural way. That is the proper way. That is the divine way. That is the way that will last and have a meaning after you pass away from this earth, because you don't live here too long.

I try to tell myself the same thing. It's important if you want to have any kind of standard, if you don't remind yourself, it doesn't exist. It really doesn't matter, whatever you say, whatever you do. It doesn't matter, because you'll never measure up to it, even to your own standard in the end.

When you look at this world, and let's say this is one extreme and this is the opposite extreme. [*Pointing to the opposite corners of the podium.*] There are takers, and there are givers, and something in between. Takers will do anything and say anything to get what they want. For what purpose? You ask those takers. And there's the opposite and what do you think normal people in general are? I hope you can make an easy model and just take a little sphere and based on the center here everybody just exists here and that's the world—that's the kind of bubble we exists in. [*Hyo Jin Nim makes a ball with his hands at the middle of the podium.*]

But do you really think that the dividing line absolutely right down the center? I think the world is a little more to this side. [*Hyo Jin Nim*

positions his hands a little more to the left, taker's side of the podium.]
That's the problem. You would hate to see a world living here
[taker's side] right? It's foolish to think it exists like this *[Hands all the way to giver's side]*. That's kind of God's stuff, a long way to go from reality. Would you imagine that it is potentially doable because that we're the children of God?

So be it, but the reality is there. So, how do you deal with people like that? How do you deal with people you can't really communicate with? There are no words that can transform these people who are addicted to that lifestyle, who are absolutely absorbed into that lifestyle. That's how they're going to find their meaning. They aren't going to change, until something happens.

And unfortunately the only way this can happen, for those people to change, is for them to hit bottom, to lose everything. Crash and burn you know? What if that doesn't happen in that person's lifetime? It will pass on to the next generation. That's the problem. That's why even in the eyes of Father it will take generations to make that happen, potentially. Why? Because you have to go through that process. Unless you can somehow change that without allowing them to hit the bottom, those people that you can't verbally transform through normal ways of communication, they all have to go through that process, and if it doesn't happen in their lifetime then it will pass down to their children, and grandchildren. It will take time. That's why it's going to take time.

So, how are you going to change something knowing that inevitably that is the only way to assure that change will happen? What can we do about it? I know it's difficult, but somebody's got to do it. Somebody has to do it if there's not another alternative. It's a long shot. It's very difficult, it's never ending stuff. But even if it's a long shot, if there's some possibility, we have to do it. That's what we have to do. There's no other way of communicating.

We have to try to communicate—try to find the best way. We have to find the most effective way to reach the generation at hand at present, the ones who are movers and shakers in the world, both the elders, and our young people too. We have to keep that line, that approach, let's keep on trying. That's the only way. Otherwise you just have to wait for the inevitable to take place. But that would be very unfortunate, because they won't change until they hit bottom. I know this. They won't.

It's too important to them to have what they want. It's unfortunate. It's all about them, but that's just the way it is, and that's real. I'm not making this up, as you know—all of you understand what I'm saying—but that's reality. The only option that we have is to keep on trying to do what we believe in and try to find a better way of communication, find a better something. We have to use what's out there to communicate and elaborate on it as much as we can.

Give more, more, more, more. It would be wonderful if we could constantly be in the presence of humanity. We could have 24-hour stuff and compete with the big guys. Look at America for instance. Look at conservatism and liberalism. To me it's about homogeneity, because it has a tradition mostly based on Christianity. There is a sense of a homogenous effect like in a homogenous society like Korea or Japan. It's easier to unite because there is a kind of nationalism. For the sake of the national interest you put aside your regional conflicts or whatever.

You have a conflict in your own family too. I have a bunch of brothers and sisters. Trust me. *(Laughter.)* You come from the same belly but you still struggle with each other. *(Laughter.)* That's reality.

In America conservatism is pretty much like that, because it's kind of Christian based.

Liberals are like, "We don't want tradition, we want less tradition. Push the boundary! Push the boundary!"

"Hold the boundary! Hold the boundary! Push the boundary! Push the boundary!" It's that kind of conflict. In America even when you deal with those kind of conservatives, as the Unification Church we have to compete with them, and with all sorts of Christian denominations, because they want to do good too.

These days it is almost fashionable to talk about moral degradation and blaming Hollywood and stuff. It's fashionable. And they are going to try to do something about it. As much as we do they will do. And how do you deal with that ultimately? You have to outlast them first of all.

So, having a standard of something beyond change is good. Father stresses absolute value. That's good. In what? In us, his blood lineage.

And all the good things that we can commonly share with the other religions who have good intent, we will do our best to support them because we need to support each other, but at the same time we are competing with them.

The extreme Muslims will outright say to conquer with violence— that's crazy. They all, in some way, want their religion to be the standard bearer, nicely put. I believe it is necessary for us to understand the true meaning of indemnity. Everything that we do even if we think that it's promised by our faith, our discipline, we have to earn it because that's the basic way
decent people communicate with each one another.

Decent people try not to take away from something, right? You don't just take, take, take, take from this guy, take from that guy, take from your sister, take from your brother, and make yourself fat right? "Because only I have the answer stuff." There is only one Father in my house. You understand me?

You have to first realize that this is a church first before anything else. That's why you don't do certain things. You can't do stupid stuff because of whatever crazy predicament you might run into. If you are systematically trying to do something with consciousness, you'd better be aware of who you are. You're church first before anything else. It's a fair warning.

We're asking for it. It's not a difficult fight. I don't even consider it a difficult conflict. It's stupidity. Anyway.

You still here you guys? *(Laughter.)*

Sometimes, to be honest with you, that's my way of putting on a defense. I don't want to be hurt.

Anyway. I'm sorry about it. I didn't mean it to come off that harsh. That's my fault. It's not yours. Take care, okay?

How Can We Earn Something That Can Last?
December 3, 2006

Good morning.

Today's topic is, "How Can We Earn Something That Can Last?"

Anything that can last has to have some kind of relevance to the human and divine relationship, right? It has to reflect your understanding, at least, your recognition of the existence of God. That's where we have to start. Otherwise it's going to be very difficult to define it, because you can't prove it—you'd be dead.

When we talk about our individual perfection, how do you define that? What is perfection, just being mechanical? What is the reference that we're using to define perfection? In the 20th century a lot of heavy emphasis was given to technological advancement and we pride ourselves because civilization benefited in many convenient ways.

What's beyond that? What is beyond what we are? How do you define perfection beyond this reference we have, convenience, and the lifestyle as we know it?

For some it's never enough. Most people appreciate the development of humankind in terms of understanding and our ability to control the advancement of knowledge and know-how into things. This ability comes from understanding, the ability to manipulate and control for the service of our use and our needs, and whatnot.

From that you have some definition of convenience, but to some people that's not enough. They want more beyond this convenience and this basic comfort that we expect in a civil society. They want more. It goes beyond that for some people. They want luxury, VIP treatment, and just the best in everything. It never ends!

To many people, earning is a concept, especially when you look at it in a capitalistic way of looking at things. It's very, very important. The bottom line is important. "Make sure the profit is decent," and sufficient for the amount of investment, for the amount you sacrifice in your mind, whatever that might be, whatever point of reference that you are using as some kind of central guideline.

A lot of people, when they use a point of reference like that, they kind of set themselves in a central figure position. Many times that becomes a problem with how everything is viewed, how everything is judged by people like that, and the people that they are influencing.

So, how do you deal with that kind of difference in things? There will be many people like that with their very strong view of how things should be, of how profit should be made, and these people will be making all sorts of different standards of judgment.

In that situation what are we competing against? Who are we competing against, and to what end, to what purpose? What kind of group of people are we competing with and why should that be important to everyone else? What if you don't believe in that thing? What if you say "My life is too short for that nonsense. I want to find something more meaningful. Is there something more meaningful than that?"

So, who sets the target? In a democracy majority rules, right? In any democratic society, if you're going to find the pulse of that society, you have to define what the majority is and you have to properly define it if you want to make a difference.

There is a way to earn things. Earning is important to you. Why, because you have to make a living. That's personal earning. Yes, there's a concept of that. But shouldn't there be a concept of universal earning? What's that? I guess that's the opposite of personal earning, something that can benefit something greater than yourself, in the extreme sense, humanity. That's big, but hey! Why not? We have to at least talk about it—think about that concept— and why not make it exist? Is that a sense of idealism? Is that how idealism is born? Should that matter to everybody?

If you think about earnings, you have to think about that too, not just you but all, if you believe in God. Otherwise, why would you want to talk about God?

When you talk about individual perfection, to me it's an awareness, an awareness of me, myself, that I exist with God, that I have a relationship with God. That's what perfection is to me, individually. I will die. I will probably die without knowing everybody's name. *(Laughter.)* If God exists and if I want to earn something on my own that can last forever, literally that's how it's going to be—it's going to be forever. Forever relationship and in that relationship forever changing and greater understanding of one another however many it might be.

Whatever that I believe God to be that keeps me good, I will forever continuously understand more, more in depth and breadth, in three dimensions forever, universally. That's the kind of excitement that I look forward to if I think about dying. If you don't have something like that it's going to be one heck of a miserable ride, right? I know it's going to be miserable.

It ought to be miserable—the more you take on the harder it gets. It's not going to get any easier. I certainly have to try to keep my sanity intact, and at the same time my humility intact. It's going to be hard. I always have to ask myself, "Why the heck am I doing this?" in whatever I do. For me, when I play something, it's just a tool for me. I'm trying to do something so that I can help the old man. I wouldn't touch it otherwise.

In terms of how Parents look at status and stuff, I'll do something else a little more overtly, but that kind of stuff is just peripheral. Music is just a tool—I don't need it. That doesn't have to be some kind of central thing in my life. It's just a part of something that I know how to use. It's a tool.

Because everything matters, in this job, in our endeavor—everything that is visual, oral, communicational, it matters. This kind of conversation matters too right? *(Yes.)* Whatever it takes—that's the bottom line. That's what I'm trying to do, to earn something that I can give for a long time.

How can you earn something when you don't have an audience? If you make a gummy bear and you don't have a consumer, you aren't going to earn anything. *(Laughter.)* You'll have a bunch of gummy bears that you made and you can eat them until your teeth drop. *(Laughter.)*

So, whatever you do, at least I can have respect for something like that. That's important. It's important for people too. People care about those kind of things. Some people just need to grow up. How much is enough? [*Hyo Jin Nim is in tears.*]

Anyway you have to love everybody right? You can't kill people! So, you try. You try every day. Because it matters—those things matter to you. When you know that this is the essence of something—when you grow in it, it matters to you. It really does because you start to see something and that something is called value.

When you see yourself in that, then you'll start to learn something meaningful and that's true earning—because that will last with you till the day you die and after. [*Hyo Jin Nim is very emotional, in tears, and speaks haltingly.*]

That's why even your burnt out soul can be reignited.

You don't need millions to do this. Even just one, one on one, a handful—that's more meaningful. See you next week.

Building a World of True Love
December 10, 2006

Good morning.

Let's talk about a topic that's a little lofty today. Today's topic is, "Building a World of True Love."

Everybody wants love? *(Yes.)* True Love? *(Yes.)* What is love to you? Can you help me out? Let me hear your opinion—what is love to you?

(Living for the sake of others.)

Living for the sake of others, can we all agree on that? Is that the definition of love?

Life is an offering right? Love is an offering. When you make a vow of love and you open your hearts in matrimony you make the vow to care, to cherish, to love "till death do us part" and beyond. Basically it's that—it's the offering of each other.

If you put "True" on top of it that then what changes in terms of the definition? Does anything change? Or is this something that you add on to that offering? I think "True" is something that is added on to the basic definition. That's the greatest that you possess.

That's what your individual truth is. Everybody has individual truth. You can't just talk about universality all the time. Before you talk about universality, you have to define yourself clearly. You have to know how to present yourself and be yourself in the best way possible, the greatest that you possess. That is your individual truth and nobody can deny that fact because we are in some way authorities on ourselves.

Look, the concept of idiosyncrasy is that little thing that makes you different—but it's much deeper than that. Based on the notion of what we basically understand, individual truth is the greatest offering that we can make for the sake of others, not for the sake of your selfish exploitation reasons.

Of course, everything can turn bad. Everything good can be turned bad. You know the Tree of the Knowledge of Good and Evil comes from the same root. It's the same tree but you take the fruit and it can give you false knowledge and at the same time true knowledge.

Basically, that's where we are in the end. That's why responsibility is crucial. That's why failure to do that causes all sorts of problems and ultimately when you are faced with problems you have to address, you have to remedy it. You have to rectify it if need be. That's when things get complicated. That's the basic premise.

So, when you talk about True Love, you have to answer that question to yourself: "What is my greatest self?" Because that's the offering that you're going to make, if you want to achieve True Love with something other than yourself. Now that you have to answer: What is your greatest offering?

I have no idea. I'm still struggling with mine. What is my greatest offering? I have all sorts of ideas about how much I can contribute in this and that, but I'm still struggling to find the greatest, at my own level. I know in general terms which direction that I should go because I have a big hint, called my name. *(Laughter.)*

That's the first thing, before I think of anything else on my own. If you accept the concept of subject-object relationship, because it's important, and because you have to understand your boundaries right?

We have form—that's why we have existence. Life doesn't exist without form. If you don't have form you don't exist. What does that tell you? It tells you that there is a boundary that you have to understand and that you have to accept. Otherwise, you're nothing. It's not even in the category of death. You just don't exist.

That's where you have to start, with the basic stuff in search of greater truth. If you want to change the world, pretty much that's where you have to start, with yourself, then your family, and realistically if you try to actually create a world like that, the next level is the local church. That's about it.

The locality, before you talk about districts and regions and nations blah, blah, blah. No matter how you section it off, it doesn't matter. You have to expand based on what is expandable in reality. How do things expand in reality? That is the key question that you always have to address, whether you like it or not. Just because you think big constantly doesn't guarantee that it's going to happen in practicality.

You can talk about the importance of having a nation and the body of it or structure of it, but that's just a skeleton if you don't have what it takes to build something that is concrete and substantial—and it has to be real. Expansion has to be based on what is fundamentally real.

That's where you actually, literally, beyond your family, practice True Love. If you practice that stuff, it's not something far away, it's right there, right in front of you, just beyond your own individual family. That's important.

No matter how good you are at anything, you constantly have to practice if you want to expand, accomplish. Otherwise your mastery is just in your head. It has nothing to do with a reality that others can touch and feel. Without that people don't change.

People force change. That's why you get a confused group of people. You create greater confusion. What has to change is something that is fundamentally based, and fundamentally can grow in reality. From that we can make something happen in a bigger way.

If that spreads, if that is the basic foundation things are focused on, and these sorts of things are encouraged, and supported, then sure, we can build our own nation. Sure! Because it's doable. It is real. The reality is based on substantial grounds for physical expansion. Expansion can actually be measured and you can actually see the change and feel the effects.

We can expand through that kind of give-and-take, because people are in it—they're sensitive to it, not just with their spirit or subconscious mind or intellect. It's real! Even the process of trying to teach your children to do the right thing becomes easier because you can say, "Hey! Look at that! Look at this!" It's not arbitrary, it's not cryptic, it's not abstract— it's there!

I know a thing or two about symbolism. What good is it if you don't have a substantial foundation in which that symbolism can be the juice that makes you expand?

Yes, it can be done. You can build the world based on True Love, but it starts with the right approach. Starting from the individual you have to ask basic questions, simple questions, and when you answer it, can you take it to the next level, and can you mean it just as much at each level? Can it stay just as important as it was to you when you were trying to find the greatest thing, the thing that you are willing to make the offering for? You have to find this, even if it's for your own good. For your goodness' sake.

You don't try to be good just because you have so many fans right? You want to be good because it makes you feel good most of the time. I don't understand how people say I want to be good because of my fans and stuff. I believe that everyone has something true to offer. True Love encourages true offering because that's what it is. I know you want it. If you really want it, that's what you have to do. Don't just talk about it. Go for it.

And if you do, others will recognize that, and if it is True Love it will be embedded in their heart. I don't know how long, eons, whatever. I don't know. I'm not dead yet.

Can we build something in True Love? *(Yes.)* And if so, it starts from what we're talking about. I believe it's important to be involved in your local churches beyond your family—it's just a step above. The more you do it will be good for you and good for the church in the end. That's what you can do to practice what you do normally for yourself and your individual family.

See how much you can expand, how much you're willing to volunteer beyond coercion. [*Laughs.*] Because when you're in True Love, it's not just a coerced act, you volunteer right? When you have a loving relationship how can it be a loving relationship when you always have to write a contract for every give-and-take? I think something else is more important in that kind of relationship. THINGS! Bill Gates and this other guy have 100 billion dollars in their foundation. In 20 years it will probably become a trillion dollars. There are so many things out there that will give you high interest. At about eight percent in about seven years it will double your money.

When you have that kind of money there are so many ways that you can squeeze money out of people that want to use your mind. If you have a trillion dollars to spend, that's pretty substantial in the physical world. Sure, you can do a whole lot of good just with that money. Unless you have that bottom line you can't even try to think like that. Don't. Because in the end you'll only get stupid. That's about it.

Why are they chosen to be that rich? I don't know. Ask God. *(Laughter.)*

Know yourself. Know your intent. Okay? And if you have desire, please check it. If you want to ask questions about yourself, who's going to? You can't be true if you can't stand up for yourself in the end. To yourself and to God. That's the only thing that is important when it comes to defense. Because that's the only thing that matters, should matter, to an individual. Otherwise, if you do everything right you don't need to defend yourself, right? Others will know.

True Love ... Don't think it's too far. It starts from you.

Okay? Take care of yourselves.

Inspiration
December 17, 2006

Good morning.

The year is almost at its end.

How are you doing?

People say that there are patterns in everything. Life is about learning patterns. There is a pattern in the universe starting with the physical universe and obviously there is one dealing with our lives.

Through religion we try to understand the kind of relationships and patterns that bring us closer to God, because that is our search, that is our path. Anytime you take—take the path of religious faith, it becomes a commitment that lasts a lifetime. It takes a lifetime to understand how things work. When you talk about patterns you start by defining formulas and then learning the intricacies. We want to see if there is more to be learned based on a cursory observation of the depth of the formula. It's a commitment that pretty much will last everybody's lifetime. I don't know if there is a guarantee that we will understand all of it.
Why? Because I don't think you can know the faces of your grandchildren when you don't have them yet, that kind of stuff.

You know that there are a lot of treasure hunters out there. They know that the diamond is somewhere underneath the ground or they go for a sunken ship treasure and they know that is somewhere under the vast ocean. History is full of people trying to find civilization's riches. You know that there have been a lot of tragedies along the way in pursuit of these so called treasures. A lot of people are hell bent on achieving that end. Even just pursuing that kind of surface stuff takes commitment. It will pretty much take the lifetime of somebody.

Let me just share with you about some people that I know. They are people who live a very simple life. They just love reading books. They spend every free time that they have in libraries. They just go read books, every free moment in a library and they come to a point after decades that their local library is not big enough because they read everything in it. I don't even know if he was interested in some particular topic or if he just read it all. So, he has to go to a bigger library.

I also know a certain type of people that just love to tinker. They love to tinker with stuff, anything. Some guys just like to play with computers, because now there are so many kinds of software that they can just tinker away all day long, because within each kind of software they give you so many kinds of possibilities to play with, whatever that represents. They just sit there all day long every free time that they get. Sometimes they even forget to eat it seems so important. They forget even about sleeping. They are just playing with that thing, tinkering and tinkering forever. That's how they live their lives. They find some kind of inspiration in it.

So, when you think about the stuff in life, for instance let's focus on inspiration today, we have to ask, is there some kind of pattern? Is there a formula through which inspiration is achieved? I think so. When you look at those kinds of people, simply put they're geeks. They're just a bunch of geeks, but they inspire themselves. Through what kind of pattern, it's a kind of formation pattern, or growth pattern. I don't know if you can say that it is completion in the way that we see it because it has to be seen by all. It has to be universal. Maybe on an individual level it might be.

Inspiration also comes in the form of stages. You have to ask yourself, "Why are you inspired?" In what way are you trying to inspire yourself? Are you inspiring yourself? Because you would be inspired if you did those kind of things. On a form stage level, just read the books if you like reading books. That's your escapism, but it's not just escapism—it's about self inspiration.

You do that to yourself. You're telling yourself, "I need that, that's how I'm going to get through this life. That's the kind of fix that I need." You have to ask yourself, "So, in what stage are you? Formation? Growth? Perfection?" When you look at everything that inspires us, it has to do with the basic fundamental things in question, with God and mankind.

We get inspired when big clues come together, right? That's the fundamental question that we need to resolve when you talk about providence, when you talk about God's dispensation. When you say that based on my religious discipline, God is a suffering God, then you have to understand that that is important to you. When that is important to you, when that happens, when extremes come together where it has been in conflict for eons, you see somehow that a resolution is coming, and you see the possibility of resolution, that gives you inspiration.

Obvious things—when you see a child sacrificing himself or herself for the sake of their parents or visa-versa. Or you see the passing of the guard, the passing of authority or whatever. You see it happening in fluid motion without any controversy, without any conflict between generational differences or arrogance, you get inspired. It's that basic fundamental relationship that makes us who we are, and makes us able to create an ideal family centered on God.

When that happens you're inspired. When you see the basic recognition of things happening and coming together, that inspires you. Those things inspire you.

Yes, they can start from even yourself, inspiration just by the possibility of formation, growth and perfection of self-love on an individual level. But, as it grows it matures into something greater in being the level of inspiration obviously much greater, powerful. So, if you want to inspire the world, okay, you just have to accept that formula.

Where do you start? How do you inspire the world? People of the world, especially in the big cities are jaded and arrogant. They like big things. Unless you can somehow break them down, getting there is very difficult. You have to start from self and make every step of the way yours and you have to somehow connect it to God. Otherwise you don't have proof in the eyes of people who are critical against you. That's the difficulty.

So, if you want to change the world, there is only one way, the old fashioned way, you have to struggle—you have to suffer. [*Hyo Jin Nim laughs.*] It's important to do more, and you have to do it not just for yourself. You have to do it for the sake of maturity, and responding to the demand and effort it takes to deal with greater value, and the greater self. When you can put that forth, when you can make that sacrifice—yes, we can move a greater world.

How far can you go? It's up to you. I don't know. I don't know about me. How far can I push? How far am I willing to push? Oh, just be straight forward—how far can I push? I don't know. I just have to keep on trying I guess. I cannot say what it is—the funny thing is till until I'm dead—and I can't say it. You'll say it. Somebody else will say it, probably my children, my posterity.

The funny thing is that the greatest and most important thing you can think is the thing that will be measured by somebody else other than you. That's the lesson. That's the lesson in life when you try to believe in God. Always something like that. You think you're in control, but you're not because even when you think, "Let's make today a good day," even that's not as simple as it sounds. I know that we deserve a chance every day. We need to see goodness in you, and new goodness from you and me. But is that as simple as you say? I don't think so.

Yes, we deserve a lot of things that are good, but it doesn't happen automatically. Somebody has to try. Somebody has to lead the way. If that is you, you can't expect one person to do everything all the time. That's why we need family. That's why we need the greater family, right? Otherwise it will be a lonely place. Otherwise why did God create mankind and give himself such misery? Even goodness is not appreciated when you have it alone. It doesn't have a concept that allows real happiness when alone.

So, an inspiration, a belief, everything in life has a formula—inspiration too. You must value the fundamentals and try to work that into your life starting from self. I don't think that's selfish. You've got to start somewhere and it's the individual, that's where we start. We all start from there.

You can't say that's evil. You can't put that kind of brand on that. Why? Because you can't even do that to yourself in good conscience. Guess what? Somebody else will judge you, because that's the judgment that matters the most. That's the judgment that will stick in the end, that will define you.

We could go on seriously like this. I know that there is a pattern in everything in life and we can find it. We can find it together and help each other. That's what makes things better for all of us. Right? I think that's more important than just you being happy all the time. I don't like that type of people. Take care. See you next week.

Happiness
December 24, 2006

Good morning.

This is the holiday season. Is it supposed to be a happy occasion?

The topic today is, "Happiness." When do we feel happy? Help me out here. [*Asking for responses from the audience.*]

(When our desire is fulfilled, when we are with people we love, when our kids are with us.)

That's true, all those things.

Happiness begins with life itself, right? Happiness can be as simple as when you see children just feeling life as they start to walk and run. If they see an open field, they want to run. They have a clear blue sky and it makes them happy like a little colt.

All those things, just life. In life itself you can start to find out what basic happiness is all about—then comes the phases of growth, and finding the meaning of life. Understanding the meaning of life becomes more important than the actual physical give and take. That is very necessary for us, however the meaning of life and that understanding, finding the meaning of life becomes more relevant as we inspire others. Because life itself is about growth. It's perpetual growth. It's constant growth.

We have to learn. One way or another we will learn about the greater meaning of God, the will of God, and the love of God, whether we like it or not. Understanding the essence of God's love is a life-long journey, and I don't think that it ends even there. That's what we're taught that we will have a relationship with God forever, eternally. In this divine relationship there is something called True Love that we offer each other. This is because the meaning of love to me is offering. When we truly offer ourselves, our greatest, of course the meaning of love, the definition of love, will constantly expand because it should. You're growing, and you have to expand.

Of course, after finding the meaning of life you come to the point where it has to be manifest some way or another. It has to be substantiated. This is the fulfillment of life that will give us happiness. We complete the course by going through the stages of growth— formation, growth, and completion/perfection as we understand it. This is the process we go through as we deliver the expectation, and in this way complete the course. That's when you understand what greater happiness means.

When you're young, just learning something new or exciting can give you a feeling of stimulation. But it becomes more when you complete something and find fulfillment that way. The fulfillment of life will give you the happiness you seek.

Of course, the final phase will be the legacy phase of your life. You will die. We will die. I believe the greater problem is the period of growth where you're trying to seek out understanding, new understanding, greater understanding, about the meaning of life. Sometimes it can be confusing.

You can say that true happiness comes from having the ability of being able to see happiness in the eyes of others. It sounds nice, but I'm not talking about a bank robber's happiness. He'd say, "I scored big and I'm very happy." I'm not talking about that kind of happiness. There are certain boundaries there. Understand that boundary; it takes time because we have to find the meaning in the end.

Obviously to a bank robber money is meaningful. That's why he robs banks! I guess he is unable to make it properly. So, happiness itself can be defined in many different ways. You can say that in the process of growth we try to understand happiness based on individual, idiosyncratic ways first. Whatever your preferences are you can say that we define happiness based on our idiosyncrasies or preferences. When we get something that we prefer over some other thing, and we have it or possess it, it gives us happiness.

The process of growth becomes difficult because you have to evaluate all those things. You have to make proper analysis for judgment ultimately because in the end you'll be judged. Prior to that you have to make that analysis. What is truly happy for me? What will bring me true happiness?

That is the period in which you struggle. Sometimes the happiness that we seek might infringe upon somebody else's existence. In the late 1980s and early 1990s my little brothers were becoming company heads and Father was putting them in charge of businesses and stuff and there were a lot of complaints. I used to tell them, as long as I don't have it, don't complain too much. And bringing that order, for me, is happiness. Because that's what you have achieved.

It's not really what that I possess that brings me happiness—sometimes it's the opposite. Understanding that kind of stuff through life, and understanding how you connect what is, understanding the kind of things you're trying to achieve, the things that you are building—all these things can bring happiness. Once you start to figure out the meaning behind it, the meaning always has to be connected to something greater.

So, until this day I try to keep that kind of concept and that way of life. That's better especially because of what I was saying. There was a time when I was struggling too on a personal level, kind of personal faith challenges. But all-in-all in the end, if you have to think about it, you are not just you who you are alone. You always are who you are in connection to something greater. There is an historical presence. You are that, a by-product of, according to Father, the providence.

So, that's a challenge to understand and try to manifest, and if you do, if you do succeed in your mind, it starts from somewhere—it starts with you. And other can recognize. Obviously, that will define happiness for you. It will substantiate the happiness to you because of your action, not just to yourself, but to others.

That kind of stuff, as it accumulates becomes something greater, and pretty much that's what you're going to fulfill in the end. Fulfillment is all those feelings that happen, all those things that others recognize, and ultimately that will be your legacy. When you're dead and gone that's all they will remember.

That will become, not just your own happiness. Why? Because you have completed something, because you have perfected yourself? It's beyond that. It becomes something to someone else too, even after you're gone. It can count as something that can make other people happy after you're dead.

Happiness is not that far away from you—it starts from oneself and how much you're willing to listen to what your inner self, your true self, is saying. Finding that is going to take your lifetime. You're not always sensitive. You have good days and you have bad days. You feel like an idiot on some days—you don't always feel sharp and smart. It's a life-long journey. Just listen to that inner self because it's what makes everybody true in the end. True happiness is the kind of happiness through which we can rejoice with God, exchange with God, and relate with God.

It has to be something that all of us can feel. True happiness is universal. Universal in what way? It is the Creator's own. You have to understand and recognize that—it takes time to recognize that. Try to talk about your inner self, your inner truth, and your inner happiness to a little kid—I don't think they'll understand what you're talking about.

There are always steps. There's always formation, growth and perfection to something just to get to a certain phase—and there will be many phases. How can you be happy with just completing one thing? Everybody says that something better is coming tomorrow. Right? Because, if you have everything today, then there is no concept of better, right?

That's why we live. We try to find happiness in life itself. We are given the opportunity to have life and constantly search for a state of greater things. People who have faith, at least try to have some kind of a pure and humble heart. I don't want you to give up. If you ask all the people who say they believe in such things, and then if you ask them to define it, they'll come up with all sorts of definitions.

The thing is, it takes time. It takes time to be humble. It takes time to be pure. It's never ending. You wash one time and you don't wash anymore until you die? *(Laughter.)* Nobody would live like that because of hygienic reasons? It's something like that. Keeping purity takes a lot of effort.

Anyway, you know that I don't like to talk too long. *(Laughter.)*

I guess today is the last day of the year. I'll be gone a few days.

It was meaningful for me personally. I feel I've made some kind of a difference. It is healing to forgive his mother, to care about her, and in the end to take care of the family. That's what I feel. I think its fine.

At the same time this has been a journey for me. It was challenging in the beginning because I hadn't spoken here for such a long time. It means something to me. It meant something to me. I learned a lot. I hope that I have shared something that helped you in some ways.

I hope you guys will have a Merry Christmas and a great New Year. And I'll see you next year. I'll see you the second Sunday. Okay? All right, take care.

(much applause to congratulate Hyo Jin Nim for speaking for one year.)

Keeping Yourself Motivated
January 14, 2007

How are you all doing? Happy New Year!

Is it easy to keep yourself motivated? It's very difficult isn't it? How do you keep people motivated? How do you keep yourself motivated? Before you talk about how you can affect others, how do you keep yourself motivated?

First of all you have to have some kind of purpose in life. Right? And you have to have some kind of belief in yourself that you can achieve what you set out to achieve. The purpose you seek has to have a certain value to you. One way or the other, I have to see the end of that course that I've chosen for myself, and I have to believe in myself. It has to be important to me that it happens, and I have to believe that I achieved that in my lifetime.

So, having said that, how do you keep yourself motivated? Sometimes you will face the ups and downs of life. It's very difficult. It's impossible to think that it's just going to be a smooth ride all the way through, that you're going to sail through without any kind of problem whatsoever, and reach your goals. There will always be obstacles. Why? Just because you think that you can do it doesn't mean that you understand the process, because you will face the process for the first time. And you will face the challenge of growth after growth and all the variables that happen.

Then you will learn as you travel through the journey that you have chosen for yourself. All the challenges that you will face one way or the other, you will somehow resolve. You might have some guide book from someone who has prior experience, and who was capable of assisting you or helping you to ease that ride in a proper manner. You need something or someone who can ease that wave, otherwise sometimes it can be overwhelming. It can be like a tidal wave at times, but those are the steep hills and valleys that you have to cross.

Every step of the way is a learning process. You have to accept that challenge because that is inevitable. You will not have all the answers as you move forward. I know that you don't want to stagnate. I know that you want to move forward. Moving forward in itself is difficult because the nature of growth itself is so challenging. Just facing a new experience is so challenging that often it is difficult to keep yourself motivated. Just that in itself, something as simple as a new experience.

So, having said that, that's your individual challenge. That's what you have to face, everyone, whatever goals you have. I don't know you or what you are trying to achieve. There are a lot of young people here. You go to school because you want to learn something—a trade or whatever. You will face challenges in learning, but going to school is just the preparation stage. After you come out of school that's when everything begins in terms of work, because you have to weave it into society. You can't just be at an experimental stage like in a laboratory setting all your life. It has to be real. How do you connect something that you have understood basically in theory and practiced in a laboratory setting to a more tangible reality, a reality that actually affects the social fiber and society in general?

You first have to answer that question—how can I keep myself motivated? What do I need? What do you look for when you're looking for motivation? It's a simple point. If you look at society in general they use two things, a reward system and a sacrifice system. If you're the central figure and you see a very talented person, you can't really use the reward system because we don't have so much money, so you take them out to dinner or whatever. What you have to do is do it literally with your physical effort. Do it with what you have. "I'll sleep less than that guy—I'll work harder than that guy. I'll do whatever it takes to provide more creativity, more productivity. I'll do something—something by sacrificing myself to motivate that guy, to inspire that guy, to hold him." If you do this you can hold that person for a while as long as you keep on doing stuff that he can recognize. That's the only way.

When you try to reach something, what you have to do is, you have to sacrifice more. Let's say you're on equal terms with another person in terms of what you have physically so you say, "I'll take less and I'll give that guy more than I have." That sacrificial act alone, a very simple sacrificial act, becomes a point of an inspiration to the recipient—and that is a motivating factor.

To keep people motivated you either reward them, like, by giving them money or you inspire them by your sacrifice. The business world is becoming more specialized and you need a specific target to begin with and based on that you have to be purpose driven. Stop making noise and start getting name recognition. Based on that your product can get known out there. You start making money and you have to spread that wealth around. With that you can take care of the guys who are specialists by giving them a lot of financial incentives to keep them motivated, to hold their dedication to the job. Otherwise, they will go to your competitor who is offering a greater financial incentive.

Either you do it with money, or you do it with sacrifice. The stuff that comes from sacrifice is more long term. Trust me. People remember that longer. Money is a short cut. It still works, but you have to keep it coming. They're always looking, "Where is my bonus?" and that kind of stuff. "How come it's not as big as last year? What's going on?" That kind of stuff.

Sacrificial stuff works, and since you don't live that long, if you just keep it up for several decades you can establish something. That's pretty much how it's done. If you're trying to change the world, which one is the better model? Which is the better way to motivate people?

Sometimes you have to consider yourself a crusader right? To me a crusader is a person who forces himself to be an optimist. Otherwise you see the glass half empty. That sucks. You think, "I don't think we're going to make it." You've got the wrong attitude for the job. You have to look at things differently than other people would, and you have to do that on your own.

It would be nice if you always had people that you can depend on, that would encourage you and each other. But sometimes you might be alone. What if you got locked up somewhere? What if you have nowhere to go, no one to rely on or depend on to kind of pat you on your shoulder and help you find solace. You have to try and find something that you can use to motivate yourself on your own. That is the key. For me, motivating oneself is the most important thing. How do you do it? How do you motivate yourself?

Like I said, it's up to you to like being a crusader. For that you have to look at things a little bit differently. Then you can find value in them. It doesn't take much, just a thought sometimes, that's all it takes. You don't need to ask somebody's permission—you don't need someone else's validation if you can find through that just a small thought alone that you give yourself. That one small thought, even for the moment, can help you see that light—even for just a moment.

It doesn't matter if it's just a jolt, or like caffeine high. It doesn't matter if it is just a little jolt if you can find some use for it. That's something because sometimes that's all it takes to make something great. That's how you get started. You were just an invisible little tadpole in the womb and then you became you.

Life begins not just from humongous things that come in the size of a King Kong or something. The beginning can be very small too. It's easy to see something that's big. You get more something I guess, confidence maybe, if it comes in a humongous size, but it's not always like that.

If you are always ready for that kind of moment when you are alone, find that small thought, just that little thing. Those kinds of moments will happen more than the moments when you feel tremendously confidant because of some giant thing that is so obvious to see.

You can find it in all sorts of different things. It depends on personality types too. Perhaps there are some things that little girls might fancy, I have no idea about those. It happens in that way. If you can value those moments for that reason then it's just like being the crusader. It's in your head.

Just because you formulate something and someone gives you a badge and goes through the ritual of knighting you or whatever it doesn't necessarily mean that much. That might be just some symbol, but for the person it has to start with this kind of thinking.

Obviously we're trying to do this not because of glory and stuff. If it come, so be it. There are a lot of people who do things because of winning awards and accolades, but more important are the people who do it because they want to do it.

People want things for all sorts of different reasons, but we must find what is meaningful for what you want to be, for what you have chosen to be. In the end, that's how you will be judged by God. That is the most important judgment in my mind. Anything else, oh so what. Judge me as much as you want because that is not the final judgment. I can tell myself that I practice being judged. Judge me more! But that's not the judgment that I'm looking for. It doesn't matter to me.

So, if you have something that you want to achieve because you have chosen a life of faith, then make sure that you get good at motivating other people. I know that you don't have a lot of money, so what else can you do then? The other way, the way of leading by sacrifice.

Those things can happen after 2012 because it's going to start all over again from the bottom up. It's a tall order to find a nation by that time. Who knows what's going to happen? But it's a different time. We're going to do it the right way, the 21st century way, doing 21st century ecumenical work. There is a way to do it. We won't have to knock on doors. We'll already be in the living room through multimedia.

There is a lot of talent necessary to keep our movement working and moving forward 24/7/365. If they can do it, we can do it too. I'll try to do my best to support the way it is. At the same time we have to prepare for the next phase.

It's difficult to find the way. We have problems fundraising, witnessing, and maintaining ourselves. Five years? Are you kidding me? I know what Father needs. In my mind it will take about 10 generations, but he's going to do whatever he's got to do. Okay, my hat is off to you old man!

What can I do? Father will do what he has to do. By that time he will be 92. Maybe he will postpone it eight more years until he is 100 years old.

We will keep on going right. It's crazy, but in five years I will be 50 years old. And you guys will be WHAT? *(Laughter.)*

Another year. God bless you this year.

Birthday
January 21, 2007

[Today is Hyo Jin Nim's birthday by the lunar calendar. Also, Hyo Jin Nim's wife gave birth to a son, Shin Jin Nim, last Friday, the 19th of January in the evening. Two cakes were prepared on a table next to the stage.

All welcome Hyo Jin Nim and offer a bow.

Hyo Jin Nim bows to the audience as he approaches the stage. He places a small notebook on the podium – he cuts the cakes and receives flowers and a present from the National Interfaith Leadership Training Program, whose members attend every Sunday, and a card signed by most of those attending before he speaks. We all sang "Happy Birthday" twice.]

Thank you.

Please sit down.

Thank you for the cake and the present and for the flowers. This was unexpected. He came out a month early. I guess he wanted to come out. He'll be coming home today. He is healthy and my wife is okay. So, thank you.

Today I see some faces that I haven't seen for a while.

Living in New York City is rather interesting.

Do you like big cities? When you see the people living in big cities they kind of have an attitude don't they? I guess you could say that it is kind of confident or to get right to the point, they're a little cocky. This attitude is almost a prerequisite for survival in a dog-eat-dog world.

You have to be arrogant—you have to have that kind of presence—you have to have that kind of pride and also project a strong sense of self importance just to get recognized.

It's almost like the big city environment provokes you whether you want it or not to have and present that kind of attitude and personification. You have to ask yourself if that is healthy. What happens to people when they actually live in that kind of mode? What kind of transformation will happen because you will be transformed based on what you are, what you think, what you want to think, and what you want to be. This will transform you whether you like it or not. You will pass through the process, the growth, and you will change into that whether you like it or not. So, you have to ask yourself—is that good? If that's not good, if that's the only way I guess you can't stop it and we have to live with the consequences. But if it is not good then how do you stop it? That's the question. If we don't address that kind of question and focus on the solution that we can all agree on, then it's very difficult.

The challenge is in ourselves, the challenges that lie ahead for what we have to do in our mission. We have to deal with these areas and that kind of arrogance. These will become a problem area and it's growing faster than any other time in history. Every big city will have that problem. It will start itself with some idealism, but it will change because of the nature of what you have to be to survive in that competitive setting.

It will change you. That modern big city life will change you. The problem, especially in China, is that the big cities are growing up, popping out, every few years. It will become the number one import and exporting country in the world in a few years. Germany is number one, America is second. and China is third right now and it will overtake America and Germany.

That's the problem, and how do we address even the problems that we have now. Think about it.

To me, arrogance is stupidity. Stupid people are people who are in a state of stupor, right? Their senses are dulled. They feel numb to all sorts of stuff. You live in today's world and are desensitized to life. Sometimes you have to question whether that is right or wrong. Many times when you start to think morally and ethically you question pretty much everything that is stimulating your senses, all that is titillating out there. That's what you're bombarded with on a daily basis. It is overwhelming and you are getting desensitized to that reality.

We're being stupefied every single way by things that are supposed to educate you, things that are supposed to stimulate you to be a better person. But actually it is doing the opposite. Why? The great excuse is that corporations have to make money. This is the land of the free and the land of capitalism. In this society you have the right to pursue opportunity. Opportunity means wealth and personal gratification.

When that aspect, especially personal gratification is not defined properly it becomes very dangerous. We do have a problem with religion in itself because the values that religion should uphold as sacred and absolute aren't being propagated. Regardless of what religion it is, there has to be some absolutes that are equal to the primary absolutes, the laws of God. But look at physics. Even that is unstable. There is no clarity in some religions. That's the problem.

There are many issues that need to be solved. We still have basic problems. And how do you go about changing that when the world is becoming more stupefied?

We have to go to the very essence of who we are, starting as a child, we want to learn. We have to bring that back. And how do you go about doing that? It's extremely challenging and it's extremely difficult. You have to really make a creative environment that is so overwhelmingly rich, productive, creative, that it provokes you so much that you become enraptured by it, and hit the point where you want to learn— you want to start to learn again.

Otherwise things will never change. They will only decay further. How do you provoke the arrogant culture into wanting to learn again? How do you restart the need for growth? How do you stimulate that? That's the question that we need to ask. We must find the solution there.

You can't force people to change. You can't force people to learn something when they don't want to learn. How do you go about doing that? Can you create some kind of art or entertainment that is so rich, so high in standard and quality, that people will change just by being part of it, just by being in the presence of it? Can that be done? It will be extremely challenging.

Can you find a truth that is so evident just by hearing it that you can clarify many, many things that you might be questioning about life itself, and the purpose of your existence?

If we can find something like that it would be very provocative, wouldn't it? Even in the minds of arrogant people I've seen it all. The ones who think, "I've been there. I've done that," the ones who are jaded to the hilt. I'm sure that you can open the door for them wanting to learn more again. Because once they did.

No matter how arrogant you are. No matter how confident you are to put it nicely, if you can see a greater quality you can go back to humble again. If something is presented to you and you can see the quality. This is something. The quality of this is better than what I've got. That's a stimulation, no matter how arrogant you are.

Being able to present that case, that moment to one who is arrogant, making that change is difficult because you need to present it. It has to be real to that person. It has to touch them in a real way physically and mentally. I don't know if that person will understand spirit yet, but at least that first part is a challenge. We must do that at least, and it will take a collective effort, not just one man's genius, because everything in the world stands on the shoulder of something, ultimately God, right?

How can you be arrogant to begin with? It should be impossible, because you can never be satisfied if you live a creative life—even in a religious life, contentment is a killer. Even in the world of art you are only as good as the last one that you did, and you have to keep it coming. You can never be content. You can never be satisfied because it is suicide. It is a suicide position. It is a suicide action actually if that is the chosen path that you are taking. You can't survive. You can't compete. You're dead by your own self admission.

You can never be satisfied. You have to want to do more, more, more. That's reality. Why, because God is like that. Don't you want to emulate him? Do you want to imitate Him or do you want to emulate Him? I don't know. *(Laughter.)* Or do you want to be Him? Oh Boy! I don't know about that. *(Laughter.)*

And when Father says up to 12, up to 35 years, you have to symbolically rebuild creation. The number six he owns and the number seven. And the other five days? He does think, "Numerically five times seven is 35 years." Maybe perhaps then you'll reestablish his name around the world substantially, not symbolically. I believe it will take 10 generations or more. It can't happen that fast.

Look people, come on! A lot of people come and they put their hands out for all sorts of reasons. You can't trust politicians, period. Right? How can you trust those guys? Some religious people, I question them too. It is very difficult. I know that a lot of people come, especially when you present things in a certain way, they do come expecting something. That's not good. That's not how you transform people. That's not how you change the world.

It might have some symbolic sense. It might have some temporary functional effect to galvanize people to do something more. But eventually what is that? Members fundraise and you spend it on what?

Having the kind of leverage we need for a 21st century church is based in multimedia, because this is the way of 21st century ecumenism. It's going to take time to develop that stuff.

More importantly we need to develop our own people. You can't just use hired guns. It will never work. It will never work in any case, in any situation, in any organization. In any system it will not work. Money is never a solution, nor power, never.

The only way to motivate people, like I said last week, is either you do it with money or sacrifice. That's the only way. Money is always a temporary measure. The long-term thing is always sacrifice. I'll sacrifice more than you. That's the only way. I'll do better than you. I'll show you a greater product. That's the only way to motivate. If you motivate the person that way it lasts MUCH longer than money! Trust me, that's the only way to do it.

We need our people who really care and can become good at something. There are so many ways in which you can become valuable, if you're good at research or even art or whatever. Even if you don't have an outgoing personality there are many, many ways that you can be invaluable in that system, because we need to compete that way to survive. That's the only way. I sincerely believe this.

I've been saying it for a long time and I believe it with all my heart and this is how I'm going to go out. There is no other way.

Please if you want to put anything into a stupor, put your arrogance into it.

Take care of yourself. I'll see you next week.

Outreach
January 28, 2007

Good morning.

What's important to us is outreach, right?

Am I reaching you? I you could make a simple slogan—I guess we could say, "If it's un-relatable it's un-reachable."

When we think about reaching out to people, we have to have some sort of way in which we can relate to them. When you focus on this relation issue, relatable issue, you have to do it in sync with people's expectations. You have to address expectations so you can relate, because everybody has expectations.

It can vary, but there is basic stuff that we all know is right and that we all know is wrong. So there is a concept of right and wrong that we generally understand and accept. Based on that understanding which is pretty much the thing that governs our lives and deeds, we have the expectation to become a higher self, to be a better person, to be a more successful person.

Before you go out and try to start doing some kind of outreach activity, you better have some of these kinds of answers, otherwise you'll learn it the hard way. One way or another you'll learn life's lessons, even if you have to learn it the hard way. So, it's better to know yourself prior to actually trying something, which is normal especially if you're trying to help people, to reach out to people. You have to answer the question, "What is my expectation?"

How do I define right and wrong on issues, and based on that what am I doing to try to be active in my life? What is my pursuit? How does it affect—how does it connect to the ultimate goal of actually reaching out to people so that I feel good about myself in the eyes of God? So, what is my expectation? What do I want out of myself and out of the life that is ahead of me?

These days the health movement is out there right? They want to get healthier—they want to put a lot of good stuff into their body and get stronger and healthier so they can live longer. More and more people are recognizing that you have to put a lot of good stuff in your body so you can have a healthier life. If you don't manage that properly, if you're not vigilant about it, obviously you will suffer the consequences. There are always consequences, cause and effect, right? Especially for children this is very important, in the maturation, the growth period it is very important for them to have a proper healthy diet. It's very important. You see in the world so many people, not just children, but even adults, are dying of hunger. There are all sorts of tragic injuries are out there. That's real.

Let's try to take it one step at a time. It breaks your heart. You want to reach out and just help everybody and change everything at the snap of a finger. That's unrealistic. So, we have to think about how we can better take care of ourselves so that ultimately we can do a lot of good things. You have to be strong right?

Good nutrition is important for children and also for old people. You can take risks during a certain period of your life when you are a young adult. You can sometimes take in toxins and experiment because of the curiosity factor and because the world is the way it is—and you have so many images out there that provoke your curiosity. Some people will dabble in it— most people will dabble in it, especially living in the, quote free unquote society.

Everybody wants to live longer. As you get older and older that becomes very important. So, as much as it is important for your body to put a lot of good stuff in there, so it is for your mind and so it is for your heart. You know we're not just here living with the body. The way we think is very important too, and it's influenced by the stuff that we put into our heads. That's the basic point of reference that you use to determine things.

It's like when you expose yourself to certain unhealthy foods, it's the same thing. You will have many side effects by putting a lot of garbage into your head. I think it's more important that we have some kind of environment in which we can expose ourselves to goodness, and the good things that people can do and say to one another, mostly good deeds. Actions speak louder than words.

If you can capture that kind of stuff and expose people to it, let the people in general see that there's that kind of stuff out there and we choose to live that way, to be exposed only to the right things that can make us healthy, we will become healthier.

When we become healthier, as a greater unit, the ability that we can project, that we can manifest in helping others, reaching and out and helping others to change for the better can also become more powerful.

How do you achieve that? That's why I believe that systematically we have to work on that question and bring a solution. And there are models out there. Television is nothing other than a living newspaper. There are columns, pages on politics, society, religion, culture, life style, entertainment, it's just there. Pretty much that's the way we're living in the modern world. That's how we consume all the information that is out there. TV is the main medium for exposure. From that medium everything gets radiated out. And based on the information, the things that are being radiated outward can form your thoughts. That is reality, and it works! It's very effective.

In the future we'll get influence in TV. It's not that difficult because more and more systems are getting cheaper, even HD stuff. If it becomes internet viable we can create a broadcasting company. It's not a star away. It's literally doable. All you need is a production crew and the capability to maintain and manage it in terms of livelihood. That's all it takes. Having a big station like the old days is a kind of symbolism of the past. You really don't need it, but you can have it because you do need some kind of centralized symbolism. It does cater to human needs to have some kind of attachment to something, like having your own house or something. Making your presence known, it's important in relationship to other people. Other people aren't going to change that quickly so in terms of politics it's necessary I guess, or, to put it nicely, diplomacy.

Sure, it's doable. If you want that we can have that. That's not a problem. We're working on it to make it happen so that it can independently achieve that. It's better in terms of offering. Take less from Father and give more.

It's doable. An annual budget of $10 million can do it no problem. It depends on where you set up shop. The cost varies. The fatherland, geographically is a promising place. It's only two hours from Japan, two hours from China and not so far from Russia because you can unite that north and south divided situation. It's not a different country—it's just a division.

We have you here. Father spent one third of his life here investing so he can unite all the archangel nations. We have more work to do in terms of the other two, but regionally it's [Korea] right there. So it can be done when we can create that kind of model.

How often have you felt lonely? What is the cure-all for loneliness?

Love!

[*Laughing.*] Love stuff, right?

There are many ways to show that kind of stuff. You can literally showcase it. You don't need a great person to show that. You can even see it in starving children. To showcase that kind of loving humanity regardless of where you come from, what region, what kind of situation, regardless of age. If we are constantly exposed to those kinds of things, how can we be evil? How can you raise your children in an evil way?

It's out there! I just need the crew to go out and get it so we can show it to you. Then it can be done. Then we can start the change. We can reach out to people. People will be reachable. Some people are just stubborn—they don't want to change. They force themselves away from change. There are some knuckleheads that live that way.

The polar ice cap is melting, so people can melt. *(Laughter.)* Maybe there is more water to drink. Billions of people are drinking every day. Billions of gallons are being consumed right? We need more water.

It can be done. We can do that. We can change people. We can reach them. The more you have those good multimedia contents the better you can reach out to people, because you have something to make that connection.

As you get older, you're going to get interested in that kind of stuff because you know you will die, absolutely—and you want to know as much as you can about what love is if you didn't know what that is. And some people are willing to give it to you, show it to you, and move you. Because love will move mountains, right? And they will change. It will take time, but you will change—you have no choice. God will win, right?

That's doable. It's absolutely doable. That's how people change. I know this. That's how I change. If I can change, people can change. So, we just have to make that happen. That's it. It's that simple! And it's doable. We're working on it. You'll be the first ones to know. You'll be the first ones to see—that stuff. Because it's for all, right? Not for me alone, right?

Okay. Take care.

Romanticism
February 4, 2007

What kind of "Romanticism" do you think that we in our church, and some other people, will think about? What is romanticism? What do you want to die for? You want to die for love right? Tell me—what is your romanticism? Romance means that you'll give up everything for the sake of love. That's what romance is all about. It doesn't matter if romance is momentary? If it overwhelms you, it will last forever. It has consequences, serious consequences. What are you willing to throw the rest of your life away for—for the sake of love. That's pretty serious isn't it?

So, having put that aside, let's say that you only had two choices—to be a prince or to be a warrior. Which would you choose?

What is a prince? In European culture there a lot more aristocrats. Maybe you need to hold on to something. Don't get offended—it's just a fact. Who cares?

What is a warrior? Let's talk about the nitty-gritty. Let's just think about how we're conditioned to think about changing the world. How are you going to change the world? Who are you? What kind of stuff do you need to change the world? You need all the extremes. You need to learn how to be both a prince and a warrior. Okay? In what sense? To what degree? Because things happen in moments. It doesn't happen all the time. When changes happen it happens in moments.

When you try to understand God, you'd better give your life for it and know everything about it because it will not happen otherwise. If you want to die and live in happiness forever, then you have to pay the price. It's that simple.

Why am I here? If you're true to yourself and you're willing to die for it, that's all you can do. I had a choice to be a warrior.

What is a warrior anyway? You have to understand this to understand Christianity. Warriors are actually glorified. All the rich nobility of the past with all their servants and wealth could only achieve the convenient things that anyone can have today through modern technology.

Modern technology gives you a bunch of servants, but what about becoming a warrior? What are you fighting for? You tell me. I don't know you that well. I know what I'm fighting for. If you think that you're a warrior—then tell me what you're fighting for. You have to start from that and you have to build on it. This is a good life a good birth a new beginning. To make things perfect, it deserves perfection. It deserves the best. You do that for what? For yourself?

I'll keep coming here just to show you ...

[*Hyo Jin Nim is very emotional, weeping.*]

I want to tell you something; you listen. Don't ever question me. You can judge me all you want about what I do, but don't question me. I don't think you people understand me.

[*Hyo Jin Nim is weeping and one sister is sobbing aloud.*]

Life is short and it can be good. When you have to change the world you can't look at everything only optimistically. I like to look at things like 'the glass is half-full' all the time, but it doesn't always work like that. There are all sorts of reasons why. Look, it's going to happen. Just think about dying. That's the smartest way, in my mind. You can't wake up and see your children running around and say, "YOU'RE GONNA DIE!" *(Laughter.)*

Time will take care of it right?

If you are so arrogant and selfish that you can't fulfill the responsibilities of your course then whose problem is that, God's problem or your problem? It's your problem. After all, I'm the preacher here, okay. Take it or leave it. I'm doing my best. I'm trying to keep it simple. I hope that I'm interesting to you sometimes. If I give you my word on it, I'll stick to it, unless powers beyond my control intervene.

I will protect my family. I will protect my kind. I will die for what I believe, absolutely. We all die, but you still have to win. There are rules and you have to win. We all still go by the rules that are beyond us. It is not that simple when you have to win like this. War might be easier in that sense. It takes more to win that—it's just a killer. That's the truth. It will not happen overnight. It will not happen just because you believe in something. You have to make it happen.

We can do it. I know we can do it. I give every glory to my folks.

[*Hyo Jin Nim is weeping.*]

That's why you come to hear me right? Do you think I changed that easily? People like me don't change that easily. I'll change in many things, but there are things that I know that I won't change. You have to be willing to die for what you believe and I want to prove that more than anyone else. Otherwise, get out of here. I don't care what you think. It's going to take a long time to change this world.

There are princes and princesses but it will take time to make them genuine in the eyes of God in terms of the ideals we believe in. That's why I think it's going to take a little longer than what people are saying. I hope it can happen, but someone will suffer more than others. Guess who?

Don't kid yourself. If you really want to look at the reality then look at what is real, treat it as such, and do something about it. Otherwise, it's pointless—whatever you think in your head doesn't mean anything.

Okay.

I have to see you next week. That's my miserable life. [*Laughter.*}

Memories
February 11, 2007

Good morning!

Another week has passed. For most of us a couple of thousand things happened last week. I guess we have to prepare ourselves for the next level.

Let me ask you a question: Do you have more good memories or do you have more bad memories when you look back on your life? *(Good.)*

I guess it's up to you right?

[A small boy sitting next to his mother on the front row says "bad memories" and the room is filled with laughter.]

You're just a kid, man, I don't think you've lived yet. Okay, at least you've got an opinion and you're honest.

I guess that memories are the building blocks of the thing that we call intelligence. If you look at the animal kingdom, memory is a survival mechanism. It's very, very important. Animals have a greater acute sense than we do because they have to survive based on that. Memory is very important. Right from birth they have to learn how to survive to catch prey and find food sources, and to navigate from point A to point B. All that depends on memory, and their life depends on it.

For us, too, memory is very important because that's pretty much how we build our lives. If you don't have many good memories, I guess that you have to build them, to find them somehow.

So, are there some things that we can rely on to help us achieve that end? Yes, according to the promise from heaven we have the greatest capacity in terms of storing memory, a capacity beyond just the building blocks of intelligence. There are all sorts of diverse applications of the intellectual capacities that we have to do the things that we want to do beyond what you see in the animal kingdom. So, how would you create a good memory if you don't have many? That's why imagination is very important and creativity is very important. Because everything that you want to do after you have reached a certain stage where you have a basic building block of creating your greater self, because you have learned, you have memorized how to speak. You know how to read, how to write, how to do basic things. What you need to do is ... you have to plan.

You have to plan your future. You have to envision yourself 10 years from now. Let's say you're a 12-year-old kid or barely a teenager, middle school, whatever. You have to envision yourself 10 years from now, 20 years from now.

It hasn't happened yet. You don't have it in your memory, but you can store those mental images that you're creating about yourself. It might not be true at the moment in physical form because it hasn't been manifested yet, however, that image that you see of yourself perhaps one day, if you do the right thing, if you are persistent and you do what it takes to get there and keep at it, perhaps the image of you that you have stored in your head when you're a sixth-grader, 10 years from now, 20 years from now, 30 years from now, will come true.

All the stuff we store, I guess we store it mostly for some reason, but some things we don't even think about it, we just store it. And sometimes it just comes up. Sometimes it can be helpful, but if you are not careful it can also harm you. Because most likely if you store certain things that you are not fully in control of you are going to create something not nice.

Now let's say that you have to love somebody. You have to love your parents. You can't hate your parents. You have to love your siblings. You can't hate your siblings. You're going to be with them forever. There are many things that make a relationship work and sometimes you have to work at it. And it's not one way—it's always both ways. And there are things that can sometimes get in the way of building a greater relationship. How do you go about achieving a greater relationship when certain images or certain memories always get in the way?

There are so many people who I do not know personally out there walking around on this planet. If I make judgment based on one casual image that I perceive in a moment then that would not be good.

So, it is with my siblings. The only memory I have of intimacy with them is Heung Jin. We shared the same room until I reached my teenage years. Other than that there is too much age gap, so I don't know these kids except when they were very young. That's the only memories that I have of them.

What I see now, in my mind I'm concerned to put it nicely. Still, I have to make that choice of holding on to that. And I do have that capacity to make greater memories, even if it is not happening now, even if it is not real now. It can happen tomorrow. And I guess that's where religion comes in. It talks about faith and it tries to teach you the importance of faith.

How can you achieve faith when obviously you can't project yourself into the future? You try to make yourself happy. I'm happy now, but if you go out and look at the world, it makes you angry. You get depressed. No matter how you try to make yourself happy you just want to hold on to your happiness. You pretty much have to do that and start blocking out all other things.

I like to see greatness in people that I care about. What you see outside should be the same as what is inside. Sometimes because you care about somebody, you do care, it should matter to you.

Sometimes, yes, you do get emotional about it. Why? Because it's not right, it's not going anywhere like that. It's not like we're fighting a war with bullets and guns. It's competition. Success depends on the quality of how you achieve it. It's not that simple. Murder and mayhem might be simpler than loving competition.

I still remember all sorts of stuff that Father used to talk about, the kind of images of fantasy that he drew in my head with his words. I still hold on to those images because I don't think they're bad. I'm not going to say because I'm getting too old for this, and I'm more practical than that. It isn't going to happen in my lifetime. I should hold on to it. Why? Because it looks nice—let me just start with that. If that can happen, the world will really look nice.

How do you get there? We have a lot of really good people doing a lot of good things all the time. It's kind of unfortunate that the number kind of stays at a certain level. It really doesn't fluctuate too much. A lot of people come for all sorts of different reasons and I guess it's important that we start to branch out on that level because it's very difficult to find quality help. Right?

Those people do make that kind of association. The make that connection because they think we're successful, we're somebody. We're great in this and that, however we commercialize ourselves. I don't know how true that is in essence, but maybe it is through all the propaganda that we make.

It is serious stuff, just making propaganda, especially in a free society, because the absolute ruler in a free society is the masses. The presidents and all the politicians are just managers. The masses can get rid of them if they don't like them. Most people like to stay away from politics because they're busy taking care of their own business.

How can we trust all the people that we connect with, especially the politicians? Even if there is a genuine person who wants to get into politics, to make laws that help society and benefit people, their power is limited. In the end you have to get permission from the masses. So, pretty much people do whatever freedom allows, and the easiest way to live free is to think about yourself, focus on yourself. "I don't want to get involved in all this stuff other than what I have to deal with in my own life. How can I change this world?"

And when you want to change, you have to try. You can't just think about it. That's a loser's way. What's the opposite? I guess that's the winner's way. You have to DO what you think is right. If you're going to change the world, you have to start changing the world trying to build that relationship that is important. Ultimately you have to bridge the gap between humanity and God and True Parents.

It has to start, genuinely from the persons that think that is the way. If everybody thinks that is the way, that's what everybody has to do, no exceptions. It's difficult. It is difficult. It is difficult to try to get more—more—more. Sometimes you don't know what more is.

I don't get anything out of this. I don't get anything out of this other than making memories, right? Some of the faces I don't think I can ever erase because I see you every week. *(Laughter.)* I don't think I can erase it out of my memory. *(Laughter.)* I don't know whether that's good or bad. *(A lot of laughter.)*

It's those things that I think that matter in changing the world. You have to think that that kind of stuff is important. Just like everybody else, not what's just important to you. There are more people like you than there are the privileged people in the world. You have to have the right attitude.

Last week I had stayed up all night talking to someone and I was a little out of whack. I wanted to call Janine and ask her to have someone else pitch in for me, but since I was awake, I came.

Anyway, what you see is what you get. I'm trying. All those fantasies that I have, all those dreams that I have, I want to hold on to them. I think it's good. I think I'm going to keep them in my memory as long as I'm here. Sometimes you need to dream. And everything that you see is good sometimes. But if we're going to win, everybody has to be real.

I have one more week. Next week I'll be here but after that I'll be gone for about two months.

Take care of yourself.

I'll be here next week. Okay.

Role Model
February 18, 2007

Good morning!

[*Hyo Jin Nim pauses to survey the audience. He smiles.*]

There are too many young people here. Okay.

Whether you like it or not, one of these days you are going to become a "Role Model."

When we talk about the reality of how society is, we're always looking for somebody to blame or someone to glorify.

Why? Because it's important whether people in general understand the concept, it starts from individual to family, and that family extension gets larger and larger. Eventually it expands to the society as we know it and to the nation and ultimately to the world. This vision on a worldwide scale happens because of a kind of individuality that can exist even within a family, that idiosyncratic dominance or preference. That's why you draw borders and that's what we see as a result in the ultimate thing.

Even if you're in a certain race framework it doesn't matter. Somehow it's going to be divided, but I don't think that is the intent of God. Every religion fails to describe God in the ideal way as that kind of being or entity who won't stand division. However, we're mystified by the reality. We are lacking in terms of true knowledge, the bottom line is that God does represent the ideal, but many times a conflict arises even among religions. They believe in a lot of these things, but they don't know the true nature of the ideal. There is a disparity somewhere. That's why it creates conflict.

So, having said that, what is the nature of the idealism of God? According to what we believe God cannot achieve the end result, He cannot manifest His will, or achieve True Love without the presence of mankind. If God represents the ideal, then man represents something else. The individual man that we start to create, and that humanity starts to become, is something important in the whole process of ultimately realizing the will of God.

When you put God as a representation, that individuality is humanity, because God is the representation of the ideal whether you like it or not. That's why we have religion. And we want to describe things better than the other guy. That's the competitive factor in religion even when it pursues one God—who in the end is more persuasive, who can prove it better.

The Fall occurred in the Garden of Eden, and because of the Fall all this chaos and conflict arose from that initial act. In order to restore that which is so crucial to the fulfillment of that ideal, somebody has to be the true testimony of what blessing is. Because, as the objects to God, so far as we're concerned the whole creation process is a blessing. We have to restore that blessing, that act of blessing. How do we bless somebody?

Unless you can bring that back into humanity, and allow humanity to understand that, and then on their own free will learn religion and manifest it to each other and to God, then restoration is just a thought. It is not tangible—it is not substantial.

If we are competing with other people to proclaim and give a testimony, a living testimony, and to bear the responsibility to rebuild the ideal world, then ultimately that blessing factor has to be brought back through our efforts into the realm of humanity. In other words, in the end we have to be blessed by humanity. Otherwise, it's not complete. It might be directional, if you give it to people, and try to educate people as to how you plan to go about achieving it.

In the general setting of Christian thinking you have seven virtues, four cardinal and three theoretical: justice, temperance, fortitude, prudence, faith, hope and charity. We have the basic kind of direction as to how we are going to represent that aspect of what God is. In terms of creating the ideal, we basically have a way in which we can try to live up to that standard as a basic guideline.

There has to be something beyond that. There has to be more than that. So, when you talk about being a role model sometimes, even on a personal level, even when you have a family, it's a daunting task if you're just pushed into it. Some people might have been longing for that kind of opportunity but sometimes it can be shocking to the system.

How do you go about achieving the ultimate end of trying to represent something that is very serious because many times the importance is lost? When you try to do anything that doesn't come from the heart it is a meaningless quest. It is a meaningless task.

That is the difficult part, trying to understand the importance of each individual thing, especially when we look at it from the viewpoint of God's idealism and God's representation. We are individuals to God, and God and humanity have to become one. It's crucial to achieve that important relationship, and to find the value in that—it takes a lifetime to learn.

When you're old, how often do you think about something, think about your potential? Many times you want to show off and practice that basic virtue stuff, self restraint. All that little stuff that's important to practice and understand. The ultimate value is what we must understand in relation to God.

It's difficult. It's very difficult when you have to think about dying, because when you talk about value that is forever and everlasting and has to do with a relationship with God, it doesn't really matter what others think while you're breathing. The value as we know it in the secular realm can't go with you after death. Valuable things that we believe as we try to idealize ourselves is part of knowing what God's ideal is all about. I want to make that relationship work out and know

God better. I don't know how much I know now but it has to be more than this. I need to know more. It has to be greater than this.

As you push yourself in the end the answer is very simple: There are only some values that you can take. There are not many out there. There are not many here. You really don't see it. Things that are going to last—you really don't see. It might be easier if money exchanged between hands and stuff and back and forth, but it's not like that.

It's about something that is of love and the effort to try to describe love. How do you love your children? Pretty much that's the basic standard. God loves you right? God loves His children. In what way? How do you love your children?

Can you take that and put it into someone that you don't know? That's difficult, but it can be done. That's the trial in fact. That's what we try to accomplish ultimately in the end. And how is that going to happen? I can't give you that answer. It's on a one-to-one basis.

You can try to simplify it, but it's also possible to over simplifying things if you're not careful. You have to know who you are. If you have to oversimplify something it's got to be in a sort of extreme circumstance, and yet you have to ask yourself, Why do I want to oversimplify this? What am I getting? What am I looking for? What am I trying to get out of this stuff? In what way?

Because unless it's war, oversimplification is not always ideal. Why? Because I don't know you, and I don't know you [*pointing to different audience members*] and I can't say that you and you are identical. That's the problem.

That is the problem of dealing with people in developed nations. The level of expectation and self value, of course varies, but it's very, very different in a developed nation. That's the problem. But that's not un-ideal. Everybody wants that kind of special attention, right?

I can't fault you guys for having that kind of desire. That's why it takes commitment. You have to realize what's right and what's wrong and it takes time. It takes time for us to figure that out even as we swim through this confusion made up of all these variations, differences, and all sorts of separate existence.

It takes time. And it will take a lifetime for some people. And it will take a lifetime of the next generation too, until that is realized. It's not going to happen overnight. That's the reality and accepting it is a big step. You asked for it and you're going to get it. There is no exception to that rule.

I question myself some times. How far can I go along this path? There are many separate ways I could get off. I've figured that out. How far am I going to stay on this path?

It's up to you. You can't force somebody to do that.

I guess to have that desire to achieve what is of true value to me, I must ask that and answer that to myself. That's the only way I'm going to be a role model to my children. One way, good or bad, they're going to use me as an excuse. Right?

So, how far? I don't know.

What is my highest or what is my greatest? I don't know.

How far can I go? I don't know.

Do I want to get there? Do I want to win? I guess so.

Something like that. That's all I can say sometimes, most of the time.

It's better than you having all the answers on that day. Then you should go to sleep, because you're no good when you're awake. *(Laughter.)*

Anyway, take care of yourselves? Okay?

I'll see you soon. I'll miss you a little bit.

Self

April 15, 2007

How have you been doing? [*Hyo Jin Nim last spoke at Belvedere on February 18th. He has just returned from performing in Korea and Japan.*]

Is everybody okay?

Let's talk about, "Self."

You know there are so many self-help books out there. Improve yourself this way or that way. What is the first step? If you read any books that is the kind of guidance that you want.
Normally if they have a proper perspective it has to focus on you. You have the answer. What is your best? What can you do best? That is the first answer you need. You have to question yourself and give the answer. You have to do that. What can I do best? For the time being just put aside the idea that, "I want to be the best, the greatest." Just what can I do best? Know your limits, because everything has its time and place.

Time ticks forward, so you have to think in the present before you think about the future. And when you think about the present and knowing the limit means that's how you lived and how you think about history. That's when you think about the past.

Finding your best if you have to make that conclusion, you can only find it today. Tomorrow might be different. Hopefully that's how you're going to get better. So, you have to ask yourself, "What can I do today, what is my best?" And if you have that insight then you can think about what is my greatest.

And even when you have that answer of being the greatest you can be, then comes the greater responsibility. If you do, and I believe we do, we live with God, in relation to God, in a relationship with God. You have to think about a greater responsibility.

Obviously, you're not just doing this for yourself, right? So, why do I have my greatest? What is it for? You have to answer that question too. That means that you give, and that's very inevitable. That's the next point. That's the next phase.

The final phase would be living that life. You have to expand because you can always do more. And more is in tomorrow, never in today or yesterday. So, from there you find your direction and you invest your life, your short life. *(Laughter.)* You have to think that even the greatest is relative. Right? Not everybody can be number one, the champion. It sounds nice but it doesn't work that way when you try to cram everyone into a time frame especially in the present. Do you understand what I'm saying?

It doesn't work. So, what are you chasing? What kind of understanding do you have toward what is greatest? It has to be real to you. You can't just live a fantasy for the rest of your life, because if you do your life will take all sorts of unwanted directions. Why? Because you're living a lie. You can say it's a dream, a fantasy, but if it is not real it can be a fantasy or a nightmare. You really have to know how to pace yourself. First you ask yourself what is my best. Figure it out! You know yourself. Nobody else does better than you. Figure it out.

Is it going to take care of me? Will this be able to take care of me being my best, give me my self-sufficiency? And from there give me the room or the possibility to do my will to my nation and to God? You have to answer that question. You have to find that best. Because now is a different kind of time.

Father's best is being the king right? *(Laughter.)* There is only one Father. Right? There is only one messiah. That's it. That's what he's best at. But that's not me. I have to find my best. I have to find my greatest. And I have to struggle to make that offering. And I have to struggle again and again to expand. That's my choice. That's the choice that I have to make. And that's the life I have to live if I want to receive what I want to receive. Because I believe in something, that's the price that I pay to receive what I believe in. It's just as simple as that.

And live life pursuing the one thing that is important, then forget what you did, especially when you think that you did something good. Why? Because it just became yesterday. You don't live in yesterdays. You don't live in memories. That's stupid. People lock them up, you know what I mean? It's better always to focus on tomorrow. You have to think about tomorrow. That's when you find your self-expansion. You want to be bigger right? You want to be greater right? It's always in tomorrow, never in yesterday or today. All you can do best is recognize that and remind yourself of that again. You should get out of your crap and say, "Hey! Calm down! Be cool! Forget it! Hold on! The better is in tomorrow." Because if you don't do that, nobody else will. Why? Because in the end, you only listen to yourself. *(Laughter.)* So, just get rid of all the nonsense and cut right to the chase.

Pay attention to someone who you will listen to in the end. If you kind of remind yourself of that you can make it a habit, a good habit, because no one is going to take care of you better than yourself. Okay? If we don't know how to take care of ourselves, that's something else, then we need something like daycare.

Well, anyway. *(Laughter.)* When you talk about yourself, what do you really, really think about yourself? Pray about it. Soul search it. Squeeze your brain until it blows up. *(Laughter.)* What can I do or what is my best? From there, move on. Okay? Build from there. Taking it from there, think about it practicality, and think about what you want to do for the sake of a greater purpose.

You need balance. There are some things that will change and you should make them keep on changing. At the same time there is something that should be unchanging, absolutely. You need to live a balanced life. Because if you don't it will skew and it will tilt. You don't live that long anyway. There's always better stuff tomorrow. Always in tomorrow. Believe it. Because that's true. That's why I want to change. That's why I want to expand. That's why I will expand and I will change. There is something that won't change, that understanding, knowing that it works that way.

Okay?

It was good to see you again.

Are People Born Evil?
April 22, 2007

Good morning.

Let me start off by asking you a question. "Are People Born Evil?"
(No.)

I have to talk about it because obviously we all know what happened.
[*The context is the 33 deaths on Virginia Tech Campus last week.*] All
those innocent lives lost. That's unthinkable. The degree of shock and
the horror is immeasurable.

We have to talk about it because it happened. The thing is that it
happens not just in America, but in places like Iraq where America is
trying to bring democracy. Dozens of people, at times hundreds of
people die every day. That's a tragedy.

Sometimes just taking care of ourselves is difficult enough in itself.
You don't want to think about other huge problems that exist in the
world where truly people are selfish and dying.
But that's another issue when it comes to you and me, when it comes to
"I." What happens to "I?"

That's what's important, right? Because from that "I" something
happens, hopefully something for the better. And even that is just a
hope. It's not a conclusion. It might be a promise to yourself, therefore
in light of yourself you want to view it as something of hopefulness.

Sometimes you don't want to pat yourself on the back too often. You
don't want to do that too often without any results. What matters
beyond yourself, right? Beyond "I." Can we stop this nonsense? Is it
possible? If none of us is born evil then how did these people become
so evil? If what happened is not the epitome of the definition of evil,
then I don't know what is. You can blame it on psychological stuff.

You can say that young man was demented, but how did he get so demented? How did he get so corrupted? How did he get so fouled that he can do something with no remorse whatsoever, even to the point at the end of taking his own life.

I thought that was easier than shooting 33 innocent people. That is serious stuff. What happened? What happened?

You developed-nation people understand the importance of diet right? You have to have a well balanced diet, right? You have to have the right minerals. You have to have vegetables, and dairy products, proteins, and whatever, healthy and balanced to keep your body healthy.
What about the mind? You see children obsessing over certain sugary stuff. You can't feed them that stuff forever. Somebody has to be looking after children when they're growing up, even physically. What about mentally? Whose responsibility is that? Are we supposed to educate children just so they can get a job. More and more in modern days you need to be specialized. So, whatever special skill it demands to get a decent job in the workforce and whatever the stuff you need to survive and take care of the business, it's there for that and it ends there.

Where else do you spend time? Hopefully you spend time in churches right? And how often do you spend time in church? You spend your waking moments after you turn six years old or so pretty much outside your house preparing yourself to make a living ultimately. That's it. Think about it.

What do you envy? Envy has a negative connotation doesn't it? But it can also be positive. Anything bad can be turned into something good. Good can be turned into bad, because we have that power. We have such subjectivity over everything under creation. Okay. You take the envy and what do you envy? Why are you envious? When you envy something just obsessively it's like you saying I want to eat just sugar, I don't want to eat anything else. Well, you're going to get sick very soon, okay?

You have to know how to balance this stuff. And what if you don't have that available then you've got to put something in your stomach. Right? So you can live. Right? So, you have to know how to do that. People that fail to recognize that aspect of maintenance, just self-maintenance, they lose the point. Many problems rise from that. Individual, personal, emotional problems arise from that. Things that are out there, they're just like things in your diet. You need minerals, fruit and vegetables, protein, all that stuff. You need to balance that if you want a healthy body. Just as with your mind, the same goes for that too.

What about the spirit? What sense of love are you talking about here when you're talking about a proper diet for the spirit? What kind of diet will you be chasing after? You should be able to be in control of everything that you have the potential of being and of achieving. Even just taking envy for instance, why can't you envy someone you love, some goodness that they possess?

Why does it have to be something that is so far from you? All this stupid stuff comes because you practice stupid things, you think in stupid ways, and you practice stupidly. Because that's what you think it is and it's not. It's not like that.

Like I said last week, better is always in tomorrow. I feel for those kids ... but I guess you have to move on, right? If you want to learn how to live you have to know how to give, right? Give what? What will last? What can you leave behind that will last when you die? You will not take money with you. You will not take whatever fame with you. What you take is what you have given to others. That's what you take. If you want to envy something make sure that there is a right way of using it. Otherwise envying things can turn people into all sorts of craziness. It is not just wrong. We just don't know how to use it properly. Don't blame God. Bad happens because we make bad, right?

And hopefully there is a learning to this and it doesn't go in vain, American people. Okay, take care.

What Do You Want To Love?
April 29, 2007

Good morning.

Let's talk about love. What Do You Want To Love?" [*Hyo Jin Nim waits for an answer.*]

Say something! *(Laughter.)*

What do you want to love? *(God.)* You want to love God, what else? *(Everybody.)* I guess this is the kind of answer you'd expect in a religious setting, right?

What about people who are not religious? What do you think that they want to love—money, fame, power, beauty?

And so I guess we all have our definition of love. It depends on a kind of tribal reality. The particulars are obviously stressed. That's why it's hard at times to unite everybody, because a lot of us all around the world base ourselves on that kind of reality, tribal reality, what we value as love, the concept of it varies.

So, when everybody knows love is good however the value of love differs. There is obviously a potential for conflict, and that difference makes it difficult at times. But certain things are fundamental regardless of how you may like a particular thing, desire a particular thing. One could translate that desire as the definition of love.

Certain particulars are universal, and anytime you talk about unity we have to understand, if it exists, what that particular is. Otherwise we have no grounds for unification. There is no foundation. There is no basis. So that recognition, if there is such a thing, that should be the ground in which we plant the seed. Otherwise it won't happen.
When you talk about love, who do you want to love, what kind of people do you want to love? Beyond the kind of material things that we

like to love is there a type of people you want to love? What type of people can we think about universally and have a kind of mutual understanding, people whom you want to love? There has to be some kind of quality there.

It's very difficult to unite something unless you have that understanding and unless you want to love something.

When you try to show love to your children, first of all there has to be a basis in which they can understand and they can reciprocate with you. That becomes the cause of understanding or realizing love.
What is that?

You can start with giving right? What kind of giving? You have to give based on the level of understanding and maturity they have. That is the first thing that teaches us of the concept of love. It might start with the frivolous things for children because they're still immature. Their maturation level is relatively low, however it still starts with giving. Giving what? It varies. But the concept of giving is the basis of learning about love or making love, the realization of love. So, what do you want to give? When you talk about the concept of giving, what is actually happening? If that is the cause, what is the effect? When you give something to somebody hopefully you give because you want that person to what? To become better, right? And that completion of cause and effect, action and reaction, makes you realize love. It has to be better. It has to make you better in the end.

When you give certain things to children, they might feel better because you're giving candy or what not, but that giving or that understanding and better feeling might be temporary. You make them feel better. They're sad and all of a sudden you give them candy and they feel better. It might be very short in terms of duration, however, through that little child, by the action of giving, something has turned in their little moment of life, in their head, something better.

So, when we mature to the point of understanding eternity or start to ponder or try to understand God obviously the value of giving or the quality of giving, the stuff that you want to receive takes on a value or meaning that is equal to that pursuit. Right? You want to learn about eternity. You want to learn about God. Then the giving, the something that makes you better, should possess that kind of eternal quality.

It changes as we mature. And as we mature to the fullest adulthood, we can start to understand those things, the things of eternal value in terms of making you better. That is what's valuable in giving. You talk about unconditional giving, but the funny thing is that even unconditional giving has conditions. Why?

It has to make you better in the eyes of God. It has to make you a better person who can co-relate and co-exist with God for eternity. You can't just unconditionally give money to terrorist so that they can kill people. That's not unconditional giving. Even forgiveness. There is no such thing as unconditional forgiveness. It has to have meaning, purpose. It has to have a purpose as a condition.

How can you forgive somebody if he doesn't have in his heart the wrong that he has committed? What is the purpose? There is no purpose then. There is no meaning. It has to have conditions. Even in giving someone unconditional love, unconditional forgiveness, it has conditions because it must serve a purpose. Purpose of goodness, right? Eternal goodness. Otherwise there's no meaning. They'll do it again and again and again, right? What is the purpose of forgiving wrong if it's going to be done over and over and over again? It has no purpose.

We want to love people who make us better, right? That's the kind of love that we want, right? Someone who can help you to be better. Because when you receive that kind of love you know it's meaningful to you as much as to the person who gives it away. And that's meaningful, that's the kind of people you want to love in the end, for a long time, the longer the better right? *(Yes.)* That's not easy. Who said it was easy, right? *(Laughter.)*

Anything that is meaningful, anything that is worthwhile holding onto forever is challenging and will be difficult to achieve, but it can be done. If God can endure all sorts of misery and pain that we've caused

Him in our lifetime, if God's allowing us to understand and make that happen, then He will assist us in every way He can.

That's a pretty good deal isn't it? *(Laughter.)*

And it can be done if we understand the value of love and how it's done. If we take responsibility to be the kind of people we should be, and to have the people around you, around us we want to truly love and have them love you, it can be done. That's the grass-root thing. You know what I'm saying? *(Yes.)*

It will grow. That stuff, if it grows that way, it will last because it will take root first and it will grow. And I believe everybody can do that, be valuable to someone else, because you can give to someone else something of value and make someone else better, hopefully better than you. Now that is the ideal world. That's how you build it. If there is a way, that's the way.

You can do it. You might get addicted to it. Who knows? Certain personality types gravitate to those things much quicker than others, right? So it varies, but it can be done. The more people like that we have, the better for our movement.

Okay? Take care you guys.

Prosperity
May 6, 2007

Good morning. *(Good morning.)*

Does everybody want to be prosperous? What is prosperity?
Do you want to be prosperous? *(Yes.)* In what way? *(Laughter.)*
Money? Money way?

I'll cut right to the chase. To me prosperity is a perception, a perception
of how one thinks about one's own contentment. So, when are you
satisfied? Because prosperity equals satisfaction? That varies. How do
you see prosperity? It's a perception of how you think about your own
self contentment.

Look at the televangelists today. These people are doing very well.
They put on a great show. They package themselves very well. It's an
event when you go there. And events have, I guess, certain kinds of
appeal or expectation. For instance, like on a commercial level, you
create an event to sell your product. In politics you create an event,
make budget promises, and ask for your vote. *(Laughter.)* At times, in
religious circles, you have an event and make a statement, make a
proclamation of some sort, representing the divine. And it's how you
use that kind of stuff to draw attention that makes the event highly
successful or not. Right? *(Yes.)*

And pretty much, that's how we communicate with one another on a
larger scale. Otherwise, it's one-on-one. You have to literally build
things one-on-one. And because of modernization, we can afford that
kind of large scale give and take using those kinds of situations,
because we all have that kind of situational awareness of how things
work.

Especially when the people who put on those kinds of things have
certain expectations. They try to make you listen better to what the
point is, and then they'll try to get you to stick to it, whether they're

selling the right product. But time will tell right? Eventually you see whether it's a good politician or not, or whatever. Time will tell.

But anyway, in the end what is all that for? Why is it necessary? You have to ask yourself, ultimately in the end, can we find something that is universal? What is that universality in which we can all share in contentment? That's important. Because when you talk about being prosperous most people are thinking about the physical mind and body. I guess people get stuck on a physical level because that's all they understand. Maybe it's environmental or whatever.

Some types of people are kind of stuck on the intellectual level. They pretty much give their whole life in pursuit of creating that and getting greater and greater satisfaction in terms of expanding intellectually.

And finally, spiritually. In spirituality it goes the same way but that's a very broad kind of reality. How do you find satisfaction, unless you have a telephone, a direct line to God, a red telephone, like Batman's phone. *(Laughter.)* It's very difficult. If something is tangible or if something is intellectual. At least you can feel it because there is give and take you can perceive and determine, and analyze it or whatever. But how do you go about doing that, how do you analyze and define a perception when it comes to having a relationship with God? How do you ultimately feel that satisfaction?

So, you have to take a leap of faith, right, and try to predict how God will think in terms of satisfaction. Not you! Not you first, but how He would think of the satisfaction. What would He feel? What would God think that will make God satisfied, make Him feel contentment?

When you chase after that notion, the feeling of God, it's not something you can determine based on yourself. That would be foolish wouldn't it? You have to think about how He would perceive it. That's the leap of faith we have to take. What would make Him content?

He wanted us to procreate and proliferate like all the stars in the universe. What would make Him satisfied in the end? What would make Him happy? Because anything that gives contentment has all that stuff in there, prosperity, happiness and all that stuff that you want. But in the end if you want to chase God, that's what you have to do. You can't ask for things just for yourself, you have to ask what would make Him contented. That's the only way, because you have no idea.

Do you truly know what makes you feel satisfaction yet? You're still chasing it aren't you? At least I am. I'm not going to live that long. I'm still trying to figure out what, to this person, defines contentment. Only then can you truly feel prosperous in my point of view.

Give a bunch of candy and French fries to children and they think that they're in prosperity. *(Laughter.)* When they grow up that perception changes. That's about it isn't it?

It's true. I still think like that. I don't know about you. In my own way, in my own stupid way, I do. The desire keeps you pushing on to try to expand to try to ask questions, what is more than I have?

Before I talk about giving, I have to know what I've got. What more do I have. Then comes the part about giving. That's the choice. It's the choice that made us fall. It's the choice that can make us successful too. Heavenly choice. If it has to come from your responsibility, me and you, then that determination ultimately falls on you, and you have to expand your limitations. If you don't, you can never be prosperous. You're going to make a big booboo. *(Laughter)* It just might be criminal.

So, prosperity is in you. It's how you perceive seeing your limitations, but at the same time, don't let the notion of limitations bind you. You can expand. The world has boundaries, sure, but expand, right? Unconditional love has conditions right? *(Laughter.)* Know yourself and that answer lies in you. Nobody else can give it to you. And if we can be the church that can understand more than just the kind of prosperity stuck on the body or the mind … maybe a little higher. Hey let the best man win, right? That's about it, isn't it?

We'll attract people because that's how we think, that's how we live and if we can showcase those more in confidence, trust me it will be beautiful. And people are attracted to beautiful things. It can be done. Others can sort of do it. We can do it to. We'll certainly do it if we put our hearts and minds together in our efforts. Faith and effort, hey, to start that's all you have. But you have to believe. God still believes that this world can become an ideal world. We have to believe right? Otherwise we will all perish, right? We can't let that happen, right? That's not an option.

So, let's see what we got! Okay?

I guess next week is Mother's Day. You guys going to be busy? (*We'll be here!*) I'll be here. *(Much laughter.)* I'll see you next week.

What Is Natural?
May 13, 2007

Good morning. *(Good morning.)*

Why are you coming? Is somebody putting a gun to your head? *(Laughter.)*

"What Is Natural?" When we think about things that are natural what do we expect from them? What do we expect from things that are natural? Let's say that God is a loving God, in His lovingness what do we naturally expect? *[A child on the front row answers, "An embracing feeling."]* An embracing feeling, you should come and speak. *(Laughter.)*

Okay. A loving God to you, I guess, is an embracing feeling. Ah, you know you need to be embraced sometimes. Even a stone person like me needs to be embraced too, if I can get it. *(Laughter.)* It's good to be embraced. What else do we expect from a loving God? What is natural? Are there stages? If we think about God in a natural sense, the lovingness that we expect from Him, on the level of physicality, what do we expect? What do we expect on the intellectual level? What do we expect on a spiritual level? Because there will be some variations.

I'm sure that the requirements or expectations can vary according to individuals, but I'm sure that there is some universality, some general outline, and some constants. If there is a sine curve or if there is a waveform, they'll be something constant that creates that form, because without that principle, that concept is irrelevant, it doesn't exist. The circle is nothing other than just one cycle of a wave, putting verticalness and pushing it together. Then you have a circle.

So, that rolls on and on and on. That's why things move in the direction that gives life, and it's linear because we live in the physical world. I don't think that we're mature enough to understand spirituality. We're barely learning how to maintain and manage our body, our mind, and it will take a lifetime to get there.

And then there's spirituality, to have a relationship with God, and to make the relationship with God natural. It's going to take a long time. It will take eternity, but you have a chance because you believe in eternity. You believe that you have spirit.

Let's think about it in spirituality, even just the concept alone, in a sense dictates faith, the simple thing, faith. Faith without an absolute is no faith, has no faith right? You must have an absolute to have faith. So, faith without an absolute has no faith. Why? Because if you don't embrace that faith concept, you can't understand that crazy stuff about the Christian tradition, the Fall of Mankind. It doesn't make any sense.

There is a limitation to God's eternity, right? The unconditional love of God, how do you describe the unconditional love of God? If there is no description, then what's the point to talking about unconditional love if you can't describe it? It has a description, so it has a condition. So, when you talk about naturalness, especially spirituality, the ultimate achievement for us is to have the relationship with God, that eternal relationship, something that will take our life to learn about, our body, and our mind, just to manage and maintain.

Our sanity, and our progress within sanity, while understanding God and spirituality will push on forever, will expand forever. This life is nothing more than giving you the idea, "That's how you will expand." That's it! Just because you say ,"Awe, I'm just about to croak," laying on your death bed and, "Now I know everything." It's not like that. If it were, then we should all just try to make a pill that would make us really old and die so we can just cut to the chase, fast forward, cut away all the nonsense. *(A lot of laughter.)*

Why not? If that were doable, I'd rather live that way. I'd rather take that course because it's too much energy living normally. So, what is natural to you? What do you expect out of your naturalness? What do you expect from nature? What do you expect naturally from yourself? What do you expect naturally from God? Somehow that has to connect.

What do you see when you see nature? What do you learn from it? Do you see just the survival of the fittest or do you see some examples of nuances that are harmonious? If you pay attention, there's a lot of stuff that bugs and plants and animals do better than men. You know what I'm saying? There are certain things that literally we have to learn from those lesser things, right?

And what do you see in you, naturally? What goodness do you think you have? Do you have it? Do you know your evil side? I'm sure that you have some goodness there. I hope so. *(Laughter.)* I don't think that anybody is pure evil. And how does that connect. How do you compare that to nature? Also, you have to ask yourself then, "What do I naturally expect from God?" How do I see my God to be? If I see my God, what is the impression that I expect of Him? Will He disappoint me or will He inspire me? At least think about it! Have that description! Forget about being disappointed. At least have a description first. You should, because you are going to die with it. You've got to know what you're dying for. At least you have to have a description of it.

Don't believe in something that you can't see, you can't feel, that you can't touch in your heart. You know what I'm saying? If you don't have those, you'll drift. You'll fly away like a little tweety bird. It is important to have that. Think what is natural. If we're good, naturally we should have a relationship with God. Who is my God and what does this text book teach me. What does this nature teach me? Hopefully, if we're good enough, if we have a definition, at least about our self in community, then we can find and we can accelerate that process a little faster. That's about it.

And you have more to share, something relevant that we need, not nonsense. Okay? Think about what is natural to you and goodness. I don't know. You know. You have to find out. There are generalities. You can talk about generalities, but look, you want to be special.

Okay? Find something that makes you special. That's the only way that we can be rich together.

Okay, see you later.

Forgiveness
May 20, 2007

Good morning. *(Good morning.)*

Let's talk about, "Forgiveness."

Have you ever hated somebody? If you have hated somebody, please raise your hand. Do you still hate that person? If you look around, all the religious conflict is based on the ability to not forgive, right? It's born out of hatred because of differences of belief. That fanatical Islamic community, they don't need any drugs, they purely hate Western society, especially America because it goes against what they believe. And what they believe is absolute. Nobody else is right other than them. That fanaticism is fueled by anger, it's some kind of self-righteous spiritual anger in the name of God, borrowing the name of God. That's why they can kill themselves and teach young people to strap bombs on themselves to kill as many as they can. And it doesn't stop there. If they could, they would create more mass-destruction if that was doable. But how do you stop this? That is a reality based on spiritualism.

What about hatred just based on an intellectual level? Let's say somebody stole your idea. Let's say somebody conned you out of your hard-earned money because they're 'weaselly' like. Whatever. You want to hate that person, and it's very difficult to forgive that person because they have taken so much from you. However, even on the intellectual level, that is doable. That can create the kind of hatred that changes your life, not for the good. Unfortunately, it will torment you. It will isolate you. You will literally live in mental hell, mental incarceration. Why? Because you're just so angry you want revenge.

What about just on a physical level? Somebody beats you up, or somebody just stole your money outright, but not burglary, and you have caught that person, and you know who beat you up. It is easy for you to forgive that person? You want some sort of retribution don't you?

Just because we have the ability to grow based on give and take, if it falls on the opposite direction, yes just that technical aspect of it will kick in too. It will affect you. That's why, in anger, if you feel that you have been victimized, you want to turn to that process. You want to turn it on and do something about it. And what are you doing in actuality? It's about retribution and revenge. If you want to forgive, you have to understand that you have the greater possibility to expand to grow.

An arrogant person cannot forgive. An arrogant person is limited to the body, limited to the mind state, spiritually limited as well. Why? Just think about it. Suppose someone takes away your whole family and brainwashes your children to hate you, hate your own kind. For whatever self-justification they might have, they feel superior to you. How can you forgive that kind of person? Because you feel the anger from the tip of your hair follicle down to your toenails, your anger is to the degree that is makes you sick, physically sick, intellectually dark.

You won't see the light of the day. All you'll see is what is in your head. It's that pure hatred, and that's what you feel too. And how do you go over that? How do you try to forgive somebody when you feel that much hatred? It's difficult, obviously. You have to recognize that. But then you have to try. If you don't heal yourself then nobody will. If you can't take care of yourself, nobody will. Why, because you'll be dependent on someone else for the rest of your life. And who's to say that the person you came to depend on to cure your anger, to help dismiss your anger, and nullify your anger. How can someone erase something, when someone doesn't know what the hell you've got?

In that kind of situation the only person that can cure you is you. You have to tell yourself, "Okay, what is going on here with me? Why am I this angry?" Physically you have limited yourself to where the hell you were at the moment of inception of this miserable stuff. You're still stuck there physically.

Intellectually, you have only entertained yourself with the thought of this tremendous amount of hatred and you're only allowing yourself to let that grow. Spiritually, pretty much, you've shut down. Why? "I've got a problem with life, breathing stuff. I've got a problem with dealing with stuff with my mind and my body and I need to somehow resolve this." I know that is crying out inside of me. The inner voice inside me is crying out, "You need to resolve this, otherwise you're going to kill yourself!"

Why, why am I stuck in this limitation? What is my limitation? You need to go back. It takes two to tango right? And basically you're trying to evaluate the wrongdoing in terms of a ratio. That guy is nine and I'm one or eight and two, that kind of stuff. It's that justification process. Because it falls into that kind of rational thinking, that category of thinking, that happens. If you think like God, obviously you can be a little more patient, more expansive, right? But that's just good enough for me. Pretty much that's where I'm stuck. Remember, we all die and will be judged. You stand for your consequences.

Some people do stupid stuff, they play games with you, and you forgive them. It's a never ending game with some kinds of people. So, you say to yourself, "Why the hell should I forgive that guy one more time?" But there comes a time in situations like that that you have to say, "Okay, I'll forgive you." And walk away. Why? Obviously that person has an issue that he needs to control. He needs to manage on his own, prior to having any kind of relationship with anybody else.

Why? Because we have to be responsible in relationships. At least if you have done wrong, you have to recognize what you have done wrong. If you don't have that capacity, what's the point? You start something and it will end the same way over and over and over again. For the sake of that person, sometimes you just have to walk away. Okay. He'll face God's judgment. They'll face their own consequences. Every individual has a responsibility for their own perfection. And the basis of perfection is knowing how to relate with one another, and make the human relationship deeper and deeper and wider and wider, that kind of stuff.

You can't talk to a wall and understand human relationships. Do you understand me? So how do you, when you're faced with stuff, deal with somebody who has no capacity at that moment in time to change? You can be patient, but the thing is, changes will happen when they will, isn't that the catch?

If God cannot control mankind from the beginning, because of individual responsibility, no matter how you try to invest in somebody, unless they understand their basic value, and the responsibility of being human and facing up to the consequences of their own actions, right or wrong, and know how to complete themselves, then don't expect every direction you take, every step of the way to succeed all the time.

The basis of humanity has to be there and understood by yourself if you are going to build a true relationship with other people. And when you don't have that capacity, why, because you don't think that is important? Then why the hell don't you talk to a wall? You're just talking to the wall! You're talking to some kind of entity that doesn't understand your language or concepts and perceptions. You've got a problem.

The only thing that you can do is pray for that person's soul. Sometimes that's all that you can do. I hope you find yourself before you die. Because it will be much easier than after dying. You will learn your lesson one way or the other. So, if you want to forgive, try to be humble. Be a humble man. It takes effort. I jokingly always say that a humble man is nothing other than a man who keeps his arrogance to himself. Know your limit. Arrogance is limitation, and you can flaunt it as much as you want, but it's only in this life that you can find some sort of audience in certain unique circumstances.

Steve Jobs or whatever, that guy in Apple, his philosophy is that "I don't particularly care if I'm right as long as I'm successful." That's screwed up, okay. You can find something in life, but you want to complete your life well, and in oneself there is spirit, mind and body.

Controlling that in union is more important than centering on oneself. You aren't going to take it with you when you die. That's for sure.

I need to forgive too. I need to be forgiven by some people too. And I have to do my best to be as humble as I can when I'm faced with that task at hand.

And so today.

Okay. It's kind of depressing but, hey! See you next week.

What Do You Want to Inherit?
May 27, 2007

Good morning. *(Good morning.)*

"What do You Want to Inherit?" Do you have any particular things? You say blood lineage, come on help me out here! You say True Love. Out of the things that you've said what is the first thing that you can actually handle? What can you actually handle? You say True Love, love and lineage, True Parents' Tradition, but what can you actually handle? Or, do we have to be more particular?

Well then, let's be honest. If you're going to find an answer to my original question you have to make the question relatable to you. It has to be rational to you based on your understanding or reason, your ability to reason. It has to be initially plausible. Possibilities will grow in it and hopefully you can develop into it, and ultimately, in the end, you can find the answer you're looking for. But even the question itself has to be relatable to you, otherwise it's irrelevant and you'd might as well just watch TV talk shows. Talk shows seem like they're relevant, but in the end they become entertainment. You get hooked on that entertainment and they drag it on to increase the production value, and it becomes more and more frivolous. That's the nature of the way things are in the multimedia realm. It can start off with some serious stuff but the whole purpose of it in the end is production value. So, how many times do you need to regurgitate the basic stuff? And if you tried to even find an interesting point of view, perspective, it becomes more and more difficult and you're just pressed for time and have to cut corners.

Once people start settling in on certain things, a lot of times. Unless you're always feeling the heat so to speak. You'll settle down. Settling down means nothing other than just trying to find the easiest way to maximize whatever gain that you're looking for. That's about it.

So, when you talk about inheritance, what do you want to inherit? Why do you go to church? Why do you want to believe in God? Before you talk about inheritance, let's talk about the reality of what people do with an inheritance. You see a lot of struggles, right? Especially when folks die or whatever, their heirs fight over whatever is left that has value, in terms of monetary value. If you were a cave man a long time ago, prior to us, being a little more intellectual, living out there was a struggle, and survival was the priority. Sometimes it was very violent. You had to deal with the environment. It was harsh and brutal and went in cycles regardless of your needs. You had to go out and gather and hunt or whatever, just so you could survive. And many times it's just like when you watch the National Geographic Channel, where they showcase the animal kingdom. It's brutal. It's very violent. Civilization teaches us that, okay. And however stupid it might be to some people, violence can exist as a last resort. We accept that premise. Some people might vehemently disagree, but there're in the minority. The majority agree, accept, and embrace that concept because unfortunately that's reality.

So, when you talk about inheritance, what is important, what is of value to you? Is there anything that you really want so much that you want to be violent to inherit it? And what causes violence when it comes to the core of inheritance? What triggers that thought of violence? You say, "I have to act upon it somehow, as it's my last resort. I have to claim my stake." But, what is so worth committing violence for? You can teach people to hate. Even religion can do that. They can justify it simply because of cultures and how they interpret the relationship between God and human beings, humanity, in such ways that sometimes and as a last resort, you can commit horrendous stuff in the name of God until you defeat your enemy, however long it takes. Why? Because they too want to inherit something. They want to inherit the divine eternal life centered on God, in His blessing, in His glory, and be eternally peaceful, live in joy and happiness forever for the mere sacrifices, however those are done. And most likely those are done in violence because you think that you can inherit all that stuff. And people teach people to do so. There are people who teach people that that is how you inherit God's eternal love.

What is important to capitalism? What is the definition of a capitalist? Let's say that we're agnostic or atheist. What's the definition of inheritance? It's all about material stuff isn't it? Either you inherit it, or if you don't then do the best that you can to gain it. Or, quote-unquote, earn it. You will do everything under the sun short of going to jail to get what you want. Nobody wants to go to jail, jail sucks. But that's reality. They say, "If I can't get it in an orderly way, then I'm going to get it one way or the other. And I'll inherit from this earth. I might not believe in God but I'll take as much as I can for it's here." We are supposedly civilized because we are inheriting our knowledge through history, from history, standing on the shoulders of others, right? That's one way of inheriting. A lot of people devote their whole life to intellectualism. It's all about that, inheriting from their knowledge. You just want to put something more on the table. That's about it, isn't it?

But what does religion try to teach you? Inheriting something from God. How do you measure that? How do you measure inheriting something from God? It starts from your attitude, knowing what is valuable, in faith as God will see it. And that is the belief that you are willing to give your life for. Because even in measured stuff, if you believe a certain concept in say, science and medicine, you will dedicate your life to prove it in the intellectual world. The thing is, I want more than just my intellect. I want to have a greater relationship because I believe in a greater being. That's a leap of faith. That's why you believe in religion. Anybody who says that they believe in God, whether they fully understand the meaning of a leap of faith or not, they challenge themselves once they make that decision. They're taking a giant leap from what they know in body, in physicality and intellectualism, into something that is absolutely mysterious in certain ways.

Why? There are so many things that we don't know even about this planet. We have only observed about four or five percent of the ocean and blah, blah, blah. We haven't named all the creatures and plants in the rain forests. What gives us the right to make that decision unless we become humble to ourselves and are willing to die for it? That is the greatest price that you pay to learn about something. You're willing to pay the price to gain a greater knowledge. Whether you like it or not, you have to do that physically, intellectually, and spiritually of course, but it has to be your life and you have to mean it. Yes, you can screw up and make mistakes. But never lose sight of it. You try. You try. If people succeed in the first shot then you're lucky. We can all be successful if we understand how we can reach that end. And that is with dedication, with our lives. That's the only way that I can grow too.

I'm speaking every Sunday because I'm getting attached to certain things,. Physically, intellectually, even certain faces. But to make this into a duty that I want to carry on, now that's the next step. I might have initially done it because of extraordinary circumstances. I forced, I willed myself to do this stuff. But in the process I changed. I know that because at least I had some experience in the past. I wanted to do this kind of stuff. And I wanted to go back and find what I lost. That's about it. Because I know what's right. You know what is right. You're finding something that is right and that is important. There is no exception. You can't be free without boundaries and consequences, right? That's right. And I want it back. That's why you try.

And what do you want to inherit? Personally speaking, if I want to inherit something, I want to inherit how my Father built this church. That's all. That's enough, because that's what's important. I know that He spent every waking moment, every breathing moment to build something from nothing to what he has now. I know that he valued every single one of those people who came in the beginning. And that's what made Unification Church what it is, if it means anything to anybody. Now that's important. That is the most important value, truth value, that I want to inherit. I could care less about anything else. If I want stuff, I do stuff. And I'll do a whole lot of stuff. What's important will last forever. Truth value, that I want to inherit. That's enough. I could care less about anything else. I can get everything else on my own. I don't need anyone's help. I'll get it in my own way. It's not about external.

Even if I do become successful, I'm trying to put it on to the table because I feel it's necessary for the betterment of all and for what we stand for, and that's the stuff we can't erase. I fear God. I fear my children. I fear history. That's about it. I don't fear anything else. You will die of disease, you will die of accident, somebody can kill you or you will die of natural causes. Suicide is out of the question, but it can be done. Life is short and I want to put something on the table. I've got to earn my way, earn my keep. That's love isn't it? You can't just take right? You've got to give, and everybody knows that.

Why do we stray from that sometimes? Because we get lost in stupidity and our values change. However primitive my value had been, it hasn't changed yet, no matter what, and I'm trying. Look I'm trying to be responsible, okay, for myself and for my expectations. This is all I can do. What you see is what you get. Well, hopefully, it can expand, it can grow. I'll do my best to make it happen. I will not, I won't stop trying. People like me, I don't think I can. I'll find a way somehow. What do you want to inherit? You want to inherit true love. Start from the thing that you know, what makes love turn around? Try to give. Try. Even people like me try. I'll keep on trying. I'll be here as long as you're here. See you.

Maturation
June 3, 2007

Good morning. Let's talk about, "Maturation."

How do you want your children to grow up? Before you talk about yourself, before you talk about what's right and wrong, before you talk about what's good and bad to children, I think that you first have to understand what kind of reality they have to face. Their reality, because they'll be in it, not you. For instance, I could send my children to the nursery here where they glorify Father and they could be in that kind of environment, but once they start to go to public school things would be very different. The glorification would be somewhere else. That's a problem. And they're living in it, not you.

So, if you think about reality, you have to think about their reality. That's the reality that you have to deal with to help them grow. You have to learn something from it, know how to control it, manage it, and ultimately transcend it to the next level. Because there are many levels in which you need to overcome, you need to first understand and then overcome so that you can finally say bye-bye to this world and prepare yourself for the next one. And many times language is a barrier.

The language parents use to speak to a child who lives in that kind of environment is often foreign to them. You expect them to rise up to your level. But there are times when you need to step down. You need to understand their reality. You have to understand their reality, what they're going through within their reality, before you talk to them about good and bad, what's cool and un-cool, and importantly, what's smart and stupid. In the end you want to teach your children something and to give them something, yet they have to be in a position to receive it, otherwise they'll never get you or understand you.

As the child, the first thing is time, the decade you are born in. You start with individual self stuff. You're experimenting with yourself, you're trying to learn your boundaries and your limitations. You want to know how much excitement, how much boredom you can take. That's what happens in a child's mind and in a child's reality. That's the only thing that's important to them. Then once they start to go to school and they reach the next decade, they move into teenage-hood and deal with what is cool and uncool, that kind of stuff. It's the social rather than individual stuff that is important to them. Why? Because they're growing up. They're just beginning to realize how it works in society. So, the fundamental thing that they seek to learn is that relationship. So, the concepts that you use to try to teach them what is right ultimately has to relate to them, not you. You're still growing too. And I know that when you get to Father's age you are only going to speak about spirit world. Trust me.

Then comes the time when they grow up beyond teens and they go to college. They become college students and they start to become more socially active, right? A lot of them become idealists. If you can become an idealist, that's the time that you're going to turn into one. You're accessing a greater society, greater relationship. The next decade is going to be more. You are literally going to try to find yourself and define yourself in a certain kind of situation. Whatever profession that you have chosen, that's all that you're going to think about and that's all that every ounce of your energy will be focused on trying to master that and trying to make a difference and to compete and win. A lot of times the jargon of your profession is important, but

In the next decade it's won't be as important anymore. When you turn 40 all those things are not as important. What's more important is finding a more universal focus, something that is more universal. Even if it has to be earthly, you want to find something more universal, and you want to expand that social base, connect to more people, not just to your existing relationships and you're just going to take it to the next level. You literally want to start to actually see the value in people, and their differences, not all the bad but only the good, because that's important to you. Why, because you're preparing yourself for the final departure as that is the completion of maturation. More and more it's going to become more and more important to you, that thing, knowing that stuff. Nothing else matters. That's how we grow.

Please, when you deal with children, just speak their language. Once they start to disregard certain things they will rail against our language one way or the other. When I was young, I was taught certain things, and when I went to school it was completely opposite. You can only take so much, but when it starts to become more and more overwhelming, you then start to disregard what you were taught, regardless. Why? Because it's human nature. It's self preservation. "I have to take care of myself. That ain't good—there's nothing good here." And you start to react. The thing is, unfortunately, when that happens you just might go down the wrong path that it will take you a long time to recover from. You're pretty much on your own then.

How difficult was it for you to find God? Did you grow up in a religious environment? What if you didn't? It pretty much will be like that. You pretty much have destroyed whatever you had in your mind and you have to build it back up. That's the problem. So, if you can, don't go that path. Success is just one little thing. Even in competition, winning is measured in milliseconds, right? That determines the first place or the second place guy, right? It's that kind of stuff. It's that little effort, a little more, that makes a difference. And it's difficult to do that sometimes. And if you have to do that all the time obviously it's going to take stuff out of you. You will pay for it. If you have chosen that path then that's your call isn't it? And how long can I stick to this? I don't know. How long can you tough it out? I don't know.

The thing is that everybody, regardless of whether they're a little kid or people that are preparing to go to spirit world, to the very end they have to face that one question. And you have to answer it. No one else can do that for you when it comes to you. Try to understand that God is in zero, right? God is in the middle. That's why He's in zero. Father talks about horizontal and vertical and God is in here. How far do you want to expand? That is your life goal, to determine how far you expand. When you expand horizontally you have to match it vertically too. What you deliver based on your horizontal expansion is up to you, because you want perfection right? Aw, that's tough. Boy it's tough! Am I doing this stuff so that I expand horizontally for myself or something greater? That's tough.

Let's say that you can do that, expand to the level that the world will recognize. But to be perfect you have to match it up vertically, right? We understand that because that's the language, the jargon that we use in the church, right? But when it comes to kids, try to understand you have to sink down, you have to go down. You can't expect them to always rise up to your level. Even grown-ups can't. You can't expect them to always do that stuff. How do you expect children to do that stuff all the time? That's crazy! So, you have to have that kind of understanding that sets the standard. It needs to be so, yes! Hey, it's your child! And it's your life, right? And we will grow to the end. It's up to you. Okay.

Change
June 10, 2007

Let's talk about, "Change."

Let me ask you a question. If you had one wish for a change, what would it be? Let's say that I have 100 million dollars. That's a lot for one man, yet it depends on the location. But on average you can buy someone a house for a quarter million dollars. So, I could buy a house for only four hundred people and the money would be gone. Something like that means something to those people. But, if you expand it, it's not enough for most people. That's reality. So, if you add a zero and now you have a billion dollars, it too would be gone just like that. That's all it's worth. You add another zero, that's all it's worth.

So, where does it end? There's more than four hundred people in the world, right? That's the problem. That's why it's difficult to change. No matter how much and how good your intentions, and however you want to do good and you try, that's about it. It depends on individuals. And you have to somehow unify people who have that same desire, that same need. It can be basic, because it's practical, because it's physical. You have to think about yourself in a physical way, and you will think about yourself in an intellectual way, and hopefully if you have that under control you then have a time to be spiritual, right?

But the problem is that most people struggle where? You tell me. That's the problem. I'm thinking about sending my children to school in some other place, maybe back to Korea during a certain period of time in their maturation. I'm thinking about it because it's very difficult to process all that unless we have something that we can provide, some kind of security that is somewhat guaranteed. But, there is no guarantee that you will not die of accident or disease.

So, how do you change? In what way do you want to change? Let's say that you have something that is important to you. Then what would that be as a single individual, or as a family? You want to have some kind of property that you can build equity in, and ultimately you want to be productive within it. And on top of that, in the same way, you want intellectual property, and spiritual property and then align the physical and the mind and the spirit. Those things are important to you because it grounds you. You can't really change unless you have something that you're sure of. You have to be absolute to have real change. If you don't have something absolute, change doesn't mean anything. Because you'll always change and you'll never have anything. You'll have change that is meaningless. And what good is that?

You have to ask: "What kind of change do I want? What kind of change can I do for myself before I give it to others?" If you don't question yourself in that way, and answer yourself and know that you have the answer, change doesn't mean anything. You'll always change, but it won't mean anything. That's the problem. Of course, you want to be self-sufficient. I don't want to go to daddy for anything. You want to be a tough guy, macho man. There's a reason for that kind of stuff, there's a reason for manhood and womanhood. That's a different topic and we'll talk about it some other time. But let's say that you have something and want to create something more. You want to give to something more in a time and place. If I have money, I can build a beautiful studio everywhere around the world, one step at a time, one place at a time. And it will be a functional one. To me, productivity matters. If you have property, if you have equity, yes absolutely I want to have the best stuff in the world, but it's going to be productive. Not just for me, for everybody hopefully. But there's no guarantee it can please everyone. But it will be as functional as it can be. And it doesn't have to be just for that purpose only. It can be for people in general even if you don't do what I do, if we're connected, sure.

The thing is, ultimately in the end I believe that multimedia is very important. I absolutely believe it's important. If we have just two dozen blabbermouths that can think on their feet, we can start. You have to have something because it's about getting your message out there. That's what church is for, especially in this chaotic situation, in this world of confusion. Multimedia is very, very important, and it has to be constant. It has to literally tick with the clock.

Even when you talk about yourself, or talk about giving, or talk about self-sacrifice. You have to see it as putting yourself in a sphere first and then see yourself against a vertical axis and horizontal axis. As you draw away and expand your audience, if you do it right it will also raise their expectations. Of course, you will suffer, and that cycle happens over and over and over and over. That's the sign of infinity, right? But that's how to expand, that's how you expand. Not just with yourself, but with others. Who cares if you exist alone? God doesn't care. That's why He created us right? That's the essence of growing.

You want change, that's growth. Some things don't change, yes, because there are boundaries. You cannot have freedom without boundaries and consequences. The thing about unconditional love is that it has conditions, okay? You want a change, any change, that's difficult. I'm just here to entertain you in your mind, but I'll be here as long as you're here. But it's difficult. That's how it goes. That's what's normal, because I believe that's the ideal. Okay, I'm done. I've got nothing else to say.

See you later.

Do You Like to Fight?
June 17, 2007

Good morning. *(Good morning.)*

"Do You Like to Fight?" Why do we fight? To dream? There's a lot of fighting going on. Right? It's sad and I'm sure that in your own ways. I don't know you individually, but I'm sure that you have to struggle and you have to fight.

So, for life in general, you're dealing with people because you can't live alone. If you want to live alone, go live in a mountain and become a hunter and gatherer. That's one way to avoid fighting, just cut off all the world, and just find somewhere you can actually live that cave-man-like life if there is a piece of land left over. You can do that. But, you're more than that, so you fight.

Okay, having said that, why do we fight? What do we normally fight for? Let's talk about physical things. Let's talk about possessions. Within the limitations of physical things and possessions, within the concept of possession, what do we fight for? We're just talking about physical stuff here, I mean literally possession stuff, authority, control, power, money, fame. They're just pure physical stuff.

What do you fight for on the next level, on an intellectual level? We fight imbalance and seek for what's called fair, what's righteous and all that stuff, all that goody-goody stuff. And what about the spirit?

Okay, before we get to the spirit, let's dwell on this physical stuff for a little while. When you break down the physical self, what are you actually trying to possess? Because it's about possession. But, what do you want to possess beyond the generalities that I said earlier about power and money? What does that give you? Why do you think that people pursue that stuff? Because they want comfort. They want pleasure. They want control. They want stuff like that. They need to feel a kind of adoration. Adoration is very physical. You know what I'm saying? Why do you want to be adored? Why do you want people to like you? It's a physical thing. If you do have a reason for it that is of the divine it doesn't matter. Adoration doesn't become physical, in that temporal sense. It really doesn't matter. And you get fixated to that stuff. How do you think any kind of addiction begins, whether it's addiction to whatever stuff is there, like sex or drugs. How do you think it begins? It begins when you become fixated on that stuff. That's it. All those things are very physical.

The thing is that physical and spiritual have some kind of reflective quality, a reflection quality. Physical stuff is very individual. Spiritual stuff, all those things, you feel them with God. What you see when you look at yourself in the mirror is yourself, your reflection in opposite. However, you should see God in your reflection, not just yourself. Stuff in the middle, the intellect, that's the problem maker. That's why we fight, because we don't know how to control that reality. We don't even know how to see that reality in order, in propriety, as God wants us to be.

All of this makes for a difficult path, very difficult. You will struggle to the end of your days, no matter who tells you otherwise. I won't see it. My children won't see it. My grandchildren won't see it. My great-grandchildren won't see it. It will take at least ten more generations. But you do certain things because you believe that you can do something about what you don't like, what you want to change because you think it's wrong. But, it's going to take time. If anybody tells you otherwise, let them do it. Give them everything you've got. Let them have everything that you have, but it won't happen. I swear to God it won't happen. But we believe in something, right? We can make it right. Nobody's perfect, right? At best we have representation, the best we can have, right? Hallelujah!

We need to move on, trying to better ourselves and making that understanding real. Think about it. You know God has a right to love everybody, right? You want things to change? Change is love. What the heck is love? "God just loves me!" Just you? No. Everybody, right?

You have to allow that to happen. You have to create that kind of environment. That's what's important. And I said what you fight about on the physical level was possessions. And on the intellectual level, you fight imbalance. And on the spiritual level, it is arrogance. You can't be arrogant. You can't just say that, "Oh your love is mine, all mine!" You can't do that stuff. When you truly love somebody, you want to love everything around you, right? Do you select among your kids, "I just want to love this kid and kill the other ones?" You can't do that. It's wrong. I don't think that anybody teaches that to be True Love.

So, everything has to get put order more and more, deeper, broader and broader, higher and higher, in all sorts of ways in all three dimensions and beyond, if we can achieve it. But, let's just think what we can do in physical terms. That's what we need to focus on. That's the kind of church that we need to be. Otherwise, it'll never happen. I want to live up to my expectation of what my name puts on me, this slavery. I'll do it. I'll do it. As long as you are here. If you're here, I'll be here. No problem. Stuff happens, every day. It's not that bad. You always have to move on and hopefully you can make progress. Quality! Quantity! Speed! That's all you can do. And then you'll die! Isn't that the absolute truth? Anyway, we'll try, right? Let's not fight, okay? Loving is difficult enough, I don't want to fight, okay?

Take care.

Masculinity and Femininity
June 24, 2007

Good morning. *(Good morning.)*

It never ends. It certainly doesn't get any easier, and it shouldn't. Otherwise you're like useless equipment, outdated. This morning, let's talk about masculinity and femininity.

What is a macho man? I guess pretty much in general, and throughout the cultures, man does the providing right? They go out and take the risk and do whatever that they have to do to put the food on the table. That's what they do. And women raise the family, the best that they can, and every detail matters when you are trying to raise children. I guess there're opposite roles. Man's responsibility expands and woman's responsibility focuses. So, basically that's what it is, I guess, that's what we're supposed to do as a father and mother if you have a family.

But where does that concept come from? God created mankind in the image of Himself, so masculinity and femininity obviously came from God, and are manifested in the creation of humanity. And when you breakdown the essence of humanity, there is man and woman. That is the essence of humanity. That is the origin of masculinity and femininity. And there is a difference between them, they are opposite. Opposite in what, and for what reason? To learn to come together. That is the most important factor, to learn to unite. Because man learns from woman something that they need to learn to become one with God. And woman too, visa versa. And that's the essence of responsibility. You have to put something on the table. You have to earn it. Yes, you have that potential. That's why it can be learned, but you have to act upon it.

It is your responsibility to make the right choices in understanding how things work best, because otherwise you can mess up your whole end of the thing. When you look at nature, it is beautiful, right? There is so much beauty, but at the same time it also has fury. The reason that nature exists in an opposite reality within the domain of the earth itself is because that's how it grows and expands. That's how it rejuvenates itself. That's how it recovers. That's life! We have to understand that stuff.

How many times did we jump to a conclusion through our arrogance without really knowing things? That's why we make mistakes. That's why the foretelling, fortune teller stuff, foreseeing stuff, gets it wrong. Understanding nature is part of the learning process isn't it? That's how you learn. But, in the end, it exists to unite, to create something, teach us something. Nature is there as a textbook of learning about basic stuff that makes us who we are, to give us the basic understanding of how we can relate to God. And to learn, we do have the tools within our physical self, our consciousness and our spirit.

In terms of volume and size, and the degree of expansion, within nature we're the highest. There's nothing greater, not on this planet. Maybe somewhere else there are beings flying around with flying saucers and stuff, but that's a different story! I'd love to meet those hermaphrodites! Even in our practical day-to-day reality, why should the government, the political system itself in America, be adversarial? You can have two opposing things, but why can't the model be that of love and not an adversarial system? Why can't we just teach each other something and try to learn and come together in union, like the model of man and woman coming together.

It is so silly otherwise. Freedom doesn't license you to be stupid, okay? I'll start from there. And what about racial relationships? What about everything? Anything that you want to talk about in human relationships, why does it have to be adversarial? Because if it is, it is like living in a home where the father and mother don't trust each other and are always doing crazy stuff to each other, and you grow up in that. That's just nonsense! How the heck do you make an ideal family in that situation? How is it possible? Just because somebody does something does not mean that it is right. Just because America, being the richest nation on the earth, says, "We have ten trillion dollars in revenue, and are top in terms of taxpayers, and our government budget is three trillion dollars. We have so much money and we are the best!" So what? Who cares? It has nothing to do with making your family correct. And that's what you need to question if you're going to question anything. You have to question that. Why? You want to be good, everybody wants to be good. But, people take advantage of that goodness.

People want to love stuff. And throughout history a lot of manipulative people in power have used that to send young people to war, because they want love, they want to become something united to something greater, something opposite, something that they're not and hopefully that is greater. Of course, you propagandize it. The reason you're being greater is because there's a relationship of subject and object. Why? Because we do have a relationship between God and mankind. That's why we go to church. Do you expect God to come to you every day? Who chases after the other more, you or is God chasing you more? So, who's the subject? And there is such a thing, but in love it doesn't matter! Because you're one, and it's a necessary oneness. You need it. Who cares if I'm the first? Why does that matter when it takes two to become one and make you whole? Why do I have to say to myself, "I am important, am the best!" What about the second that I myself need to be whole?

You have to be humble and keep your arrogance to yourself. That's a humble man. Because you want to grow, you want to learn, you want to love more, I want more, that stuff. That's why you want to be humble. How can I say that I know everything, that I have everything? Then I'm gone. I'm a dead man walking. Might as well be dead, right? Anyway, you have to learn to come together. We exist for a reason. But that stuff, that opposite stuff, that's the way to family. It might initially be the simplest stuff we'll experience in our human life, but there is a whole lot more out there beyond that stuff. That's just the fundamental stuff.

You have to be willing to be whole, to make oneness, so please don't be arrogant. It's a constant job. It never ends.

Okay, take care.

What Are We Dying For?
July 1, 2007

Good morning. *(Good morning.)*

It never gets any easier, and it shouldn't. "What Are We Dying For?" People here, including me, are dying for faith, right? And life is about proving the faith that we have. And what is faith? How much do you know about God? How much in terms of percentage? Do you know him absolutely 100 percent or what? Life is a risk and we choose our path and that in itself is a risk, the choices that we make. And we have chosen to follow faith.

What is that faith? And if I ask you individually, almost like a job interview, I'm sure that everyone has a different degree of answer. You might say something general like, "I want to know God." But there are all sorts of variations. That is reality. And how do you conclude and say, "This is faith." You like changes. That's why somebody who stands here has to live a miserable life, one of unchanging misery. Yes, life is miserable, but you have to change.

What are you dying for? Look at yourself as an individual. Father is always talking about us being the microcosm of the universe. And just on a social level, a societal level, yes, we are law makers. Individually speaking, we are managers. We make things. We are creators. We do make laws for ourselves, don't we? We give ourselves laws and say, "Okay, this is my standard. This is my law, and I will do my best to follow it." And as you grow, those can change. But at the same time, once you make the law you have to manage yourself and what you do. What you see in society is just a magnification of what you actually go through in your own individual life. That's it. And some people do get carried away in body mechanics. That's just pure physical things. That's just body mechanics.

But what's greater? When you can set a standard and then manage yourself to live up to that standard and prove yourself. Then what happens afterward? You have to take yourself to the next level. What is that? Expansion. And where does that come from? How do you expand? You have to educate yourself, right? Education is important, right? Knowing the beauty of God and all His creation, that takes a whole lot of education, to understand God's beauty and purpose. It takes a whole lot of effort to make that expansion. How much do you know about your own potential? Education in its ideal sense provokes people to reach their potential. Because if you don't, you can't expand. And if you can't expand then how the heck can you know about God who Himself is expanding in love? Who do think you are to say that I know everything about God's love? Based on God's love, a new face that I see is part of that plan, that realm. But how can I know you automatically? What kind of arrogance is that?

When you talk about dying for faith you really have to understand that the risks we take, we take for a reason. We want to grow. We want to expand. We want to ultimately understand how we can unite with God. Many times on a physical level, you know, immediate reality, sometimes it's difficult just to get to know the next person, even a friend. How sociable are you? And if you're not, why aren't you that way? I'm sure that you have a whole lot of excuses and blame. And I'm sure it's justifiable in the way the world is. In this age, if you look at secular politics, the presentation is more important than the deed. You see so much pretentiousness and all that stuff. People say that a picture is worth a thousand words, but action is worth a thousand pictures. How's that? Putting something into action for the right reasons, for the sake of others, for the sake of stuff we believe that is good, is difficult. And you're going to do it till the day you die? Difficult. Because like I said earlier, it's about proving your faith.

Having said that, I want to thank those of you here because you are changing my ways. I used to be detached. I was indifferent. I was vulgar. I lived in rage. I am grateful to you too, for you are helping me to change my ways. Little by little, I've got a ways to go. How can you change without give and take, without relationships, opportunity, reality? Some things you just don't want to change if you're by yourself. You know what I'm saying?

Changes come when you reach out, when you want to reach out, for whatever reason. That's how changes come. And that's how you grow in faith. It doesn't matter if you have to serve a purpose in a position of unchangingness, the symbolism of it. Still you need to have that give-and-take relationship so you can change too. Because you have to expand, right? And as it takes time to do so, you need that unchanging stuff to balance the change and then you go to the next level. Then you go to the next level. It's that kind of stuff. But finding gratitude in misery is difficult, but if it comes with the territory, you can't complain, right? Everybody suffers, right? One way or the other, right? There is no exception.

Please, know what you're dying for and prove that ultimately you have the greatest faith. That's a good competition slogan! Take care of yourself.

Moving Up
July 8, 2007

Good morning. *(Good morning.)*

Let's talk about, "Moving Up." America is the most powerful nation in the world I guess. Is it? You say kind of? Is it Russia? How many nations are there in the world? Over two hundred something, right? The number goes up and down, but there are hundreds of nations. And those hundreds of nations, do they follow America's ways and values in every which way? I don't think so. They have their own way of dealing with quote-unquote democracy, the greatest gift from white people to mankind! And there are all sorts of versions of that.

So, starting with yourselves, you make your own rules, right? You decide what is right and wrong, you make your standards and you manage your life. And with the ability that you have, that all God's children have the ability to imagine, to create, you try to envision yourself as something more than what you are now. Obviously you always want to look forward. You always want to move ahead. Because that's life, that's physics, time ticks forward. I don't think it goes backwards does it? Maybe in fiction, with a time machine or something and maybe that's doable when you're dead. As for what is real for us at this point in time, what it is, is what it is, and what you see is what you get, and that's it. And from there, you start. You make your own laws, you make your effort, you have your standard and you manage your life. And based on that you try to do the best that you can to envision yourself in the future, and based on that imagination, you use your creativity and try to make your ideal real. Unless the ideal becomes real, it doesn't exist. If you don't have some platform to stand on, you can't move up. You don't build the Empire State Building from the 100th floor down, okay? I don't think that's doable. It's that kind of stuff. It's just basic physical things.

We have to remind ourselves how we can relate to how things function and deal with physical reality. The more that we are realistic and approach it the way we can, knowing our limitations, the better. You have to know your limitations, for if you don't know your limitations, nothing works. Power doesn't mean anything if you don't know your limitations. Remember even God, the almighty God, the omnipotent God, He has limitations to His power. That's you! And if you don't understand that limitation, and even if let's say you want somebody to help you, and you go to somebody who is powerful, if you lie to them, you compromise them too. Do you know that? You truly have to know your limit. You first have to be true to yourself. And obviously I hope that you're a good guy. I don't think that you should shove goodness down somebody's throat because we all know what it right and wrong, basically. You should have that basic decency, basic propriety, even if you're asking for help from somebody else. Because if you don't, you'll destroy them too. You'll compromise them too. So, what good is that?

So, how do you move up? Ask yourself, "How can I move up?" What do you think will last, you or a good deed that you might have done? The good deed that affects something else, something greater, that will last more than you, that's for sure. So, what is the kind of stuff that we can do to make our lives more meaningful? Yes, it is important to make laws, manage, and to create stuff. And that's stuff on a physical level, stuff on the intellectual level, and stuff on the spiritual level. That stuff is there. It doesn't matter on what level you're struggling. That's irrelevant. Why? Because in the end of all the things that you can do, the greatest that you can possibly do is something that can last longer than you. For your sorry butt will die! I have to remind myself every day, I have to die well. I know I'll die. That's what's important to me. And life is nothing other than proving my faith. That's about it. That's the meaning of my cause and in every man or woman's life.

In that short period of your life, what are you going to do? What can you take when you're dead? The funny thing is that you can only take what you leave behind. What is meaningful in the stuff that you leave behind is what you can take. That's so funky! That's the irony isn't it? Well, that's true! Pretty much that's about it. That's what faith teaches you. That's just the way it is. What you got is what you got, and more power to you! Spend it here. You aren't going to take power and money and all that stuff with you. What is that meaningful stuff? To me, it's education, something in the arts and science and God. Hey! Make a pill that cures cancer. Be a billionaire, more power to you, but its money then, right? Build a flying saucer, more power to you. Be a millionaire, okay. Something like that, and you want to create, okay, so more power to you. Inspire people, and be rich and famous and be good. I'm not going to tell you what to do. You know what to do if you had that stuff, right? But it takes effort. It takes time. It takes time to take money from outside people!

For projects like making movies, I need millions. But anyway, I'm working on it. You have to start somewhere, and you do it for a cause, you have a purpose, and certainly it's not just for the sake of money. People have billions of dollars. Bill Gates has enough money to buy everybody, all humanity, a McDonald's' Big Mac meal! He's rich, but that's it, one time. Yes, he is rich but who cares? Are you going to change your life because of one Big Mac meal? It's very difficult to persuade. It takes time. And that's why it's important. It takes time. It takes time. If you have family, you know how it is, right? It takes time. It's just that, and then you have to multiply that on a larger level, and nothing changes. Nothing changes. You might have changed, but nothing changed. The standard did not change, that's what you literally get pulled back into.

That's why it's difficult. You think, "I've done my stuff and I'm ready to go to sleep, I'm ready to retire." But no, no, no, no, no, wake up! It's that stuff. That's why it takes time. Something precious doesn't cook overnight. What matters is something that you can change for the betterment of humanity based on your beliefs. That's what's the greatest. And if through your effort, through your sacrifice, you can leave something behind that can help other people, other than yourself, that's what's important.

So what can you do? Go make some medicine. Go do something, build something great. Teach your friend something that they need to know. If you know what is right better than your little friend, a friend that you like to be around, you have something to offer, something to share, and do it whether they like it or not. And you keep on giving it to them. Why? Because it's going to take a long time to persuade. Don't give up. Nothing happens in just one shot. You want that, then walk on water! Okay, see you.

Politics
July 15, 2007

Good morning. *(Good morning.)*

Let me start off with asking you a question. Can you please everybody? Well, you may try to out of the goodness of your hearts, I guess. But is it doable? I want to talk about politics. The topic is "Politics."

People normally want to go into politics because they want to change society. So they have to get involved in law making and have to become a law maker. That's the basic reasoning, right. People become politicians because law can change, forcefully if it has to, certain social behavior. And by changing certain environments and personal behaviors, and by having the authority to do so, they can perhaps create an ideal world without measure. What the heck are the Founding Fathers then? Why do you call them Founding Fathers? People want to emulate the Founding Fathers if they want to become a politician, right? But it took several centuries to come to a point to recognize that there's an irony, the position of political authority is not something of a parental position or a stature of some grandeur, it's being a civil servant. You're a civil servant. You're not the Statue of Liberty, or stuff like that. You're not a symbol that lands on a mantel piece somewhere. Functionally speaking, you're a civil servant. That's what politicians are, right? That's how we think, don't we?

Children are taught that in public schools about politics. So, what happens to the politicians? Okay, let's talk about why we don't like politicians. Why don't we like politicians? They're hypocrites! We all say that they're hypocrites. When they talk, they have two tongues, a forked tongue, you know. They're the devil incarnate. They say one thing and they do another thing. What is the nature of their hypocrisy? What layers of lies do they commit? Fundamentally, there are politicians out there, but especially these days, there's no place for them to hide because there are eyes everywhere, ears everywhere. It's becoming more and more apparent that there are no secrets anymore. Good! So, literally speaking, there are criminals out there. They're just out there to take as much as they can, steal as much as they can, using that platform. And there are people who have lied for their agenda. And there's some who trump that, who want to be God! And that's the tragedy. That's why we don't trust politicians. How do you become God to begin with anyway? Why the heck do you want to be God? He is the most miserable entity in the universe, right? If He is supposed to be the Parent of all humankind there is more suffering than glee, right? Obviously, He is the most miserable person and you want to partake in that misery? Why the heck do you want to do that, for what reason? You know that your life is short, and why do you want to do that? Why do you want to play God? The thing is, at least God walked the walk. If you just tell people to do something and you yourself don't walk the walk, that's not cool. You can do that just sitting in a lawn chair, right? Anybody can do that. Just flipping through TV channels, or surfing the internet on your laptop, and seeing something and saying, "That sounds like a good idea. I'll tell people to do that because I have the power." Well, that's not going to last. That's the problem.

A lot of people play those various levels of lies and that's the reason that we don't trust politicians. Because of that kind of hypocrisy you will do some things to a certain extent, but everything else is just self service. All the propaganda is just self service. That's a problem. And there are the outright liars and thieves. That's why we don't trust that parental position on a national level. Because that's the reality. In one form or the other, politicians fall into those basic categories, and that's sad.

Now, how to change this kind of world? It has to be real! It can't be just spiritual, okay? Otherwise God would have done it a long time ago. There's no exception. You might have a moment of reckoning, a final reckoning you might say, okay? But still in the end, it has to be done, and done the right way. And guess what? It has to be real. No hocus-pocus stuff! I'm sorry, but that's the only way to do it or it's not going to happen. How are we going to change the world when we can't even bring together people that we know, for a reason, for a cause, something, anything! That's just silly stuff. And I hate to say it, but I'm worried. Even if you have a vision, it has to be realistic, right? Just having a vision doesn't mean anything. It has to be implementable to be implemented. Otherwise it's useless. And what kind of influence do we have, and to what degree of persuasion, in terms of our belief and purpose? And based on it, how prepared are we to effectively deliver to the people that we're reaching out to? Where do we stand? We need to measure ourselves properly. If we don't know our limit, then we can't grow. Everything has to line up. There has to be proper alignment to achieve proper growth. You have to know your limit especially if we're undertaking this stuff. Aw man, we've got to know our limit! It better be packed, it better be perfect within the range that it operates if it's going to be worth anything. Otherwise, you're going to grow up mutated.

I started this because of my son, my dead son, nothing else. And I just got to know you, some of the faces. Now I know their names. That's about it. I'm here because I want to be here. It's a pain it the butt! That's about it, nothing else, and you know that.

All of you, in a way, you're politicians in the way you take care of your children, right? You make the law, right? You say to your kids, "As long as you live under my roof blah, blah, blah." So, from that kind of ordinary innocence, something good should come out of it, ay? That's about it. The only way that can happen is if you don't lose that innocence, no matter how 'snakish' you have to be just to survive, say? Because you have to be a snake to survive, right? You have to be a snake, a bigger snake than the next snake, so you eat that other snake! A lot of snakes eat other snakes, you know. They have to. But that's just survival stuff. As long as you believe in idealism and want to hold on to it, that's what you keep, something of original essence. It's going to take time to change the world, a long time. I don't know everything, but everything has original essence. That's what you hold on to as best as you can, because in the end you'll be judged. Judge me! See you next week.

Your Wish List
July 22, 2007

A thousand more of these and 20 years will pass, right? How are you doing? Sometimes I want to say certain things, but there are too many young people here so I have to kind of hold back. If you have a wish list, what is it? Do you have a wish list?

If you do have a wish list obviously you're going to need some kind of practical anchor or something for it. You've thought of some kind of practical anchor, something based in reality, because not every reality is our wish. Even a drunkard can say, "I wish for world peace." Is that world peace? That is not world peace. So, what is your wish list? And what is the practical reality that you're trying to anchor yourself to? Unless that is clear you're just going to be floating around, and you'll get lost at times. That has to be the kind of fundamental question that you always ask yourself, because if you don't others will do it for you. In the end you are responsible. People will say, "Hey, you have to be responsible for your consequences." That is the nature of responsibility.

You can talk about responsibility in religious terms, social terms, but there are always consequences and they can be severe at times. Nobody likes to go to jail right? Do you want to go to jail? Have you been to jail? [*Someone responds,*] *(Yes.)* Okay, good for you! Because it's a great experience? Now don't, don't—I shouldn't talk like this to you! So, what is your wish list? How many people here in this room have a father, have parents, who are considered by many in the world to be billionaires, have a lot of material wealth? How many people? Would you be here if your parents were like that? And what if that so-called materialistically well-off person is a religious leader, and a misunderstood one at that, still to this day? Because I know for a fact that there is a different law for you if you're a Moonie, and especially if you're Father's children, and that's reality.

So, what good is all that material stuff, and what does it represent? Who is Father to you? Who is Father to me? Let me ask myself that question. I don't like to talk about myself because it is inappropriate at this platform. Why? Because every give and take has a subject and object relationship and it should not be about me. That's why I don't talk about myself too much. Can I talk about myself? Oh heck, yeah! But it's inappropriate, it's not right, it doesn't serve the greater purpose, and that's what I'm trying to do. I'm here as a human being trying to give and take with another human being. And this platform calls for you being the subject, not me. That's about it.

There is proportion for every little thing in the world. Just look at your body. If it is not proportioned properly you are going to be retarded, mentally disturbed, sick or something. That's reality. You can have your wish list stretching out the wazoo, but there are certain things that you just can't do because of your practical circumstances, because of your reality. If you do not understand where you stand, you will never have your wish list, because your wishes will only come true based on where you stand, okay, knowing where you stand.

What the heck is your wish anyway? What do you want? To me, this life is jail to me. I just want it to go away. But you have to let it follow the natural course. In other words, follow what God has planned out for you, and do the best you can to make it work, and make it prosper. Make it better if you can, but that's very difficult. Everybody wants to be somebody, but how many people actually become somebody, even if you have talent?

So, let's talk about practical stuff about you, "What can I do as a parent?" There are a lot of young people here, you're going to be parents. You do practical stuff. You get educated so you can have a profession, so you can make a living. Having said that, and all that is good, but why do you do that? So, you can have a family and hopefully so that you can give something more than you had to your children. And then you will die. So, what do you want your children to be? I think that realistically speaking, we lack in practical reality in this church. I think that we should teach our children to become healers, to get into some kind of medical profession, something practically speaking, something to do with healing, something to do with making life better for mankind, something to do with inspiring mankind, and, most miserably, something to do with educating mankind. That's what we need. We need to give that kind of encouragement. We need that kind of reality. Otherwise there is no future for us.

How long did it take you to get to know Father? And how long did it take him to get to know you. I saw him at the start, because I'm a little older than my younger brothers. It was a miserable life. All day long, all day long, everyday, it never ends. The less that you have for yourself the better. That's how you impress people. That's how this church was built, his church. There's only one messiah. My Mother is not a messiah, she is the messiah's wife. None of my brothers and sisters can be the messiah, they're his children. And if there's an exception to the rule about what I explained earlier about using this platform to say "I", only one person has that distinction. I guess that's the prerogative of the messiah, no one else, no one else. Do you think that when my Father is dead and gone I can tell young people to go suffer for me? I don't think so.

What you're learning is a tradition. If you're going to keep on keeping on, you have to do the basic things correctly, no exception to the rule. That's why it's going to be a miserable life. Do you want that? I mean that is the greatest gamble that you can make with your life. And why not? If you make it, it can be the greatest thing. The more you get involved, you're going to get more miserable. Trust me. So, what is your wish list? What is your reality? What is your practical reality? You have to answer that stuff, nobody else. You! Why, because I've seen so many people betray Father, and say, "I'm the Father!" I hope that you make the right decision. Take care of yourself, okay.

The Parental Role
July 29, 2007

Hello. (*Good morning.*) Let me ask you a question—Do you need more money? Do you need more inspiration? Do you need more love? In which order? You want everything at the same time!

Let me start with something personal I guess. I came here to America in 1973. I'm not going to say the last name but Earl was a kind of funky kid. I was in a kind of period where things were changing in a dramatic way, with a lot of persecution, you know, and the only friend I had was this guy called Earl. He's the one, I think I was in seventh grade or something like that and we had lockers and stuff, and he actually brought a beer, and he brought a cigarette, and he brought a "Playboy" magazine to school. That was my first exposure to "Earl-ism", and I was like 14 or 15.

So, what I'm trying to get at is that these days you're worried about your kids, right? I've got kids. And today's world is a different world. Internet schooling is becoming more and more popular, because you can get a basic education via stuff like that through home schooling. Home schooling has certain limitations, but you have that option. And you then have to deal with the argument about how kids learn to relate to other people, about the social skill level stuff. That's where you have the church. So, when you have a kind of basic parental foundation you don't have to compete with that kind of stuff. You can literally take initiative and take control of your situation. You don't have to rely on someone else, because you can compete when you're ready. It takes time to get ready. Nobody is ready right from the start. That's too much to ask when you're not in control. And it is way, way beyond logic to expect your children, all of them, hopefully, ideally, to take care of themselves somehow. That's just unrealistic.

So, if you're supposed to be in control of something, you have to find appropriate measures. That is your responsibility, whether you like it or not. That's the parental role. If your children screw up, who are you going to blame? You're going to blame you, right? And because it's your children, society will blame you, and it is your responsibility. You ought to be the best and you've got to get involved. So, that's just about children. That is the essence of life isn't it, your life, your future, your everything when you're dead and gone. So, are we in control? You want money? How are we going to get money? How are you going to become useful to somebody in life, in general? Like I said, you know it is important that you become someone who can reciprocate to the rest of the world based on essence.

Do you know how to heal? Do you know how to make things better? There are all sorts of things, science, technology, and chemistry, whatever. There are so many things available. Do you know how to inspire? That's hard, and to educate? Joe Kinney here, he sends his email notes of what I say here to a lot of guys, I guess. I guess there are some members out there fighting the war in Iraq who read those notes. What do you think is important to them? Money? I don't think so. Maybe inspiration, maybe love. Coming home! It's that kind of basic stuff. If you don't address that stuff you don't build anything. You cannot increase if you don't strengthen the essence of stuff. It might be money, body, spirit and mind, something, but, it has to be something relevant to you at that moment otherwise there's nothing gained. It's sad, but true.

So, what's important to you? Everything right? You want the spirit mind and body aligned perfectly, right? The desire of the mind is more important than the desire of the body! The desire of the spirit is more important than the desire of the mind! That kind of stuff, right? Ultimately you want the spirit to line up somehow down to the body. I wish that upon you. And if I can help you, I'll help you as much as I can. If three hundred million Americans say, "I want ten thousand dollars", that adds up to three trillion dollars. But, you can't do things like that, right? Otherwise you'll go belly up very quickly, you're dead. Do I see you as a black person or do I see you as humanity? Do I see you as a white person or do I see you as humanity. Do I see you as Japanese or do I see you as humanity. It's that kind of stuff. That's what we need to revisit, and teach our children too. They can learn from us, from that point, from that fundamental aspect. If we don't do our job correctly, it isn't going to work. *[The sound of flatulence is heard in the room.]* Somebody is blasting off! No problem. It happens. Thank you, you made my day!

If you want that perfect alignment—spirit, mind, and body—don't ask somebody else, ask yourself, okay. Where are you? What is the most important thing to you? And don't blame it on anybody else. You answer that question first before you try to find a solution. You have to know your limit, otherwise expansion is futile. Ask yourself sincerely, "Where am I? What do I want?" and from that you start. Okay, see you later.

Whom Do You Want To Love Forever?
August 5, 2007

Do You Want To Love Forever?

Did you say garden and wife or God and wife? God and wife, okay that's a start. What else? Is there something else? *(Kids.)* What else? *(True Parents—the messiah.)* The messiah? *(Yourself.)* Myself? Yes, you can love yourself, you can try. You know people try that every day and they're trying very hard to make that work for the rest of their lives say.

(Parents.) Parents—that's a difficult one isn't it? But, where did you come from? So, we have to know exactly, at least the basics of who do you want to love forever. You have to talk about that stuff before you talk about anything else. So, you want to love God. You should love your parents forever. You want to love your wife. You want to love your children. Who else? *(Brothers and sisters.)* Brothers and sisters? Do you have people other than that kind of lineage orientation? *(Friends, all mankind.)* All mankind, okay, this is the stuff where people make money in religion!

Why do you want to love something forever? What's important in that kind of relationship? What makes it work? What do you expect out of that kind of relationship? And if you do, what makes it work? The Principle says that everything is of give-and-take, right? It says that it is reciprocal love that makes things, that makes love work. So how do you find that reciprocal love? How do you find it in a real situation? Not something in the conceptual realm or something beyond, but how do you find it in reality? When do you feel that reciprocation of love? When do you feel that somebody is giving something to you that you feel good about taking and you want to do that back to that person? So, how would you find that sincerity? How do you know it? Where do you find that trust? Because when you talk about sincerity, you have to go into trust.

How can you trust something? For it is them that you're supposedly reciprocating. So, from there you start. If you don't answer that stuff, if you can't answer that stuff, you can't start. So, what is your relationship to something that matters to you? I can't answer that for you. All I can say is that that's where you start. You have to find your own answers. Why? Because it's your life. Nobody else can live it for you, nobody can tell you how to live it. Because you live your own life, not me. I live mine, you live yours. That's it. It's as simple as that. And because of that absolute truth, when you ask the basic questions, when you're seeking an answer to make your life better, you start. That's about it, whether you like it or not. I don't care how old you are. It doesn't matter whether you're a teenager, whether you're middle-aged, or whether you're old. My Father wants to live to be 120, so be it. You answer that question, nobody else.

So, start asking questions about yourself and start seeking answers and start counting those I want to love forever, okay? Count them! Write it down if you have to, start with that. How can I make this better? The list may go on and on. Somebody said humanity, okay. I don't know humanity. I don't even know you, not all of you. I know some of you. It's up to you. So, what's going to make me better? What's going to make me and at what level? Eternal level, forever stuff? Okay, write the list. Make the list. And you answer to that, no one else. That's why you struggle, okay?

Peace, and happiness, okay we all want those. Yeah, that's why you go to movies, right? Sometimes it's something like that. But it takes a process to make things happen. Do you know how important alignment is to make your body perfect? It's important, it's a process. Something has to be true to be what you idealize. No matter how screwed up you are, you want that stuff. That stuff is very difficult to get, and it's not going to be given to you, okay? Trust me. Nobody can give it to you, not even God. So, where do you start? Answer that stuff, that basic stuff.

Whom do I want to love forever? If you want to be good, at least know that stuff, and that's where you start. I don't know how big or far you'll make your list, it's up to you. So, when you start, you'd better know what you're doing because you're going to die for it. True love has no choice. Selfish love has a choice. That's why you want to be a patriot, right? Those poor guys. There are members out there serving for America, for this country. Those guys, I wish them well. You have no choice in certain things. That's the irony right? The truth of love.

Okay, see you next week.

Judgment

August 12, 2007

How are you doing? Do you like to be judged? Do you want to be a judge? Some people try hard, they go to law school to try to be a judge. I guess that's something that means something to somebody in finality. But, how do you evaluate somebody's worth? I was talking to somebody the other day and I just came up with a line that I like. I will share it with you—"I'm cheap, no I'm dirt-cheap, no I'm free!"

Why do we need to judge? It's because we have a lot of questions. You seek an answer when there is no answer that you can otherwise accept or that you're hearing in terms of balancing extremes. You always have to deal with that. Life is about answering, trying to understand the extremes in whatever level you are at, in whatever it is that you do. It doesn't matter. So, when you're questioning yourself sometimes, if you don't have the answer and if you don't have the patience, you'll eventually answer it yourself. Whether you like it or not you just became a judge! Pretty much the free market thrives on this kind of mentality. So, that's why things shift in all sorts of unpredictable ways, because people are judging and you can make money out of their judging. Is that good or bad? Who knows? Do you like to be free? Well, that's your freedom.

But, what is the ideal world then? Is there some kind of design? Well, obviously that's what we're trying to figure out. Our whole life is about figuring that out. That's it, figuring that out. We spend every single second, if you're conscious, being about that. If that's what you want to know, every second of your life you'll spend trying to figure it out. And unless somebody can give you some kind of consistent inflow up and down, you're going to be judging, and many times you can make a bad judgment. That's a possibility.

It's not just about faith. It's about action too. It's not about the foundation of faith, it's about the foundation of substance. It's about action, demands, something like that. You need the answer so you can move on. Whether I have it or not, I need that answer. If I don't have it, I'm going to give it my own answer, that's about it. That's why we commit ourselves to things that sometimes we might regret later on. Why? Because you question things, I question things. You question things and you need an answer, and if there's no answer, you'll make your own judgment. In other words, I'll give myself my own answer, whether you like it or not.

Do you want to create an ideal world? Okay, then keep something moving forward. Make it flow. Make it flow and keep it moving. It doesn't always have to be big, just something so long as it becomes more and more and more meaningful. Meaningful in the end, it's not subjective stuff, it's objective stuff. It's how you, the audience, feel in the end. It's not what I say. To begin with I don't want to be here. It's not what I feel, it's what you feel. It's that kind of stuff that's more important. Why do you have kids? Why do you want a family? Because it's all about you? No, it's about something greater. Whatever you do, the judgments that you make, if you have to make judgments, it's not about you in the end. It's about something else, more than you, bigger than you, right?

Hopefully you want to be a superstar, right? Whatever, you want to be, be the best, because that's the kind of natural progress in understanding God. That's where you start. That's why you need that answer. But the world can be very confusing at times because it's messed up. You have questions, and hopefully you can find answers around you. But, just because you don't doesn't mean that the answer that you give yourself because of those circumstances, because of your predicament, is the only answer. Otherwise, you are truly the judge and that will kill you.

Judgment, yes you're going to be judged. That's what you do to yourself every day. If you want a more embracing, warmer kind of climate, then try to understand that there's the opposite too. Life is about control right, earning control, balancing the extremes. And you go step-by-step upward! Balance is just horizontal stuff. You are just levitating, that's about it figuratively speaking. You want to move up, if you want to do so then keep that in mind. Then you go to the next level, the next level, the next level. Wherever your consciousness is at it doesn't matter. I don't care, because that's irrelevant. It can be at zero and you're still a human being, okay? It could be at one hundred, a thousand, it doesn't matter, a million, who cares? When you move up, you move up because you know how to balance something, the extremes, in your own way. Even horizontally you can go far too, right? If you want to move up, that's how you do it. If you want to judge yourself, then judge yourself because you're the one who is going to give yourself the answer and say, "I can do this! And I did it." Who's that? That's you, not somebody else, not me, it's you. And that's what it is, that's how you move up.

There's a purpose for everything, so don't use things for stupid reasons. Know how one thing affects another, okay? Even if you want to heal something, you have to know how things are connected, right? It's just that. Focus on that stuff, not stupid stuff. If you want to change the world, then try to get to know what is real about God. I don't know who's providing that knowledge, but that's what I'm chasing too. That's the only way to do it. I believe that. We try. My reason is a little more personal so it might be a little different, but it's the same thing in the end. We want that stuff, all of us. It doesn't matter how you get there, how you come to that conclusion after trying. That's all we want in the end. That's the universality of it all. That's what love is. Love can bring every person under the sun to life, so try, okay?

Quality of Life
August 19, 2007

Good morning. *(Good morning.)*

Another day of the grind, just another day.

Today's topic is, "Quality of Life."

Can you give me some idea of what you think quality of life is to you?
[*No response*]
Oh, you have no quality of life? That's terrible! [Laughter] Okay.

I was watching TV the other day and there was a documentary about conservationism. I guess they summoned some economist and a geologist to estimate what it would cost for the clean water and clean air that we take for granted that nature gives us for free. Their conclusion was that humanity would have to cough-up annually about 30 trillion dollars for something that we take for granted. Because when we spoil these things, it's based on that kind of logic.

Obviously, something is trying to provide us with quality of life, even with the fundamental stuff, just your sustenance, the vital stuff that keeps your body working. So from there, what are you chasing? What is quality of life?

Let's say that you're locked up in a prison in a six foot by eight foot cell. It's much better for you to try to somehow get into a work program that you volunteer for. Let's say that you wash thousands of dishes every day, they'll pay you about two dollars a day. Because, based on laws, if they don't pay you, it's slave labor. So, you get paid about two dollars a day for doing that kind of stuff, washing toilets or mopping the floor, washing dishes, that kind of basic stuff. The most that you can get is about ten dollars per day being a nurse's aide or doing some clerical work for the bureaucrats.

But at least that's better than being locked up 23 hours per day in a six foot by eight foot cell, because if you're doing stuff, at least you have a purpose. When you have a purpose to life, the quality of life changes.

And where you find purpose, it's up to you. You can complain. I mean people complain when they're locked up. "I'm innocent!" Everybody's innocent right? "I shouldn't be here!" But if you choose to find a purpose your life can change, the quality of life can change, because you know that you're going to be stuck in there for X amount of time, and you know what you did wrong and what your sentence is.

The funny thing about jail is that if you're not sentenced, you don't even get paid. For instance, like if you're in jail for contempt of court, you don't get paid. But it's better to do something than not. That determines, when you're in that kind of miserable situation, even in the worst hell hole, that's hell on earth, living in places like that, if you have something, if you have some meaning, some purpose, it can change the quality of life, because you're going to do it whether you like it or not. You have no choice.

There's another thing that I believe is important. I took my kids down to Boston for a week. When I was young, all the entertainment that I had was just reading books, because in Korea when I was a kid, TV came on at five o'clock in the afternoon and went off at midnight. Right after the war Korea was poor and couldn't afford to broadcast stuff and spend so much energy and money needed to have 24-hour programming. What you got was just one cartoon every week. [*Laughs.*] I really looked forward to that.

What are you going to do? You read books. That's why I hate reading books, *(Laughter.)* because I read too many books when I was little. I read the same book over, and over, and over, again. In those fantasy books and stuff, all sorts of little story books, they depict something beautiful. It kind of sticks to you, something beautiful, because we all want something beautiful, something more, when they depict something like a beautiful beach, let's say I'm reading a pirate book or something.

Of course, you don't have the kind of white sandy beaches like you find in the Caribbean in Korea. Just going there, there are some beaches with very course sand. One time Father took a bunch of leaders to a place like Kang-Nung on the East coast of Korea and he took me with him. I still have that memory, and it's still wonderful to me. Because of that it doesn't matter what happens. It doesn't matter what the current situation might be, that's the quality of life for me, when it comes down to it. Based on the memory of Father and me. That's it.

And the more that you have it the better, right? The clock ticks forward, it doesn't tick backwards. It's done, it's history, it's a memory. Whatever you do. and moving on.

To me the greatest thing that can define the quality of life for me is how much love do I have, how much love can I give, and how much love can I get. That is the ultimate thing that will determine the quality of life for me. So, you ask yourself how much you can give, are you being loved by others. How much? God will judge you in the end. The thing is, don't waste time judging each other about that kind of silly stuff, but focus on what you can do.

The funny thing is when you're first growing up, when you're a little kids, just physically testing yourself, speed matters first right? You want to be a little Speedy Gonzales always racing each other around, literally speed wise, you know. Then you get into a little more of the, "I'm smarter than you" stuff to try to determine intellectual quality and try to measure each other and try to compete with each other.

I guess when boys get a little bit bigger they literally start to get AWWWW QUANTITY! *(Laughter.)* I have a bigger quantity than you! It's funny. And even girls too, "I have bigger quantity than you!" [*Gesturing toward chest and hips.*] *(Laughter.)* But all that is during the maturation process to the point of quote/unquote adulthood, it's like that. But when it gets to the point when you have to choose a profession, something that will give you sustenance in life, make a living, make money so you can live, it goes opposite.

You have to know how to deal with volume, you'd better have the highest quality possible, and you'd better do it in the fastest time possible. That's how you move up the ladder, whether you work in corporate, or whatever, in any competitive situation. That has to do with sustenance. It's all about sustenance isn't it? It's about making a living. When money is circulating, that's all it is.

When you retire, all that stuff doesn't matter except for one thing, quality, quality of life. And what the heck is that? What have you learned? Because what you take when you're dead is what you leave behind in goodness and what you learned. That's all that you take, doing good. Everything else is meaningless.

Once you get older and older you will start to feel that more every single day, because you know that time is ticking forward and you know that you're going to die anytime soon. So, what is life?

Make sure that you know what you're dying for. Make sure that you have a quality of life that you can be proud of, facing death, because you will die. And that's the lesson of this world, learning the quality of life. You make the answer. You make the answer, not somebody else, because everybody will be responsible for their answers, because your answer is who you are and you will die.

Choice? Yes, you have a choice, make a good answer. For yourself, not anybody else, start with yourself. Don't worry about other people, other people have the same worries like you. You want to help other people? Okay! I commend you for it. That's noble, but that's very difficult.

At least be sure what you're dying for first, before you try to help somebody else. Be sure, absolutely sure. Otherwise it's just a game you're playing. And if you think that life is just a game, well, okay, that's your opinion. But I think that it's a little more serious than that, because you will die, and you have one life to live.

When you're young you think you can play around, hey so be it, but in the end, you've got one life, that's all you have. You want to play with it? So, play with it, it's up to you.

It's a pain in the butt process, learning what's right, when there's so much crap out there that is luring you, dragging you, and pulling you from here to there to whatever, all over the place. I'm sure that you face that stuff each and every day and that you feel that pressure, but it is not a game. Okay?

You make that call, and you make that answer, and you're going to stand by it because no one else will. That's it. How many people do you think would be willing to do the time for you that you deserve? How many people do you know around you who will do that for you? Even if you have people like that, still in the end, you'll stand alone in final judgment.

The quality of life, what is it to you? Think about it.

Okay, I'll see you next week. [*taps podium twice*]

Change
August 26, 2007

Good morning. *(Good morning.)*

How are you doing, okay?

We all know that changes are in the future, right? If anything is going to change, it's going to happen in the future. Is all change good? Is it all just good? Sometimes changes can be bad. So, how can we determine the change to be the change that we want? How do you go about achieving that? What's the kind of change that you want? What is an ideal change?

Do you have a relationship with God? You do? You talk to Him every day? Really?! Okay, that's your opinion. We all have opinions. You can believe whatever you want to believe. This is America, right?!

Do you idolize something, idealize something, and does that have something to do with God and humanity? Or is it personal? Can you make something that is ideal personal? And if you can, and if that is doable, then how do you go about achieving that? What has to happen to make ideal personal? What do you have to be to actually achieve that? Because when you talk about ideal, in a way you have to talk about the relationship between God and humanity. It's God and humanity. Even when you talk with the little information that there is about Jesus, he is a representation of humanity, it is the relationship between God and humanity through our representation, a single representation. And obviously his course was tragic. And through that something was manifested called Christianity.

What is Christianity? There are so many versions of Christianity. There are many denominations, close to 500 and growing every day. They each have a different interpretation of that single person who represented the relationship between God and humanity. So, when you idolize something and you try to make it personal, you have to know where you stand. Why do you want to make it personal? Because only then can I have some kind of give and take that I can feel, that can give me some kind of satisfaction or something! And why do you want that kind of satisfaction with the relationship between God and humanity? Change, change for the better.

You know, the first thing that goes against change is arrogance, right? There are so many experts out there that say, "I know everything about this, and unless you pass me, you aren't going anywhere, whatever you think you have." And there's another opposite group of people, the insecure defeatists, doomsday-sayers, the naysayers. And then there are people in the middle, the skeptics and cynics who say, "I don't trust you." Trust is a very difficult thing for the cynics and skeptics. Why? Because they say look at history. And that's all they need to say as they go down the list, blah, blah, blah, blah, blah. And then they say, "Who the heck are you?" And how are you going to prove anything to them? It takes time to prove something. Right off the bat you have that kind of challenge.

Change is difficult just because of the way we think and where we are in reality. I mean you have to deal with all that stuff. I mean you can separate them into all sorts of other levels, but basically that's what you have to deal with in order to make change real. You can talk about change, but first of all you have to go up against that hurdle. How do you do that? How do you convince those people? How do you convince the so-called experts, the arrogant people who say, "I know everything in this field, so unless you prove to me that you know better than I do, I'm not going to move. I'm staying here, this is my authority." And you go to those people who are absolutely insecure and who respond, "No! It isn't going to happen, it isn't going to happen, it isn't going to happen. Just living with my neighbors, no it isn't going to happen!"

So, what is the ideal? What is the ideal relationship between God and mankind? What does God want from us? Do you feel His love? Really? It's a concept isn't it? Okay, everybody feels the same? No? That's a problem! The ideal relationship is love. And how do you teach somebody that stuff? How do you learn about that kind of stuff? How do you have the kind of feeling that you have, and that others can have as well? How do you do that? You have to be honest. And you have to try to be as transparent as you can possibly be. Even if it means that you have to be vulnerable, so be it. So, what you see is what you get, nothing else, that's it. And from there you can start. If anything is going to change, it's going to start with a very simple goodness. That's about it. That we all know, but many times we don't practice because of all sorts of reasons.

You can find your own thing living in this pretentious world. You can pretend and try to take as much as you can when the opportunity arises, right? That's the way, right? That's the way of capitalism, isn't it? You gamble with your life in that way. And it's a short life. But, what do you want to change? How long do you think it's going to take to change the world? We haven't even found the proper communication, proper ways to communicate with other religions that are warring in the name of God. That's a big homework isn't it? And it's a very important one because it affects everybody. What good is freedom when you live in terror? What's the point? And how do you go about addressing that issue? It has to start from very, very basic things. You have to address those. If you can't, there's no way you're going to change the world. I want to change too. All my life, I always expect things to change for the better, because it was promised to me. I'm still waiting. Most likely, I'll die for it. That's pretty much what I see, the price that I have to pay for the change. So be it. And it's not just me, you too. As long as you are here, that's the price you pay.

So, what can I do now? You tell me. You want an ideal relationship with God, you want to learn about the greatest love, the eternal love, all the blessing and joy and happiness, everything that was promised, everything that is ideal that you can fantasize about. I want that. I want that with God. I want it forever because that's where forever comes from. Because I want that forever, I need to make that relationship with God. So be it.

How do you go about starting that relationship? What are you going to do? What is your first step? What is your second step? What is your third step? The first step is understanding basic vows. That's about it. The promises that were made, you have to understand that step then go to the next one. What is the next one, after the basic vows? It's your blessing. Make the blessing work. And what is the final step? And I'm simplifying things. You give your life for it. And I'll do my best as I learn these things. I'll do my best to help you so that I can help myself achieve that ultimate end, that I'll give my life for. Judgment? People die every day, people are born every day, right?

So, that's how you change the world, knowing the absolute basic stuff. First of all it's necessary, you have to live it, and I try to live it. That's the pain in the butt part, because it lasts your whole life. What else can I say? Life sucks! But it can be good, it's just the way that you look at things. It varies in different days. Okay? All right, take care.

Power

September 2, 2007

Good morning. *(Good morning.)*

What is your definition of, "Power?" Who do you think is powerful? What is power good for? Lawmakers, they're powerful, right, generally speaking, in their idiopathic way? Do you think that they can be changed simply?

How does one become, let's say, a U.S. Senator or a member of the House of Representatives? They have their own history and they know it. They are aware of every step of the way that they struggled to get to that position of power. When you try to assert yourself, you do that because you're basically saying, "I'm here." That's what power is. Right? "I'm here, I exist, and this is me. What do you want to mess with me for?" Basically that's how it starts.

So, how do you change somebody who knows exactly how well he has earned the power to become a member of the House of Representatives or a U.S. Senator? And how do you change them? What kind of greater power do you need to transform those people? Is there such a thing? Do we possess such a thing? If there is such a thing, then how do you possess it? Where does it lie? What is it? It can't be a miracle. Right? It has to be real.

So, where is the true power? When God blew Himself up and started this creation process, only He has that ability to divide Himself and literally create a counter-action, a counter-part, with whom He can reciprocate and start the creation process. We're just a by-product of that divine ability. We think that we have that ability, but I'd love to see it. If you think you have it, then blow yourself up and start creating your own universe!

But we do try in our own head, and starting with our head, I don't know how tangible it can become in the end, and actually make matters different, but you try. People do that all the time. That's why there are mental hospitals, and a lot of drug companies that make a lot of money treating those people, and all sorts of stuff. So, having said that, how do you change those people? How do you change those people who think that they are powerful? They know exactly what they want to do, they know who they're catering to.

I have my faith. We all have faith. Right? Especially, in America, you have to have faith, you've got to have some kind of religious affiliation. And how do you change those religious people? When people come, they come because they think they can be helped, whatever their agenda might be, because they think you have money, access to money. When I went to Africa, I saw a lot of incumbent African politicians that were attending the tour. Their assessment is based on whatever we have projected to them, and it looks impressive to them because this is America.

A whole lot of stuff went into America. What do you think that whole lot of stuff was? A lot of sacrifices from a lot of people. But ultimately in the end, what did you build? What do we have to show for it? And still to this day, with the symbolisms that we have, how do we keep it running? Can we maintain it ourselves individually, self-sufficiently? You tell me. You should know as much as I.

That's as far as it goes. And that's what they're looking at when you're in Africa. Not in America. Because all those people in Africa want to be president too, if they're just a member of Parliament. That's about it. There is no other connection, that's the problem. And how do you make any connection real? How did those people become elected to begin with anyway? It's because of people like you, the voters. That's where the power is. The voters have delegated the power to those people in democracy. Right? People's power was delegated to those people to represent them because they need that kind of representation. People need representation to make their lives greater so that they can focus on an individual level and take care of themselves. And by delegating the responsibility to those representatives, hopefully, ideally, people expect that they are going to make their individual lives better. Because we all struggle to find ourselves, at a certain point in time we choose that representation to expedite the process because it's necessary. Why? Because we all want to be happy.

Power is not there to be abused. "Arrrgh, I'm going to use this power to punish you." It's not there for revenge. Power is there for what? Making love greater. And when you think about love, what is love? The definition of love can be myriads of things that bring you closer, that bring you happiness in the eyes of God. Right? That's the thing. You can be happy with all sorts of sick stuff, but that's not where power needs to be.

Sometimes you know, sometimes you have to kind of reserve your own power, because there will be a time, individually speaking, when, "Hey, I'm going to feel helpless one day, someday. I'm going to feel powerless one day. I'm going to feel sick and tired of this stuff someday. I can't take it anymore. I'm too tired." If you think that you are powerful then sometimes reserve something for yourself, because you need that stuff. Nobody, nobody is that perfect. Power just gives you a flash like the light of a firefly. It is just there to remind you of your existence in times of nothingness. And if you abuse it, you're an idiot because you're not that powerful. You don't shine that bright like the sun. You made that stuff? You think you can? Okay, then go do it!

I believe that the thing that can bring people together, and inform people together, and create communication, create the kind of basis in which there can be human give-and-take in real time, if there is such a medium, that is the thing, that is the kind of powerful thing that can bring change, change to us all individually. And that's what we need to focus on. Because we need to change ourselves all over the place.

Okay, I'll be out of the country for a while. Why? Because I'm in the process of making a movie and I have started casting so I have to be elsewhere. You've got to start somewhere, right? You've got to start doing to get there. But to me sound, sight, and words are important. It takes time. So, I'll be away for a while.

I'll see you when I get back. All right, take care.

Tradition
October 7, 2007

How are you doing? I feel a little restless, a lot of routine. So, how have you been doing? Hanging in there? Let's talk about, "Tradition."

These days we have a lot more church holidays than we used to have, right? It's almost like every week there's some ceremonial days, right? Is that good? Does it make you feel better? What does tradition give you, what kind of feeling does it give you? What do you do with tradition and what happens to you when you face tradition? What goes through your mind? "Today it's this celebration, on this day we're celebrating or 'ceremonializing' something" What does that mean to you? And you want that every day? So, every day should be a ceremonial day! We have to find some kind of ceremonial topic to celebrate 365 days a year! When are we going to work when we're always celebrating? I mean it's all good, it's just that give-and-take stuff I guess. That's what these celebrations are trying to emphasize, I guess, to symbolically try to teach us.

When we celebrate something, we take something, right? And we have to give. That's about it, isn't it? How does one celebrate something? How does one make something that is important into a tradition? How does something become a tradition? Let's say that you're Japanese and that you're proud of something. You like a certain tradition. Why do you like that tradition and why do you think that tradition is important? Because it gives you pride. It gives you pride in something, whatever you identify with, whatever it means. Without pride you can't have tradition. So, how does one become proud of something? So, how do you inspire pride, how do you go about achieving pride? It's inspiration, and then there's the degree of it. But, before pride there has to be some kind of provocation. And what inspires us to go to the next phase? How do we feel that something, "Hey! I want to be part of that stuff!" Of course, it can be good and bad. It depends on where your head is at. But if it's going to last, it should be good. That's safe to say because we're good people in the end, everybody. We can make bad choices because of the problems that we face, as we know, but we're all good in the end. We want to be good, and we want to inspire each other in goodness.

So, what is good inspiration? What is the inspiration that makes us better? We have to know the basic things that give us our quality as a human being that I can say, "This is me!" This is my innocence, this is my truth, this is my humility, this is my sacrifice, this is my offering to you God, because all of us have to do that. Some people will inspire you a little more than others. There'll be fluctuations, but that's life. That's how we grow and that is the way. You want absolute, then that is the way. You want a way to make everyone good, that is the way. So, that's how you try. It doesn't matter what you have left. You will grow. Children can bother you when they're crawling around, and then they grow up and start to complain and give you a hard time and try to overcome you, and try to ride on your shoulder. Especially in the secular world, after a child reaches 18 years old that's basically it, you know, good riddance. Are you having a jolly good time, little there [*to a 6-year-old boy sitting in the front row*]?

We need to make more good traditions. We have a lot of traditions, but if we want to compete and win, we need good traditions, more good traditions, more new good traditions. Why? Because without them you can't build a culture. You can't build a society. We need to have that stuff. We need to be strong. Without that kind of pride and tradition, you can't be strong. Unfortunately the physical world is a physical world. We need to face it as it is and that's what we have to do. We need to focus on those things, that's what's important. Unfortunately, a lot of stuff that church has done in the past was done in cash. And a lot of people are no-good fallen people. They try to stay in certain positions for that reason. Before the eyes of Father they speak well, but in the end they have nothing. Why? Because it's just about that. It takes basic stuff to make you good at anything, and it takes time and it takes a whole lot of stuff just to be good at one thing. And who are you kidding? I know my Father's urgency, but that does not give people the right to do the things that some people do. That's wrong and because of it we'll suffer in the end. There are always the consequences. You will suffer.

Tradition, what kind of tradition do you think that we need to create? A new tradition that can change, little-by-little, the world. Okay? What is that thing that can change the world a little bit starting from you, your friends, your work place, whatever. That little change, what is that little change that you can make? That's what you need to focus on, because that's something that you can do. We have to do it. You can't just allow somebody to make a lot of noise and talk and talk. No, that's wrong. What can you do? What kind of tradition can you make that is good? Think about it. And if you're part of a certain group then talk about it. Talk to each other. If you're on a fundraising team or a witnessing team, talk about it. You're not going to be there forever, right? You have to do something. Just try to think in a way that makes sense to you in reality. Okay? But it will grow that way, it should! And that's how you're going to get bigger, and better. And you will die.

It's good to see you. Everything is going okay, I'll tell you later. I don't like to talk too much about stuff until it's done. Anyway, if it's done right you can see it for yourself. See you next week.

Time

October 14, 2007

Good morning, *(Good morning.)*

On my last trip to Korea I went and met somebody, somebody that I really didn't like. I have my reasons, but I am not going to get into it for you. But I really did not like this guy. He is in every sense of the word, 'snake-ish,' that's about it. But he is struggling with malignant cancer, so I went to see him. And I told him, "Hey, just drop it all." And he was repenting and was trying to say a lot of stuff. But I told him, "You don't need to say anything. Let's just end it here, forget it and move on, and I will do my best to find more courage in me to forgive you."

When you think about time, how long do you think you're going to live, 100 years? Are you going to live 100 years, 120, 200? We all know that most people spend two-thirds of their life doing something other than work, right? Most people sleep seven or eight hours a day, right? One third gone like that! You go from point A to point B, and that kind of stuff, waiting, hygiene, eating, gossip, whatever, taking care of business, whatever, studying, and then gone! Even if you live 100 years, you've got about 30 years to work to try to do something.

What are you going to do? Why is the concept of time so relevant to us? It is literally held to our head like a loaded gun. And we're supposed to learn about eternity, right? Love, eternal love. How do you take something that has no time constraint and put it into the frame of time? That is the greatest paradox, isn't it? So, when you think about love, what do you think about? What do you want, something that lasts forever? What is that basic stuff? To me time is about studying. It's about going to a class. Okay, whatever 101 will start at 9:30 and it will end at 10:30. It's that stuff. Time is about learning something, it's about study. That's about it. And what are you studying? As I grew older that's what I felt. The moment that I said, "Let's forget about this" when I met that guy, I realized, "Why the hell did I hold all this hatred if this was inevitable?" Without the concept of time I would not feel what I had felt, the learning that I felt in my heart. It wouldn't be something to me, it would just be a concept that would go in one ear and come out the other ear. But I felt it. Some things God wants you to feel, that's why you have time. Because it's important to feel something, and that feeling should last forever. Why, because that's the basis of what you are, what we are, what God is. And from that we can grow forever. Nobody wants to study forever! I want to enjoy myself for a million years. But, okay, I'll go to school for the next thousand years, okay two million years. I promise.

We all have somebody to connect to. And you find that somebody to love, you should pay attention to those moments. There are some things, in the end, that will be inevitable whether you like it or not, things that you must learn. I know that you don't have time, but take time, take it easy. Some things are inevitable, don't rush.

We have to learn. We're learning. Life is about learning. It's short, thank God! He just wants us to learn about the basics. The basics, if you can give, if you can take, if you can love, if you can forgive. Basic things, there are things that are inevitable whether you like it or not, you will learn before you die. And if you do, you are the fortunate one. Time, yes, it seems long sometimes, especially when you're miserable, and of course in the opposite case it's too short. Life itself is too short, and it's about learning the basics. You've got plenty of time, cause that's what I believe. Life is way too short for me here. A lot of stuff is happening, but who cares? I'm going to leave it behind. That's about it. No matter how much you build, no matter how much you do, take that time, make that moment count when you feel something.

I know some guys here wanted to be missionaries for the rest of their lives. You know that's beautiful. Giving is better than taking. We all know that. We'll try. And I will be graded, just like you. Okay, take care.

Communication
October 21, 2007

Today's topic is communication.

I need a haircut, right? It looks like I'm wearing a helmet!

Did your parents read you stories when you were young to put you asleep? Did you have that experience? If you did, was that important to you? What if the opposite happens?

[*Pointing toward a brother*] Hey man! Do what you got to do! Make the best with what you got—do what's right.

And I'm known for making short statements, but sometimes when you're a little kid, when your daddy or your mommy reads you a story, that's important to you. Why? It is nurturing. That's the way we grow in body, mind, and spirit. What a parent is saying might not mean anything, might not be significant, but just the action in itself, that adds the value that can guide a child into the direction that ultimately any parent would want the child to go.

You know, you kind of have to look at communication in a spherical way. What I mean is that you have a forward and backwards, you have to have some kind of historical background and tradition and think about putting emphasis on that, and future thinking, outward thinking, and balancing the left and right, whatever. On a reality level, for lack of a better term, liberalism and conservatism, and up and down, God and selfishness. You have to build from there, and as you try hopefully the sphere gets bigger, as you blow more air into a balloon, so to speak. Love is elastic, so it's like the balloon that doesn't pop. Although it has boundaries, it will expand and it shouldn't pop. It won't pop, theoretically.

The most difficult thing for me is being humble. I always jokingly say. "A humble man is nobody other than a person who knows how to keep his arrogance to himself." It's very difficult. The things that make the vertical work are things that are basic: humility, self-sacrifice, unselfishness, love, forgiveness, compassion, all that goody-goody-two-shoes stuff. But those things are very difficult to achieve unless you can control the forwards and backwards, left and right and balance them.

You know there's a fine line in everything, even in the extremes, right? What about righteousness? The opposite is self-righteousness. What is the fine line that divides those two? When you destroy, "destroy" is a very strong word, but I'm going to use it anyway, the union of the blood, that's self-righteousness. Loyalty is important too. Sometimes, even if you can't deal with yourself in the moment, at least you may have the sense to walk away, right? I'm a good fighter, and when I see some jackass and he's provoking a fight, I can kick his butt or I can walk away. Now that's difficult. Walking away is difficult. Humility is difficult. I know that I can be very arrogant. I know that I can be very self-serving. If you do that long enough, you get greedy. I've seen that happen many times. But that's reality. That's what we face every day. You see people, good people, go down because of that kind of stuff because they allow themselves to let something get the best of them. And what is that something? That's what we need to communicate about to each other.

You can't live alone, right? No matter how smart you are. God doesn't want to be alone, right? So, let's just end it there. You don't want to be alone. So, you need to communicate. That's why we form a group, that's why family is important. That's the building block of a greater society, right? Tribe, society, nation, world, right? So, if we want to establish an ideal kingdom of God on earth, basic sense has to be met. And you have to know what the hell the basic is and then communicate, have give and take.

Look, love and forgiveness are an opposite aren't they? That's give and take isn't it? Why? Because when you forgive somebody, you will receive greater love. You will take greater love. Take sounds strong, but basically that's what it is. That's why we forgive, because we will take greater love because we will in turn receive love from something greater than ourselves, or even from each other, even from peers, even from your friends. Just because you know how to forgive, friends might think of you a little more differently. Even in a group they'll think that you're a little more special than everybody that they know. Now that's something, isn't it? That's called growth, and that's what matters. Nothing else matters more than that.

Ultimately, you want to communicate with God. How many people talk to God regularly? Oh, please don't raise your hand because I'm going to chop it off! At least, be in control of yourself. And give the best you got to the ones that you love, the ones that you care about. Start from there. Think about the future, think about the past, think about the left and right, think about God and your selfishness, and give. If you've got something to say, say it. Share it. And make that little balloon grow, and make sure it's true.

Let God judge, Okay? Let Him do the judging. You don't want to get into that mess. Do what's right. Do the best you can. Do that first, and don't even think about anything else. Let God do the judging when you die! So, speak the truth from your heart, because when you do that you'll die for it. Because the heart lives on, right? Spirit lives on, you die. Your arrogant ass will die! And let's all be judged by God. Okay? It's all equal there. You can forgive somebody, but still there's a judgment for that person. You know what I'm saying? So, I did my best. I tried to learn what is right. So, I'm all yours. Do what you want. Isn't that what it is? Isn't that the Christian belief? Isn't that the essence of religion? You fear God, right? But no man, right? Okay, I'll see you next week.

Hope
October 28, 2007

Good morning. *(Good morning.)*

Is everything okay with you?

Hey, long time no see, good to see you. [*Hyo Jin Nim recognizes one brother.*]

Do you have hope? Hope in yourself? Hope in humanity? Hope in the future? I guess hope means something that's going to be better. Right? For all of us, right, for all of us, not just me. Because hope has a greater range than just self-awareness or self-existence. Okay.

There are a lot of dooms-sayers you know, apocalyptic stuff that they propound to a religious community and that's based on revelations and stuff. It's based on a dream-state kind of babbling. Because what you see is what you get. That's what you see.

When we can see something, we can change it. That's the nature of mankind. That separates us from any other creatures in creation. If we can recognize something, in absolute terms, we can change it because we have that control. That is the greatest blessing. We have that control of that absolute as if we are a divine creator. So, when it's absolutely, undeniably obvious, in-your-face, everybody wants to be good, for not everybody wants to be bad. Put the principle words "original mind" aside. People want to be good in the end. How can you deny yourself the ability to change, the opportunity to be better, the blessing that you can have when you know that this kind of stuff is in your face? Of course you can see the horrible atrocities that people can commit on each other in a maximum range. In terms of degree, it's maximum. You can't go beyond this, you can't do more evil. Men can't do more evil to each other and it's apparent, you see it every day on television and stuff, the internet or whatever. Thank God for multimedia. Right? But, once we can recognize our wrong, that's when we can truly change. You have to truly understand your wrong to truly change.

So, why do you have hope? I see hope in my youngest kid. He's a bug, you know, because he's little and just slithers around on his belly all over the place. It's a bug. To me it's a bug. It's not human yet! And the little bug will turn into a monkey and then start to somehow turn into a human someday!! Well, he is a little bug and so independent. If I drop dead tomorrow, he's going to make it. So, that's hope for me. That's not to say that I plan on dying tomorrow. I want to see that little kid grow up and see him make little bambinos. I want to see it. You never know. That is what I wish. You take it as it comes. But that's a hope for me. And you go to a third-world country, and just any little thing that you give to a poor child, you see that face light up. That's a hope right there. You can do a ton of that stuff.

Many times it's the subjectivity that we all have that clouds us about the visions of tomorrow. Why do you want to take something that is so cloudy and dark when you can also choose the opposite? You make that choice. That's the problem. You're subjective. Individual responsibility means that you have to make decisions sometimes, and sometimes the decisions that you make can screw you up.

Why? Because a decision starts something, it starts the wrong cycle of stupid thinking. And who are you going to fault for what you have done? You can't fault anyone other than yourself in the end. So, even when you seek objectivity, you can't always just be objective. You have to have some kind of center and finding that stuff is difficult. How do you balance your subjectivity and your objectivity in balance and have that center. Because you know it's that stuff you will feel up, you will feel subjective, you will feel objective. You will naturally have that kind of rhythm.

But how do you balance that stuff? Sometimes you force it, sure. But beyond that point, even without you knowing you have that natural rhythm, how do you balance it? That's why you have to find that center. I don't know what your limitations are. I don't because everybody has limitations. You have to know your own limit. You have to figure it out. Otherwise. you're not going to be anything because you're trying to get something beyond what you can provide for yourself. That's why understanding your basic limitations, yourself, is much more important than anything else, and before you do anything else. Otherwise, how can you help somebody? Even trying to better yourself, you have to know your limit so you can choose the proper stuff for yourself. Right? You don't want to be a rock star do you? Maybe some people do, some people have that kind of desire. But not everybody can be that. Choose your stuff. In order to choose your stuff, you have to know your limit. Just because it looks good, sounds good, that does not mean it is for you. See your limit, you're responsible for it. Know your limit, you're responsible for it. That's individual responsibility. From there, you start. From there you can nurture yourself to grow. You mature, and ultimately grow into perfection, and become something that is you. And we need a lot of stuff like that to make a great, greater society.

When you look at America, this is the greatest nation. But basically people want stability, security, and continuity. And you think America is an ideal world? You think it can provide that, the basic stuff the citizens demand, forever? I don't think so. It will change. It has to change. Obviously it's not perfect, to say the least. Okay? It will change. It has to change. But that's what people basically want in civilization. And you want to create an ideal civilization? So, how do you go about achieving that? You have to look at yourself individually. And you have to know your limitations. You know what I'm saying. You have to first know your limitations before you start demanding stuff from others. That's the most important thing. When we can do that, when we can control ourselves to that degree, yes, there's hope for humanity. If I can start to do that, starting from me, there's a hope in me. And if that can be synchronized, then there's a hope for whatever that is greater. Okay? Hope. You build it! That fate is in our hands, our fate. You build it, nobody else. Don't pray to God, you build it. God is showing you the way, you build it, and then don't blame anyone else. Okay?

Hey! We have hope! We can do it! Just take it easy. Be patient. Take it step-by-step. You don't need to hurry. You aren't going anywhere. We're trapped on this little marble until it changes for the better. Don't get ahead of yourself. Pace yourself, look at others. Okay? Because we all have to do that to change the world, not just me. Okay, so pace yourself. Yeah, I'm sharing my personal kind of stuff, learning and whatever, personal realization, observation. But God, through my Parents, gave birth to me so you don't get credit for just anything. If I did something for you, you don't want to do that stuff. Some things you just want to walk away from. You have to know how to do that. It's not yours. Don't be selfish. Because it's so easy to be selfish isn't it? You aren't going to make it to the top taking the easy way out, right?

So, take care of yourselves and I'll see you next week.

Conditions
November 4, 2007

Good morning. *(Good morning.)*

All of us at anytime are on some kind of condition, right? I want to go on a diet, I'm going to lose 100 pounds, whatever. I'm going to do this, I'm going to do that. Try to make a condition, because a condition represents something that you want to change that will come in the future, something that will bring change. And how do you go about achieving that condition? What normally has to happen? Obviously you have to have a goal, right? You have to know what you're aiming for, you have to have direction. So based on that, you make a condition, and obviously what follows that is your commitment, and ultimately your action. Maybe you need to improve your grades so you go on a condition and you make a commitment to study a little longer. If you study maybe one hour per week, then you jack it up to maybe 100 hours or something so you can improve your grades. Well, that can physically happen, but how do you change something that is beyond you? How do you change the Spirit World? How do you go about changing something based on a condition that you can make to make a difference?

What do you call that big lotto stuff with millions, hundreds of millions of dollars to be won? Let's say that there is a lottery jackpot of 300 million dollars, and you're going to pray, you're going to make a condition that you'll pray every day to God so you can win that lottery. Do you think that's a good condition? Conditions only have to be about something that's centered on love, and if it's that, then it's not for you, it's for somebody else.

Through my wife, I heard about a person that was struggling because she joined the church but her little sisters didn't. And she was struggling because her little teenage sisters were doing stuff that she was concerned about. And I told her, "Hey, if they go down that path at that age there's nothing you can do to stop them from doing what they're doing except locking them up. If locking them up is unrealistic then obviously you have no control. I know that you feel powerless, but you want to do something." And then I saw her trying to make some kind of condition. I saw her praying in the wee hours of the morning, praying for something. That may have some kind of effect, rather than just praying for yourself to be better, because to God love is first before yourself, right? Yes.

In setting conditions, that's what you have to think about. What kind of condition am I making, why do I need this condition, what am I looking for, and what do I expect? I know that you expect something anytime you make some kind of condition. You go pray at the Holy Rock, to make a condition and you're going to pray for 120 days because you want the world to change. Do you think the world will change just because you want it? That's overly inflated in your head. You've got to know your limits. You have to know that. Don't be that godly all of a sudden and expect stuff to change just because you made a condition. That's nonsense! If that happens, let's all go to Sin City, Las Vegas, and pray for God to allow all the gamblers to win and to make Sin City into Bankrupt City. Then that city would change because they'd have no more money. You can't pray for things like that. Wouldn't it be nice if some aliens, we all like alien stuff, would land on the White House lawn and say, "Hey, listen to me Bush, otherwise I'm going to make you into a burning bush!" Or if a UFO would land in the Kremlin and say, "Hey! I'm going to put Putin in the pudding. Let's put that Putin into the galactic oven and make him into a nice pudding, and eat him!" I'm sure the world would change. Well, that kind of magic is not going to happen.

So, in conditions you have to ask yourself why do we make conditions. Because we want to connect to the heart of something. That's about it. We want to make that heart connection to something. That's why we make conditions. It can be to connect to money, to intellect, to spirit. But ultimately in the end, it is to whatever is highest, is the highest. That's the bottom line and that's what you want to connect to. That's why you make conditions. Because you want to be something, you want to be somebody. And if you want to learn about anything, you have to make conditions. "I'm going to learn this stuff, and until I learn it I'm not going to quit!" You make that commitment and you put it into action and until it's done you don't quit. You make that condition work for you.

And what are you connecting to? You answer that, no one else. Ultimately, I know that it has to be about controlling the body, the mind, and the spirit. That's how you grow. And whatever connection that you're making, that's your problem. However old you are, whatever, that sets your level. Accept that. Except note that you're trying to make progress in body, mind and spirit. And you want to make that connection because you want to know, you want to be better, you want to grow. And only you know when the condition is done. Only you know, no one else. Because only then will you move on to the next level, and you will feel good about moving on to it, to the next level, because it's a natural process, it's a natural process. You complete something, you go to the next, for your betterment. Your betterment, only you know. Your perfection, only you know. Whatever it is, it doesn't matter, only you know. Try. Try to listen to yourself, your inner voice, because arrogance will kill you. If you want something of love, how can you be arrogant? Okay, I know you make conditions every day, but make sure it's from your heart, it's of love. Otherwise, don't even call it a condition.

Okay, see you later.

Having Faith to Fate
November 18, 2007

Good morning. *(Good morning.)*

Today's topic is having faith to fate. Do you believe in fate? According to the dictionary, I guess, fate means a prophetic declaration, or something like that. Do you have some kind of inspired thing about yourself that you're willing to die for? Do you have it? If not, then you have no fate, because that's the definition, that's the standard. We try to understand who we are. We try to understand our limitations, and that's important, because that's when we can grow. Truly knowing your limitations defines the expansion that you're willing to make, to make sense and to make something in the end, to make something substantial in the end. Otherwise, it's all just foolish nonsense, it's just a dream.

A lot of people end up in jail because they had foolish dreams. I saw many people in jail because they really never clearly understood who they were, their limitations. That's why they ended up in jail, making all sorts of crazy and nonsensical sense of themselves that they can never measure up to. But they kept on pushing it for whatever reason, whether due to peer pressure, or it can be out of lust or greed or something. Things like that are always out there, and that's why such folks keep on pushing themselves to some nonsensical sense of themselves. They crash and burn. And you can't blame anybody else when you do that to yourself.

So, you have to think about your fate, you have to believe in your fate. You have it because you're children of God. So, you have something to offer, to bring to the table, to bring it all to the pool beyond race and nationality. Fate, think about your fate. What is your destiny? What is your prophetic declaration? It starts from understanding your limit, expanding it, one step at a time. And you should be checking whether it works or not for you. You know what I'm saying? You should be monitoring that stuff because when you say that you're an adult, pretty much that is your responsibility to do, right? There's not somebody always looking over your shoulder, tapping you on the shoulder and saying, "No, no, no that's not right, do it this way." You're not going to have that all the time. That's the problem. That's why take it easy, even if you want to rush forward pull yourself back. Know your limit first. Knowing your limit means knowing whether you can be effective or not in pursuit of something that you want to achieve, that you can actually accomplish, because without it, nothing means anything in the end. If you set out to build something yourself and you build nothing, and then you say, "Hey, do you see what I see?" No, I don't see it because there's nothing there. You know the story of the Emperor Has No Clothes, it's that kind of stuff. There are all sorts of fables like that. Unfortunately, if that's how it is then it's not just me that's going to see it, it has to be you too! That's why it's a pain in the butt.

So, having faith, now that's another factor. I try to have faith in my family. Sometimes it's difficult. It's very difficult. Oh, the ride is hard. But you believe. You try to believe that in the end some good is going to come out of this, in its own way, in its own way, because they're all unique. And I must have faith, because it should mean something to make a difference in the world and I'm trying to do the same thing.

So, what is my fate then? Ideal family. And what is that? That's where all of you belong, where everybody belongs. That's what ideal family is. And when my children get older and they get married, I like to see all sorts of people come into my family so that I can call them my son or my daughter.

Have faith. Have faith in yourself, and know your fate, your good. You will bring something to all. Believe that, and bring it. And that will define us in the end. You want to compete and win? So be it, and let that be the benchmark. Okay. Take care of yourself.

Independence
November 25, 2007

Good morning. *(Good morning.)* America is the most proud nation on earth, right? They're proud of their strength and they believe it came from independence. How does one feel independent? What is independence? I mean, you can't really separate yourself from anything permanently. You are always attached to something, otherwise you have to live like a hermit. But, living in a society or being civil, you're always connected to something, absolutely. So, how are you independent? What is the nature of independence? And why is that important to you? And why is that important to everybody? Because that's what you wave as a flag to the rest of the world.

How do you teach yourself? How do you get taught? The first step is that you have to accept something. That's the first step. If you don't accept, you don't get taught. No matter what other people try to drill into your head, if you don't want to accept it, you can't learn. They can torture you, they can imprison you, you will not accept it. If you don't accept it, you will never be taught. If you can't accept something that comes from somewhere else, you'll never be taught. So, as part of that process, what is important is acceptance. That's the first step.

And the next step is belief. You have to believe what you have accepted. And you have to be willing to act upon it, and to practice it, to try to live by it. And the next step is faith, you have to be willing to die by it. Otherwise it doesn't mean anything and you haven't learned anything. What is the point of being independent when you have nothing that you can represent yourself with?

Anyway, there are many things that we can do in terms of choice making. But think about where that choice making stuff comes from. Think about the process of you making a choice. Think about what triggers what. Am I making a choice in a nasty situation or a good situation? Think about the process. Think about you, where you stand.

Okay? If there's a conflict, where's the conflict in my acceptance? Where's the conflict in my belief? Where's the conflict in my faith? You have to know how to determine that, especially in times of trouble. Because if you don't, guess what? In the end you're at fault. You will live with the consequences, nobody else. It doesn't matter how many fingers you can point to other people, you will face the consequences. It doesn't matter how many people you can dupe because you are slick, but you will face the consequences. Ultimately you will face the judgment. You will die. This is a short life. Okay? Thank God there are not too many old people here! If you get old, you feel you're going towards that. And it is true, whether you like it or not, you have to think about that every day, every day. For whatever reason that you may think your life is short, you have to think about life being short every day and accept that as real.

So, what are you going to do with your independence? You have to answer that question. Because it's you, you want to be independent. You have a name. If I look in a phone book in Korea, I'm sure that there's Moon Hyo-Jin somewhere, but most likely it's going to be a girl. There are a lot of girls named Hyo-Jin. [*Laughing.*] So, it's going to be you. When you practice anything, all you're doing is you're trying to re-enforce your belief. That's about it. You're teaching yourself in belief. That's why you practice, in any technical stuff or whatever, otherwise why do you practice? That's what you're doing.

When you accept something, there's a stage of growth. Okay? And when you practice something, that's all you're doing; you're just teaching yourself your belief, reinforcing your belief. So, it gets stronger and you feel, "Okay! Okay, let's go. I'll compete! I'll be number one!" But, what are you going to do when you're number one? What is your faith? What are you dying for? Your life's short, so it had better mean something! Having faith is recognizing that I am something, something that is eternal, something that is greater than I. I want to be there. I want to make my steps towards that! And I will have earned it.

There's lots to change, okay? That's a different story and there are practical problems that we need to address. But, we have to have the right attitude, you know? You want to be independent, the key to victory is in your hand, so hold on to it. Believe in it. Okay?

Gratitude
December 2, 2007

Good morning. *(Good morning.)* Crazy day huh? [*It had started snowing heavily.*] *(Laughter.)*

The topic is gratitude. What are you grateful for?

Until you are a young teenager you have no concept of gratitude. Because if you have just left the nipple I don't think you have a concept of gratitude. It's when you start to struggle to find yourself that you understand the concept of gratitude. And you ask yourself, "What are you struggling for?" I mean you can be fortunate enough to become the richest man on earth. But, how do you start to feel that gratitude? Let's say you're going to inherit billions of dollars because your parents are so rich. How are you going to feel gratitude? Let's say that you came up with some kind of scheme and it's making lots of money, and you feel rich. Why? Because people are buying into your scheme. So, how do you feel gratitude?

Think about even the simplest scenario, how does one feel gratitude? Does someone actually feel grateful about anything? And why? Think about it. How do people feel those things? What's the trick, what's the thing that will make those people, and you if you're in that situation, feel grateful? These are basic things we need to question and answer for ourselves. We have to do that, and it has to be clear, because no one else is going to live your life. Some things are basic and you must know the answers. Only then can you understand what gratitude is. Because you live, you live. You don't live by someone else's name. You don't live because of someone else's existence. You live because you live, and that's important, and that's what you should be grateful for. That's where it starts. You can't be somebody else.

What am I grateful for? You tell me. If you want to build an ideal world, then understand that first, and from that, you move, you build, and that's a step. It's a long process, but that's what you have to accept, because finding yourself is a difficult process, something you can be grateful for. Do you feel that? So, keep on looking. Everyone does this, everybody has that stuff. You know what I'm saying? What am I grateful for? What is that process? What is my best? I know you have it!

God is fair and God is good. He gave you goodness. What is that stuff? That's your duty to yourself. Because if you don't understand that, there's no possibility for anything what's the point of trying. You're going to fail anyway, unless you understand the basics and give yourself the opportunity to succeed. You have to know what you're grateful for in life, while you're breathing. Okay? So, if somebody asks you that question, you'd better know how to answer that stuff. Otherwise, don't believe in God. So, do that first, because you don't live that long you guys! I'm telling you! So, you need to be grateful for what you are.

You want something more? Why? Why do you want something more when you can already feel gratitude? Because you want to be like that guy, or that guy, or that guy, or that guy, that guy, that guy? [*Each time pointing in a different direction with both hands acting as if shooting two pistols.*] You're an out-law, huh? A gunslinger, huh? Don't be stupid. That's what you're doing, basically, if you do that. You're gun-slinging. You're acting like an outlaw. Why? What's the point? Do you want to go to jail in the end? Do you want to kill yourself because you can never reach that goal?

People do plastic surgery. There's a lot of TV shows about that, it's crazy stuff! And it's popular to some people. Why? There's actually a show, "Beauty to the Beast," or something like that. They literally just cosmetically transform people and then they rate who's better looking in the end! It's crazy stuff! That's the ideal world, huh? Well, that's the ideal world, I guess, in America.

You can do that, but is that how you're going to make everything ideal? That's just the definition of crazy stuff. That's what makes young girls sick. Right? *(Yes.)* And you watch that stuff, and why do you watch it? Because everybody wants to be like that. The cool kids. What the hell is cool anyway? I used to chase that stuff too, when I was very young, but you get older and that stuff doesn't mean anything to you anymore. Why? Because of what you start to think of. You try to live for the sake of others. Right? That's what's good. Right? And that's why. And it is difficult. Trust me, I know how to take care of myself. I know how to service me good. But as you get older, that's not important. You know you're dying and the basic questions are more important than what you immediately see. And you will die.

So be grateful for what you have and the life that you live.

Surviving Loneliness
December 9, 2007

Good morning. *(Good morning.)* The topic is, "Surviving Loneliness." We all feel lonely sometimes. Right? *(Yes.)* Most of the time. Why do you feel lonely? People have an expectation of us. And we have an expectation of ourselves. It's not other people's expectation. It's our own expectation. And when we fall short of our own expectation, we feel lonely. So, what do you do with that? I know that you don't want to be lonely, so what do you do with that? What do you do when you feel that?

So, let's cut to the chase. Okay? Your existence is a miracle. Your life is a miracle. Your physical existence, your intellectual existence, your spiritual existence, it's all a miracle. There are so many things that can happen, it's up to you. But, just within yourself, your existence is a miracle. So, when you fall into that kind of loneliness, basically you're disregarding your existence, your reality, which is a miracle. You should not expect a greater miracle beyond what you've got. Why? Because life is too short. And in this short life, all you're doing is learning something about you! Nothing else! And then you try to prove that you have learned something about yourself that is right, that is good. That's all you're trying to prove, nothing else. There's nothing beyond that. And how we come to understand this kind of understanding, yes, that's the religious struggle. But in the end, that's the conclusion. That's all we're trying to achieve in our lives, in the end, nothing more.

Do I fear loneliness? We all have our stories, but that's not important. If we have learned that lesson in our lives just to understand our essence, that basic principle, that's all it means.
You're not that lonely. You understand something. And when you understand something, you're part of something. And what you are a part of, who knows? But that's what's important, nothing else.

Anyway, try. And as we try even people like me can get attached to people like you! So, are you lonely? You figure that out. So, hey! Everybody is lonely, okay? Everybody is lonely. But we'll find somebody to make us feel a little different, and that's where you start.

Okay?

The Greatest Self Control
January 10, 2008

If there is a purpose for the existence of mankind, we must discover what that is. What is it? If you already know what it is, a path for discovery is not needed. But because you do not know what it is, there is a need for a path for discovery. So, what is my purpose of existence? Life is short, and I am now forty-five years old. I have never thought that Hyo Jin would turn forty-five. When I was young, I did not have a concept of being forty-five years old. I thought I would retain my youth forever.

Now that all of you have aged you will understand what I am talking about. Do you want your children to grow up like me? What I mean is, do you want them to grow up in a harsh environment like I did? Although there may be no choice, would you want them to grow up that way? Do you think that you have control over that? If you cannot control the surrounding environment, what will you have control over? Controlling the environment is the basic step.

We must learn how to do this in our short lifetime. But if we are not equipped with the basics of learning, what can be properly done? Whatever anyone says, it will become child's play. If we cannot control the education and entertainment that educates and inspires the public, we will lose in the competition. If we cannot control the multimedia, we will lose. That is the conclusion. We will lose in the competition.

Our movement is a religion. If we are a religion, we must win in the competition. In the end, we must popularize it. We must attract more people to our side. Instead of calling it a fight let's call it a competition. We have to pull the people to our side. We must put ourselves in a more advantageous position. We must become more awesome. We must become popular. This does not happen in a moment. It takes time. It does not happen in my moment only. That is how you must think and prepare. If you do not, you will become handicapped. We will not be able to reach the end.

In an age of constant change and rapidly evolving trends, we will not be able to handle the competition. We cannot change positions with our competition and we cannot overtake them either. That is because we do not have the best capability. We do not have anything with which we can control the environment. We need to have at least one thing but we do not have it. That is why we cannot win in the competition. So what is our plan? First, we need a plan to preserve our foundation. From there we can start.

So what is everyone imagining? It is up to you. However, you must know who you are. I, Hyo Jin, have nowhere to go. Even if I want to run away, I have nowhere to run. I only have myself. In the end I will be judged by who I am. Do you understand? There is nothing more than that. Do you understand what I am saying?

The important thing is, you must die well! You have to die well! Dying well is the greatest self-control! That is the best self-control! There is no better self-control! One thing you at least need to know properly is how to let yourself die well! Then you will have some kind of possibility. How long will you really live? Everyone! Die well!

How Are You Going to Change the World?
January 27, 2008

How are you? Good morning. *(Good morning.)* Happy New Year! *(Happy New Year!)* [*This is Hyo Jin Nim's first Belvedere speech of the new year.*]

How many years do we have? One more year is gone, what does that mean? Okay, what it means depends on how you think about the way things are and what you are in control of in reality. How are you going to change the world? Do you know how to change yourself? Do you know that your ways are the right way? Are you absolutely sure, whatever you think that you have talent in, that you know what perfection is in it? Are you a master of it and can you control it?

How are you going to change the world? You ask yourself that question. We're trying, but how are we going to do it in actuality? You have your ways, right, and you have to start from there. But, you have to change the ways of other people if you're going to change the world. So, you have to know what the ways of the world are, and the ways of the people that you're focusing on are, and from there begin to make a difference.

What is your way? How do you live? What do you live for? What is your goal? I know that you want to be somebody. Everybody wants to be somebody. So, what is your way? There are many, many, ways. That's the problem. We have to know all those ways to change the world. Yes, the different ways come from cliques, so to speak. They start from some kind of tribal reality. But that's what you need to know to change the world. You have to know human ways, otherwise you will not change the world, right? And that's what we need to focus on, otherwise it's meaningless.

I'm trying to understand my little kids, okay? I'm sure that they have a hard time understanding me, a crazy guy like me.

But that's the way it works, you have to know why humans are the ways they are. For the more we know, the more we can get closer to that ultimate goal that we all talk about in religion. And where do you start? If you tell yourself, "I start now," then what can you do? That's what you do. You think from there, one step at a time until it gets holy and mighty. All the time just start from that, and you build it from there. See if it works. Try it out on people that you know. I don't know you. You don't know me. But you have people that you know around you. So, start there. Try it out. Change the world.

Okay, take care.

What is Love?
February 3, 2008

How is everybody? *(Good! Good morning!)*

Good morning.

When you think about love, "What Is Love?" You will die for love or you will kill for love. It can happen, right? When you really love something, it makes you want to die for it, at the same time in the extreme opposite, you will kill for it. That's what love is, right? And everything that exists under the sun pretty much has both extremes stemming from it. Why is it like that? Is it for you, or is it for me? It's that stuff, it's that struggle, it's that basic struggle. I'll die for something, or I'll kill for something. It's that stuff. It's the "we" or "I" struggle, because when I'm dying for something it's not "me" it's "we." It's as simple as that, everything starts from that. And that you need to know how to answer. That's your quest in this short life. However long you think that you can live, it's short! It's not long enough for me! I know I'm dying, getting closer to my death than to my living, and that's for sure. And that is the truth that I can never deny.

And that's how it begins. Know what you want to do with your life. Is it going to be "we" or is it going to be "I"? You make the choice, and understand that life is what you got, and what you got isn't that much. And that's where we're equal. So, it doesn't matter what you got, it really doesn't matter.

Okay, you have to do your own thinking. Look, I'm not going to read a story book for you, okay? You make your own stories, that's your life. You write your own songs: You write your own stories. That's all we do. That's the best we can do. And hopefully somebody can be inspired by it. Okay? All I can do is what I do. That's it. It's up to you what you do.

So you take care. Okay? I may be gone for a few weeks so I'll see you later when I come back. Okay?

Take care of yourself. Okay?

Why Do We Want to Love Somebody?
March 2, 2008

Good morning. *(Good morning.)*

"Why Do We Want to Love Somebody?" Why do you want to be loved? What is love to you? What do you love? And if you have a definition of the love that you want to have, how are you going to get it? There's a need and want in life that drives us in action to make life. That's what we do because of that drive, no other reason.

So, what is that drive? Based on history, and what there is that teaches us, it is that we seek the highest love. We all want to be the best in whatever we do. You want to be number one! We don't want to be number two. Well if you live long enough, you at least want to be in the rankings because it's not that simple to always be number one.

So, what is love? What is love for you? What do you want, why do you need, why do you want love? If you can't answer that to yourself, you haven't understood about yourself. Because the next question, the next step is, that if you need and want love you're not going to have it alone. Then something else comes into your picture, and when it comes, what do you think is going to happen to you? What word will occur to you? It's called sacrifice. And that's going to mess you up for a long time, until you get it right. That word is going to mess you up until you get it right. I know what I want. No, I know what I need and I know what I want. But, sacrifice? That's a different story. That's going to mess you up.

So, how are you going to make that right? There's no magic answer. You have to persevere. You have to understand where you stand and you have to persevere. That's the only answer, till you make it right. You make it right. Because in the end, you stand alone in judgment.

I wish I could have had a little more time with my son. I'm not the kind of guy who regrets things, but that's one thing that I regret and that's going to hurt me to the day I die. Why? Because I loved somebody.

You don't live that long you guys. I will be 50 soon, you know. I'm trying to take care of myself, you know. But, in a few more years you'll be dead! Right? What the heck is that? What are we learning in this life.

Find yourself, okay? And die well. Because you don't live that long. And I hope that you want to be good, okay? Because we can learn from each other, okay? Find good, find you, and die well, okay?

Commitment

March 9, 2008

Good morning. *(Good morning.)*

Is everybody here committed to something? *(Yes.)* When you think about commitment, what does it mean to you? Why do you want to commit to something? It's because it defines you. That's why you commit to something. Any kind of commitment that you make will define you, and ultimately you'll be judged. You know that life is about learning something and life is short. Very short. How about what makes you good, what makes you right? Even in business, if people give you money you have a responsibility, you have a commitment. You have to make them profit. Otherwise I don't think you're going to get another opportunity.

So, even just dealing with money, you're committed, that's what it is.

Now think about yourself. What are you thinking? What terms of thinking are you committed to? What are you reaching out to understand? Even if you do understand something, achieving it is very difficult. Now, take that to the next level, spirituality. How are you going to answer that question? You have to have spirit, mind, and body together to be perfect. That's crazy stuff! That's what you have to do, basically. So, where do you stand?
You don't want to look at the person next to you. Answer that for yourself. You ask that question to yourself and you answer it for yourself, and that's where you stand. Have I seen crap? Yes, I have. I'll probably see more.

That's where I stand. And how do I get better? Following the basics, doing the basics, doing what is right, there's no other way.

Do you feel big sometimes? Yes, but who cares if it isn't real? It's only then just about you. Do you think that anything worth living for is just thinking about me? That's not the lesson that we should be learning.

And that's the reason why this world sucks. It's not about me. It's about us. That's why it hurts. Because if we all start from "I," we have to understand "We." What is family anyway? Man and woman come together and make family. What is that? Is it, "I" or is it, "We?"

And then you will die. No matter how great you think you are, you will die. Anything that makes you arrogant, keep it to yourself. Okay? I'm a very arrogant man. So, just keep it to yourself. If you love your children, if you have children, if you have a family, that's what you do to be a good parent. Everybody does that. So, try to be good and keep it to yourself. You want to be arrogant, keep it to yourself. You need commitment because it defines you, and in judgment you had better know what that is.

I'll be away for about two weeks. Okay?

Okay.

www.ingramcontent.com/pod-product-compliance
Lightning Source LLC
LaVergne TN
LVHW091212080426
835509LV00009B/958